'What is Truth?'

GW00580214

The Western philosophical tradition and mainstream Christian theology have a common flaw: both have failed consistently to appreciate poetic truth. Plato proposed to ban Homeric poetry from his utopia while St Augustine wished to 'shun the company of the poets entirely'. However, nineteenth- and twentieth-century philosophy has seen a move towards rejection of this prejudice, pioneered largely by Heidegger and Nietzsche.

In this groundbreaking theological work Andrew Shanks argues that the rebellion of Heidegger and Nietzsche is also deeply flawed and proposes an alternative strategy for reconciling Christian theology with poetic truth. Heidegger's ideal prophetic poet, Friedrich Hölderlin, is rescued from the Heideggerian interpretation through being set alongside his equally prophetic contemporary, William Blake, and also alongside Nelly Sachs, arguably the greatest religious poet of the twentieth century.

'What is Truth?' forges an essentially new form of 'mythic theology', opening up a fresh approach to the deepest nature of poetic truth. In a culture where the status of institutional religion is in decline, there is a pressing need for new theological strategies. Not least, theology needs to seal a new pact of alliance with the very boldest forms of prophetic poetry. In arguing for a fresh 'theological poetics', 'What is Truth?' represents an eloquent and original move towards meeting this need.

Andrew Shanks is a Church of England priest in North Yorkshire. He is the author of *God and Modernity* (Routledge, 2000), *Civil Society, Civil Religion* (Blackwell, 1995) and *Hegel's Political Theology* (Cambridge University Press, 1991).

'What is Truth?'
Towards a theological poetics

Andrew Shanks

London and New York

First published 2001
by Routledge
11 New Fetter Lane, London EC4P 4EE

Simultaneously published in the USA and Canada
by Routledge
29 West 35th Street, New York, NY 10001

Routledge is an imprint of the Taylor & Francis Group

© 2001 Andrew Shanks

Typeset in Sabon by
Curran Publishing Services, Norwich
Printed and bound in Great Britain by
MPG Books Ltd, Bodmin

All rights reserved. No part of this book may be reprinted or
reproduced or utilised in any form or by any electronic, mechanical,
or other means, now known or hereafter invented, including
photocopying and recording, or in any information storage or
retrieval system, without permission in writing from the publishers.

British Library Cataloguing in Publication Data
A catalogue record for this book is available from the British
Library

Library of Congress Cataloging in Publication Data
A catalog record for this book has been requested

ISBN 0–415–25325–X (hbk)
ISBN 0–415–25326–8 (pbk)

To Jack and Marjorie Leppington

Contents

Acknowledgements

Grateful acknowledgement is made to Suhrkamp Verlag for permission to quote extracts from the original German version of poems by Nelly Sachs originally published by them, and to S. Fischer Verlag and the Anvil Press for permission to quote from 'Zürich zum Storchen' by Paul Celan, the original German version of which was published in *Die Niemandsrose*, copyright S. Fischer Verlag, Frankfurt am Main, 1963, and the English translation rights of which are held by the Anvil Press.

Workers need poetry more than bread. They need that their life should be a poem. They need some light from eternity.

Religion alone can be the source of such poetry.

Deprivation of this poetry explains all forms of demoralization.

(Simone Weil, *Gravity and Grace*)

Part I
First principles

1 Faith: poetry versus metaphysical opinion

I

> Pilate then went back into his headquarters and summoned Jesus. 'Are you the king of the Jews?' he asked. . . .
>
> Jesus replied, 'My kingdom does not belong to this world. If it did, my followers would be fighting to save me. . . . My kingly authority comes from elsewhere.'
>
> 'You are a king, then?' said Pilate.
>
> Jesus answered, '"King" is your word. My task is to bear witness to the truth. For this was I born; for this I came into the world, and all who are not deaf to truth listen to my voice.'
>
> Pilate said, 'What is truth?', and with those words went out again.
>
> (John 18: 33–38)

'*What is truth*', said jesting Pilate; And would not stay for an answer.'[1] But Christian theology is the discipline that stays where Pilate would not.

II

And so what then *is* truth, in the sense intended here?

In the fourth gospel Jesus's conversation with Pilate follows shortly after his farewell discourse to his disciples at the last supper, during which he is represented as saying, 'I *am* the truth' (John 14: 6). The truth in question, it would appear, is a truth requiring not just that one assent to it, but that so far as possible one actually becomes *identified* with it. It is the truth of a certain form of self-identification – which Jesus symbolizes.

That is to say: it is a certain ordering of *love*. For are we not most deeply identified by what and how we love, and how we receive the love of others? The discussion that follows this momentous formulation, 'I *am* the truth', is all about love. As the evangelist poetically presents the scene, Jesus goes on to speak of his disciples' love for himself; his own love for them ('There is no greater love than this, that a man lay down his life for his friends'); the mutual love between himself and 'the Father'; his disciples' vocation to 'dwell in' his love, and so to love one another.

Jesus 'is' the truth for Christian faith – not only truth's herald, but the truth itself – by virtue of the way he thus comes to symbolize the love which 'is' God. What faith finds, and celebrates, in Jesus is a symbolic paradigm for the love which is truth.

There are of course a great many other very diverse phenomena which get given the name of 'love': impulses of affection deriving from all sorts of different need. But the only needs in question with regard to love at *this* level are, surely, those which derive from the desire for truth. The particular benefits to which such love is responding are the benefits of truth. If we rightly thank God for other benefits, it is because we want to be truthful about our general neediness. But faith is not properly conditional on any other benefit received. It is simply a response to the revelation of truth; a truth-producing love of truth; a voluntary opening up of oneself, in trust, to the truth of the beloved other person's critical perception of oneself – and ultimately, thereby, to the truth of God's judgement.

What faith finds, and celebrates, in Jesus is a symbolic paradigm for the truth which is love. That is to say: truth as an ideal quality of willing; a systematic discipline of the passions. Truth as pure honesty.

But in what sort of thinking does this truth come to expression? Surely it is in that particular form of thinking which works most directly with emotion. It is both a vivid evocation of emotion, and at the same time a critical affirmation of – or resistant wrestling with – what is evoked.

In the broadest sense, therefore, the truth which Jesus 'is' is first and foremost *poetic*.

For, after all, no other form of literature can be so direct or so evocatively vivid an articulation of love as is the finest love-poetry. After Jesus's death (it seems to me) his truth is resurrected as an essentially poetic vindication of the love which is pure honesty.

III

There is however a rather widespread error, to the contrary, that religious faith is a form of metaphysical *opinion*.

The term 'faith' is persistently misused as though what it meant was any sort of 'sacred' metaphysical opinion adopted prior to, and clung to independently of, whatever rational justification there might be for it. So one hears people say that they reject faith because they do not want to commit themselves to believe anything except what they have good rational reason to believe. 'Faith' for such people is evidently just a term for arbitrary opinion, obstinately held.

And yes, I quite agree: one ought to be as critically rational as possible with one's opinions.

Only – faith, in the true theological sense, is not a metaphysical opinion. Faith is what 'saves'. But no metaphysical opinion, not even the most orthodox or the most enlightened, can ever save.

The confusion is, to be sure, quite readily understandable: faith is always conventionally *associated with* certain opinions; in each religious culture, a different set. Let us, though, be quite unequivocal. *In itself*, it contains no element of opinion at all.

Thus, what is faith? I go back to what I said above: faith, surely, is *a community-building or community-transformative appropriation of the very deepest poetic truth.*

In other words: it is the appropriation of that particular form of poetic truth which has the greatest power to serve as an authoritative basis for, or influence on, community life. It is poetic truth appropriated as sacred insight – and hence as that which 'saves'. Faith, in this sense, cannot properly be called a form of 'opinion' for the simple reason that an 'opinion' is a prosaic thing.

Opinions are either correct or incorrect. And by 'metaphysics' here what I mean is the onto-theological science which distinguishes false opinion from true knowledge only in the sense that true 'knowledge' is a name for correct opinion.

But the truth that belongs to the poetry of faith is not exactly a matter of correctness. Far rather, it is the truth of a true *challenge*: to imagine more, to feel more, to think more – in short, to love more. And so to be inwardly changed. Changed, in the sense of saved.

Faith, as an appropriation of poetic truth, is not a metaphysical opinion about God; it is an encounter with God, in the experience of that sort of challenge. Nor does it *depend* on any metaphysical opinion. All it depends on is a basic initial willingness to take religious tradition seriously. *Credo ut intelligam*: I opt for faith in order that I may understand. I open my mind, in other words, to the potential poetic truth of religious tradition so as to be troubled by it, prodded by it, inspired by it. Authentic faith – the faith that saves – is not a mind-settling and emotionally reassuring metaphysical opinion. (As people evidently suppose when they say, 'How I envy you your faith!') Quite to the contrary. In principle, it is precisely the poetic *dissolution* of any merely mind-settling or reassuring opinion – to open up the way for transformative grace.

IV

This elementary distinction between faith and religious opinion is, indeed, no new insight. It has always been implicit in all good theology, and is already rendered perfectly explicit in mediaeval scholasticism.[2] And yet – maybe, even so, it is still partly the theologians' fault that the confusion still persists, in practice; at any rate, within Christendom. For of course the church has always *also* been so fiercely obsessed with the importance of 'correct' metaphysical opinion. In my view this essentially needs to be seen as a very deep-seated corporate neurosis, in the first instance deriving from the formative experience of persecution suffered by the very earliest Christian communities within the Roman Empire.

The trouble is, in that context the institutional church originally took shape very much as an armature, designed for protection against the pressures of persecution. Already almost from the very outset, in ethnic and cultural terms, a pluralistic community, the church nevertheless needed to cultivate strict unity, in resistance to the divide-and-destroy pressures of a hostile environment. Such unity could not come direct from a shared commitment to faith, purely and simply as such, since faith, purely and simply as such, is far too much a matter of pure inwardness. For the purposes of external armature there was in fact no other real option but to insist on a closely prescribed, carefully policed uniformity of metaphysical opinion. But – alas! – habits learnt so early in a tradition's development are very difficult then to unlearn; even long after the original justification for them has disappeared, as is the case with Christianity today.

My basic aim in what follows is to try to make some contribution to the, in my view, urgently needed systematic disentangling of faith from its resultant long-term entanglement in metaphysics. The more that faith is entangled in metaphysics, and the supposed 'correctness' of 'correct' opinion is given effective precedence over poetic truth, the less free access there is allowed to genuinely *fresh* poetic stimuli at the level of religious practice. For lack of this, faith starts to wilt like a flower without water. That, I think, is the real epidemic problem now. What is therefore required – I want to argue – by way of remedy, is a theology whose whole initial focus is on the sheer *freshness* of the very freshest, that is, the most profoundly original religious poetry, in its distinctive challenge to faith.

Everything, for theology, depends upon its being so far as possible opened up, as a discipline, to the re-energizing power of great, strange, wild poetry – in testimony to the truth which is love.

2   Confessions of a traitorous *clerc*

I

What follows is an essay in theology. One might define theology as the intellectual discipline of faith, which systematically interprets history as a field of divine revelation: an attempt to analyse the history framing, or rendering possible, the poetic truth which faith, with its various community-building or community-transformative projects, appropriates.

Theology is a particular species of response, in other words, to the power which certain historical experiences, properly attended to, have to transform one's whole sense of moral priorities: one's perception of one's own vocation, and of the world as an arena for that vocation.

But what if the innermost moral of the most deeply significant – because most deeply traumatic – historical experience were precisely such as to *outlaw* a theological type of response, and compel us to shift over to some other level of thought? This would indeed be the most radical possible sort of argument against faith, and therefore against theology in general. For it would be an attack on theology right at the heart of its own territory.

The thinker who has perhaps most interestingly developed a philosophical argument of this sort, it seems to me, is Julien Benda.

II

Benda's chief concern was not with the criticism of theology, as such. He belonged to that generation of French intellectuals whose thinking was largely formed by the experience of the Dreyfus Affair. In his youth he was an enthusiastic Dreyfusard; and in all his subsequent work he is preoccupied with devising strategies to combat the various impulses which were eventually to feed into the politics of fascism, Nazism and Bolshevism. So he became a leading critic of the emergent propaganda culture of twentieth-century mass democracy – essentially for its sheer propaganda-quality.

At the same time, though, he draws moral lessons from that struggle which are absolutely inimical to theology.

As a theologian, of course, I think that Benda is wrong. He was always one of the world's great oversimplifiers: a crude thinker, often perhaps a downright silly one.[1] He has largely now been forgotten. And yet such thinkers – with their obstinate collisions against muddled common sense – can sometimes help clarify issues even when they are quite wrong.

Indeed, if Benda had not existed I guess that for my present purposes I would have had to invent him. He was, after all, responding to a set of historical experiences which remain of the most profound concern to any contemporary theology. Moreover, the anti-theological crudity of his response also seems to me to draw to the surface some of the very deepest traditional prejudices of mainstream Western philosophy in general.

Thus, what interested Benda first and foremost was the role of those he called '*les clercs*'. By this he meant free-spirited intellectuals of every sort, but he preferred to use the antique term '*clerc*', harking back to the medi-aeval past when nearly all intellectuals were Christian priests, because he wanted to insist upon a sacred vocation, analogous to that traditionally ascribed to the Christian clergy. In so far as he is remembered at all, it will no doubt always be above all for his little book, first published in 1927, *La trahison des clercs* (*The Treason of the Clercs*).[2] And rightly so. But the theme encapsulated in that title actually runs right through his writings: he is for ever like a prophet calling back the chosen people – in this case *les clercs* – to the vocation which all too many of them have betrayed.

So how are we to understand this charge of 'treason'?

The crucial first step in Benda's argument, in fact, already appears in an essay of sixteen years earlier, entitled *Mon Premier Testament*.[3] *Mon Premier Testament* is framed as a systematic unmasking of the way in which, as he sees it, people's political and religious ideas arise out of their emotional needs. It culminates in a fundamental contrast between two opposing types of emotional need: on the one hand what he calls 'the need for pathos' and, on the other, 'the need for ease'.

The need for pathos is 'the need which some people feel for a racing pulse, quick breathing, impetuous gesticulation'. Wherever one encounters ethical doctrines presented in terms of tumultuous drama – whatever the actual form such drama may take – there the need for pathos is at work. It is, in Benda's hostile presentation, the desire to be morally horrified, alarmed, filled with righteous indignation and scorn, for the sake of the pleasurable stimulus this provides; and so to have the further delicious thrill of feeling summoned to heroism. It demands morally authoritative identity-defining narratives full of abrupt transitions, sudden reversals of fortune, revolutions – in short, a morality consistently packaged to be as *exciting* as possible.

The need for ease is the opposite in each particular. Physiologically, it is the felt need 'for a slow pulse, gentle breathing, flowing movement'. It generates a taste, both aesthetic and moral, for all that is quieting, calming, conducive to a mild benevolence and meditative detachment.

There is in Benda's thought a strong apparent contradiction between substance and form. He writes with a polemical ferocity full of pathos – and yet it is all directed, precisely, against the cultural products of the need for pathos. The need for ease, not the need for pathos – he argues – is the true need of Reason: issuing as it does in a detached *impartiality* of insight. Its cultural products are much rarer and less conspicuous than those of the need for pathos. Yet this is the need to which the true *clerc* must cling. In order for ideas to have any impact on a wider 'lay' public they must satisfy the need for pathos: there is no scope for propaganda in any ethos determined by the need for ease. However, the rise of modern mass democracy has brought with it all sorts of new temptation for the *clercs*, to seek a share of power by betraying their vocation and collaborating in various propaganda-strategies designed to exploit the 'laity's' need for pathos. That is the basic corruption Benda is denouncing in *La trahison des clercs*. It is not that he is opposed to mass democracy as such. On the contrary, so long as it is reasonably liberal he approves of it. Only, he is insistent that the true *clerc* should conscientiously abstain from any sort of active involvement in projects catering to the need for pathos.

Clearly, that must include theology. For is not theology, by its very nature, always in quest of some sort of reconciliation between the two needs? To be sure, theology is constitutionally responsive to the need for ease – inasmuch as it seeks to school its practitioners in the radically detached perspective of eternity. And yet it also takes shape as a contribution to the self-understanding of popular religious communities, bonded together by the dramatic pathos of their communal perception of salvation history. There is no way a theologian can simply spurn the need for pathos, as Benda advocates.

III

In these terms – I must confess – I am myself a quite unrepentant 'traitor'. Because, deep down, it seems to me that this argument of Benda's rests upon an elementary confusion. Surely we have to distinguish between two different *modes* of pathos.

In so far as Benda's critique is valid, it is I think valid as a critique of that particular mode which I would call the '*pathos of glory*'. I use the word 'glory' here in the specific double sense of *the reward conferred by the official approval of a ruling class, or (within any sort of community) an established group of leaders, and the glorification of those rulers and leaders themselves.* The 'pathos of glory', then, is an emotive celebration of values and aspirations serving the interests of power. And one may very well be suspicious of it.

But such pathos is by no means to be confused with pathos in general, as Benda seems to do. The primary targets of his polemic in *La trahison des clercs* are all of them, in fact, clear manifestations of the pathos of glory. He attacks it, first, in its form as a rhetoric of nationalism. Much of the argument is directed against the leading French nationalist intellectuals of his day: Charles Maurras, Maurice Barrès, Charles Péguy. Maurras, the founder of the Action Française, and Barrès had both of them been anti-Dreyfusards; Benda loathed them for being militant anti-Semitic nationalists – Barrès in particular with an especial aesthetic flourish. Péguy by contrast was a Dreyfusard, a genuine and passionate Gentile defender of Jewishness, who however in the years of escalating tension leading up to 1914 also became a no less ardent anti-pacifist, a convert to his own idiosyncratic version of intellectual catholicism, largely built around a cult of Joan of Arc. In the first month of the war Péguy died a hero's death on the battlefield, and was buried with two hundred others who fell the same day. Benda was also, in his way, a patriot. But the France he loved was a *patrie morale*, not these nationalists' *patrie du sang*. That is, he saw France as the proper homeland of cool reason, denouncing the pathos-laden nationalism of these others precisely as a disease which they had caught from abroad, from the Germans.

He is equally critical of the pathos of glory in its socialist forms; the primary representative of which, for him, was Georges Sorel. Not that Sorel is easily pigeon-holed in conventional terms. An anarcho-syndicalist who flirted with the Action Française, and who was able at one and the same time to be a fervent admirer of both Lenin and Mussolini, Sorel was in fact entirely at one with the nationalist 'traitor'-*clercs* in his basic advocacy of warrior-courage and warrior-loyalty as the highest of virtues. It was just that, unlike them, he was altogether indifferent whether these virtues be exercised in the struggle between nations or between classes. Either way, his chief concern was simply that politics should be rendered as colourful and exciting as possible.

Benda's attitude was the exact opposite. He valued liberal democracy above all for the very things Sorel most despised in it: its sheer, safe dullness. The duller the better, in his view. Within that context, he himself was by no means unsympathetic to the Communist Party – as a 'lay' enterprise. For he was also a radical egalitarian. But his one objection was to the revolutionary excitement of Marxist doctrine, as a seduction for *clercs*.

In short, what he opposes – and what he thinks all *clercs* as such are duty-bound to join him in opposing – is not either nationalism or socialism in themselves, but only the element of pathos in their propaganda. At the end of *La trahison des clercs* he actually goes on to imagine a possible future in which all the current ideological conflicts of his own world have finally been superseded. Suppose, he suggests, that one fine day the various propaganda-driven enterprises belonging to different nations and classes were somehow to be blended together into a single grand propaganda-driven consensual enterprise of *the species* as a whole:

> In this way humanity would attain 'universal fraternity'. But, far from being the abolition of the national spirit with its appetites and arrogance, this would simply be its supreme form, the nation being called Man and the enemy God. Thereafter, humanity would be unified in one immense army, one immense factory, would be aware only of heroisms, disciplines, inventions, would denounce all free and disinterested activity, would long cease to situate the good outside the real world, would have no God but itself and its desires, and would achieve great things; by which I mean that it would attain to a really grandiose control over the matter surrounding it, to a really joyous consciousness of its power and grandeur. And History will smile to think that this is the species for which Socrates and Jesus Christ died.[4]

Maybe it is already now beginning to happen – at what Francis Fukuyama, for example, has called 'the end of history'.[5] But as Benda sees it, the trouble is that this too would be a politics of pathos, run rampant.

I certainly agree, it is a depressing prospect. Neither would I especially wish to defend any of the particular figures Benda focuses on in *La trahison des clercs*, as examples of the 'betrayal' he denounces. Only – I want to protest – all of these are very much examples of the pathos of *glory*, pathos in the service of manipulative power.

Benda's diagnosis, the conclusion which also informs so much of his other writing, that the real problem derives from the very need for pathos *in itself*, seems to me to be a truly fundamental error. For what about that other sort of pathos: the pathos-laden celebration of high-principled dissent against popular, officially sanctioned prejudice, not as part of any project for the gaining of executive power, but solely for pure intellectual integrity's sake, in itself?

Here, still within the domain of that which caters to the need for pathos, we have the absolute antithesis to the pathos of glory. Let us call it the *pathos of shakenness*, for it is the pathos concomitant to being shaken out of rigid prejudice, and also out of the unthinking distractedness which, passively, goes along with such prejudice – often in ways very troubling to those who rule.

My basic question, then, is: what does the pathos of shakenness look like – at its most vibrant, in poetic-theological terms?

3 The 'pathos of shakenness'
Its three defining marks

I

'What is truth?' asked Pilate, encountering truth and abruptly turning from it. The question, as asked in this context, serves to frame the essential distinctiveness of the Johannine literature in the New Testament. The truth is the gospel of Jesus Christ – so of course all the New Testament teaches. But in the Johannine literature a further distinctive emphasis appears: the truthfulness of the gospel is made manifest, crucially, in the way it *intensifies* the very issue of truth.

For the evangelist, the religiously highest truth belongs to a particular type of *moment*: wherever truth is most intensely rendered problematic.

The moment of Pilate's question, in other words, is paradigmatic for all decisive moments of truth. Pilate is put in a position where he has to judge the one who paradigmatically *is* 'the way, and the truth, and the life'. But something not altogether dissimilar recurs wherever we are, likewise, again confronted by the Christ-like disturbance of the Holy Spirit. We too are, each in our own way, obliged to judge; and, by our judgement, are judged. For the truth which Jesus 'is' recurs as the truth which the Holy Spirit 'is' (1 John 5: 6). This is, after all, the promised 'Spirit of truth' who will guide us into all truth (John 16: 13). The same truth.

At the heart of the Johannine literature is an elemental play of light and dark. The theme is introduced right at the beginning of John's gospel: 'The light shines on in the dark, and the darkness has never mastered it' (John 1: 5). But the darker the darkness, the more spectacularly luminous, by contrast, the light becomes; which the darkness, after all, cannot overcome. The moment of truth is, first and foremost, a moment of starkly intensified moral chiaroscuro.

Herein lies the whole narrative dynamic of the gospel. Thus, as Jesus stands before Pilate the darkness has reached unprecedented intensity. Pilate asks Jesus about his *basileia*: his 'kingdom' or, perhaps better, his 'jurisdiction'.[1] 'My *basileia*', Jesus replies, 'is not of this world'. The *basileia* of this dark world stands face to face with that other *basileia*, which is the luminous jurisdiction of truth. Nor could there be any starker confrontation, to highlight the darkness of the dark judgement.

Yet the metaphor also serves to generalize the point. 'The light shines on in the dark': the context in John 1: 5 is the creation of the world, it has shone from then; and the present tense indicates that the same light shines to this day. What the fate of Jesus dramatizes is a truth about the interplay between the light and dark of the two jurisdictions everywhere and always. The same basic pattern is surely typical of every authentic moment of the Holy Spirit's resurgence into the world: according to the Johannine logic, the religiously highest truth is in general that which appears above all at moments of intensified moral chiaroscuro. Such moments do not *simplify* matters; that is, they do not make it in any way simpler to distinguish the bad from the good. But they do help *clarify* the sheer moral urgency of what is at stake – by ripping away the concealments of ordinary normality.

It is the same, for instance, with the intense moral chiaroscuro produced by the most murderously totalitarian forms of modernity. In the Third Reich, or in the Stalinist Soviet Union, people became mass murderers who, in other more normal times, would have spent their lives quite quietly, as nice respectable folk like us. Others – who in more normal times might have appeared almost indistinguishable from these – were, on the contrary, revealed as extraordinarily courageous upholders of conscientious principle. A new intensity of darkness descended on the world; and at the same time a new intensity of light also entered, here and there, in response. This, as John sees it, was also just what happened with the coming of Jesus – only, so to speak, in reverse. Wherever 'the light of the world' appears it rips away the concealments of ordinary normality; and what the Johannine literature speaks of as 'the truth' is, in essence, everything that such moments of divine judgement lay bare.

In its impact, it is all that serves paradigmatically to differentiate Jesus from Pilate; or from the religious leaders clamouring for his death. Pilate and the religious leaders – considered both together, as they are brought together by the story – may be said symbolically to represent every sort of political or ethical establishment-mindedness. But gospel truth is the elemental opposite. Thus, establishment-mindedness clings to fixed and clearly codified values, in perfect harmony with the perceived self-interest of those in power. The truth of Jesus, however, is 'good news to the poor'. It is not just addressed to any particular group of the poor – John is especially concerned to make this clear, by way of corrective clarification. It is not the promise of future blessings which will help lift a particular group of the poor, in some sense, out of their poverty; nor, therefore, is it just the sort of promise which is represented by the charitable giving of material goods to the poor. But, far rather, it is addressed to the poor *as such*: the poor 'whom you have always with you' (John 12: 8). For it is, quite simply, the good news inherent in the symbolic overthrow of all establishment-mindedness, culminating in the resurrection of the crucified. In short: it is – precisely – the gospel of what I would call 'shakenness'.

And here, then, is what I mean by 'the pathos of shakenness'. Such pathos is that paradigmatic quality of the gospel story which John reflectively expresses, above all, where he writes of darkness and light; and which recurs wherever, through art or ritual, the Holy Spirit is at work carrying forward gospel truth in new expressive ways.

As *pathos* of shakenness it is a registering of the sheer intensity of moral chiaroscuro belonging to any really decisive moment of truth. As pathos of *shakenness* it is a registering of the intensely urgent need of thought deriving from such moments, consequent upon the weakening and collapse of all the old fixed reference points of establishment-mindedness.

The Christian gospel represents the pathos of shakenness at its most serene. For the intrinsic bitterness of the clash between darkness and light is tempered, in the evangelists' narrative, by an overriding assurance that everything which happens is fore-ordained and necessary. Jesus is shown as always knowing this; and hence as a model, for us to follow, of perfect inner calm, above the fray as well as in it, loving his enemies after all, even under the very greatest pressure.

In what follows I will be discussing the work of several poets who seem to me to be especially eloquent and ambitious advocates of the truth-claims of the pathos of shakenness – but let me straight away concede that nowhere in the writings of any of these poets do we find the same ultimate serenity as appears in the gospel portrait of Jesus. Inner trouble, not serenity, is what inspires great poetry of the specific sort I want to discuss. The unique beauty and truthfulness of the gospels may indeed be said to lie in their special juxtaposition of the most intense pathos of shakenness with a portrayal of perfect serenity. Jesus is, in this way, a saviour equally responsive to both the needs of which Benda speaks: the need for pathos and the need for ease. Again, a complete Christian theology must no doubt try to do full justice to the symbolic implications of both these primal aspects of its subject matter. And from that point of view my argument in what follows is, it is true, quite one-sided.

Yet it surely remains the case that the serenity of true faith requires a background of the most vivid shifts and nuances of dark and light, fully to bring it out. For which we need – I would argue, above all – the help of shaken poets.

II

'What is truth?' Clearly, we have to distinguish different levels.

At one level there is the common sense notion of truth; which also informs both metaphysical and positivistic philosophy. Thomas Aquinas for example, following Avicenna, defines truth as *adaequatio intellectus et rei*: the correspondence, likening or coming together of intellect and thing.[2]

The common-sense notion may be said to have two aspects, an objective and a subjective one. In its objective aspect it is a quality, directly, of propositions. In its subjective aspect it is a quality of ideas: the process by which the truth of propositions is recognized, grasped and assimilated. Where the 'things' in question are facts, it begins with the accurate reporting of what is observed and the construction of theoretical interpretations with maximum explanatory power; where the 'things' are values, it begins with the making of judgements properly consistent with what are accepted, by the 'truth'-assessor, to be authoritative first principles. But in either case, at this level, what is 'true' is first of all the set of propositions which express correct observations, explanations and value-judgements; and then the set of ideas which those propositions convey, in so far as they are existentially appropriated. First objective correctness, then its subjective recognition.

Of course! What else should truth be? asks common sense.

But let us reconsider what is actually involved in the *recognition* of truth-as-correctness. Is there not, after all, something else – besides the intrinsic persuasiveness of the correct proposition itself – also required, in order that it should indeed be recognized?

That, as is continually to be observed, one and the same expression of truth-as-correctness should impose itself more on some people than on others is not always, only, down to differences in intelligence. For are there not also very often problems of resistance? And smoothing the way for the recognition of truth-as-correctness, therefore, there is surely first required a proper *readiness* for it. Before all else, one has to be ready for truth – or, as I am inclined to say, shaken free for it. Shaken free from any repressive attachment to prejudice. And from every sort of distraction: freshly attentive, genuinely wanting to learn, patiently waiting.

But is not that initial predisposition of readiness, already as such, itself an embodiment of truth?

It is, I would argue, the primary level of truth. And this is also the level to which the pathos of shakenness belongs. *The truth of the pathos of shakenness is nothing other than the aesthetic solicitation of this mode of truth; which is, moreover, that which is religiously highest – because it is existentially most fundamental.*

Thus, on the one hand there is the level of truth which belongs to good science in the broadest sense; to wise moral and political judgements; and to metaphysical doctrines, in so far as these are able to do justice both to the demands of science and to society's real spiritual needs. On the other hand, there is also the level of truth which *precedes* science; which *precedes* any extended moral or political code; and which *precedes* metaphysical reflection. For the truths of science, of ethical and political codes, or of metaphysics are all of them, in their various ways, truths of propositional correctness, requiring first to be formulated, then to be recognized and internalized. Yet, more primitive than any form of truth-as-correctness – more primitive than that whole interplay of objectivity and subjectivity – is this other mode of truth; which is, simply, the original turning of the will to genuine thoughtfulness.

As I have said, one might perhaps call it *truth-as-honesty*. Such honesty may well remain quite inarticulate, subliminal, in itself. Or else it is what comes to expression, most directly, in the sheer pathos-laden evocativeness of truthful poetry. Far more directly in that form, at any rate, than in any sort of philosophical prose, which sets itself to labour first and foremost for correctness – accuracy, explanatory power, consistency – instead. For here, in short, we have truth not so much as a quality of propositions, simply as such; nor as a quality of ideas, in the sense that true ideas are simply the appropriation of propositional correctness; but, far rather, as a quality of *revelation*. That is to say: it is the revelatoriness of a certain basic disposition of the will, towards experience. And hence, also, of a certain pathos; prodding and pulling at the will.

In suggesting that we need to revalue this most primitive level of truth, I am by no means saying anything new in philosophical terms. Thus far, I am only trying to reiterate what Martin Heidegger for instance argues in his classic little essay of 1930, entitled 'On the Essence of Truth'.[3]

The essay does not actually deal with the relationship of truth to poetry (although it does, nevertheless, mark a key stage in the general evolution of Heidegger's thought towards a radically new openness towards poetic truth). He begins here with the common-sense notion of truth, and then proceeds to move back towards what he considers more 'essential'.

'The essence of truth', Heidegger boldly declares, 'is freedom'.[4]

The way he describes this 'freedom' (what I would call 'truth-as-honesty', freedom from the impulse to lie) is in fact quite strongly reminiscent of traditional religious notions of salvation. Yet it is at the same time a very distinctive description, inasmuch as he is determined – when speaking of that which is intrinsically *pre*-metaphysical – so far as possible completely to avoid any terminology with inherited metaphysical overtones.

Thus, as a Christian theologian, I would want to say, for example, that the primordial form of truth, truth-as-honesty, is essentially a shaken waiting upon God's grace. In so speaking I have taken a concept, that of 'God's grace', which mainstream theological tradition has endued with heavily metaphysical overtones, and am trying, nevertheless, to apply it post-metaphysically. That is to say: by contrast to the usage of meta-physical theology – in which 'grace' is first and foremost a term for what God gives to the inhabitants of one particular domain of cultural 'correctness', namely the Christian church – I am using it, far rather, with reference to *any* achievement of primordial honesty, anywhere. However, Heidegger will not do this. He is far more of a linguistic puritan. Therefore, he will not speak of God's grace at all; instead, he speaks of the essence of truth as being a freedom, not that we possess as our prop-erty, but that on the contrary possesses us.[5] In his account, the authority of God disappears; to reappear as the proprietorial creativeness of 'freedom' itself. The substantive point is really the same. Only, the terminology has been purged.

It is this linguistic puritanism, cut loose from the internal conversations of any metaphysically informed community, which gives Heidegger's writ-ing its peculiar flavour. Another example: I have spoken of primordial truth as a quality, not so much of propositions or ideas, but rather of 'revelation'. Heidegger, wanting to draw essentially the same elementary distinction, carefully works his way around it, anxious not least to avoid all entanglement in the traditional connotations of 'revelation' as a term of Christian metaphysics. Hence, he says things like this: 'Freedom for what is opened up in an open region lets beings be the beings they are. Freedom now reveals itself as letting beings be'.[6] Revelation, as an event made possible by a particular historic *kairos*, becomes for him '*what is opened up in an open region*'. And the whole associated dialectic of redemption from sin becomes a matter of '*letting beings be*'. Heidegger has no interest in trying to disentangle the pre-metaphysical core of the Christian gospel from its metaphysical wrappings – he is trying so far as possible to decamp, instead, into an entirely fresh vocabulary.

The literal meaning of the Greek work for truth, *aletheia*, is 'unconceal-ment'. Yet, Heidegger remarks, every moment of unconcealment is equally a moment of concealment: 'Precisely because letting be always lets beings be in a particular comportment which relates to them and thus discloses them, it conceals beings as a whole. Letting-be is intrinsically at the same time a concealing.'[7]

The 'letting-be' in question might also be described as a special intensity of concerned *focus*. But truly to focus on anything is, straight away, to leave all else aside. Unconcealment can, in this sense, only ever be partial: an opening up of that which is immediately focused upon, but by the same token a concealment of all that is not immediately focused upon. All truth is ambivalent, an insightful seeing mixed with the untruth of peripheral not-seeing. And the honesty of true 'letting-be' is fundamentally a frank acknowledgement of the full extent of that necessary ambivalence; which, in our fallenness, we would prefer not to acknowledge. The 'essence of truth', then, lies in this sheer openness to the inevitability of truth's belonging-together with its own untruth, the impossibility of final answers to any question about 'beings as a whole'. That is to say: any question of religious significance. Here we have what Heidegger simply calls '*the mystery*; not a particular mystery regarding this or that, but rather the one mystery'.[8]

For Heidegger, indeed, the whole problematics of human fallenness – or, in his preferred terminology here, human 'errancy' – derives from a fateful historic withdrawal of 'the mystery', into forgottenness. Thus:

> By disavowing itself in and for forgottenness, the mystery leaves historical man in the sphere of what is readily available to him, leaves him to his own resources. Thus left, humanity replenishes its 'world' on the basis of the latest needs and aims, and fills out that world by means of proposing and planning. From these man then takes his standards, forgetting being as a whole. He persists in them and continually supplies himself with new standards, yet without considering either the ground for taking up standards or the essence of what gives the standard.[9]

The thinking of fallen humanity is a continual 'proposing and planning'. It is never, in other words, a proper *stopping* to think. Still unshaken, in its prejudices and distraction, it is no doubt a pursuit of correctness; yet with no real feel for honesty in the deepest sense. And can any form of metaphysics, as such, adequately challenge this? Inasmuch as metaphysics is itself a pursuit of correctness, leaving the issue of honesty in the margin, surely not. Hence, the linguistic puritanism.[10]

Clearly the puritanism of Heideggerian vocabulary is intended, not least, as a sweeping implicit indictment of Christian metaphysics in particular, for its prevalent failure properly to respect 'the mystery'.

Now, I certainly have no interest in being a general Heidegger-apologist – and will come back to what I think is wrong with his working-out of this doctrine. But I would by no means want to deny that there *are* real, major difficulties facing those of us who, unlike him, seek to be, in the fullest sense, true to 'the mystery' even while still remaining within the ambit of traditional theology. In fact, that is exactly why I think we need to seal a new pact of partnership with shaken poetry, to help us out.

III

'My *basileia*, my jurisdiction, is not of this world', said Jesus, to Pilate, symbolic representative of the jurisdiction which is of this world. As I would understand it, the confrontation here, between the two jurisdictions, is essentially pre-metaphysical. The dark 'this-worldliness' of Pilate is not simply a matter of his pagan metaphysical belief-system; for in this paradigmatic conflict he is thrown into a direct alliance with the Jewish religious leaders, people with a very different metaphysical belief-system from his. They too are caught up into the dark untruth of 'the *basileia* of this world', just as much as he.

No, if we are to follow the implicit logic of the story itself, 'the *basileia* of this world' is surely definable in pre-metaphysical terms, as the domain of those who, in general, forget 'the mystery'; the busy 'proposers and planners'; the unshaken. For these are the qualities which Pilate and the Jewish religious leaders most fundamentally have in common.

In this case, however, Jesus's '*basileia* not of this world' is just the luminous jurisdiction of pure truth-as-honesty. As a pre-metaphysical phenomenon such truth may be expressed in many very different metaphysical guises. (It is, to that extent, the rendering-true of all sorts of contrasting metaphysical systems – although without in any way diminishing their differences in metaphysical terms, or requiring them, at the metaphysical level, to coalesce.) But 'the *basileia* not of this world' is, I think, what appears wherever people start to make pure truth-as-honesty, *in itself*, the ultimate basis for community-building.

Or it is what elsewhere (following Jan Patočka) I have called 'the solidarity of the shaken'.[11] And by 'the pathos of shakenness', then, I mean that special quality which is the defining characteristic of the art and ritual proper to this sort of solidarity.

The pathos of shakenness may be said to have three key distinguishing marks:

1   *It is the expression of a radical unease with any sort of establishment-mindedness; an urgent calling into question of all establishment dogma, as such.*
2   *Yet it is by no means just an easy, complacently individualistic agnosticism, of the sort that merely dismisses ultimate questions as not being worth the fuss. It is really the exact opposite. Thus, shakenness differs from agnosticism in that it is always oriented, in yearning, towards an appropriate solidarity – no matter how frustrated that yearning may be.*
3   *Neither, on the other hand, is it merely the opposing of mainstream establishment dogma with the even more regimented counter-dogma of*

a sectarian, or revolutionary, counter-establishment. For that which shakes is also, very much, a yearning for fresh air.

Wherever any form of art or ritual manifests these three negative qualities – there is the pathos of shakenness.

For is not this what Jesus symbolically represents? He is a true prophet; an impassioned community-builder; yet, at the same time, the absolute opposite to a sectarian – never laying down any laws. And indeed I would also see an essentially Trinitarian logic at work here. That is, if one considers the three Persons of the Trinity in the order Second Person, Third Person, First Person: God made manifest in the resurrection of the crucified dissident / God the Holy Spirit at work in the passion of an evolving traditionality / God the universal truth beyond and behind all culturally particular truth.[12]

It seems to me that the core, pre-metaphysical truth of the gospel consists in the extraordinarily direct and dramatic way it invests such pathos with serenity. (All other great religious traditions, I would argue, likewise owe their greatness to their own, different admixtures of the pathos of shakenness and serenity.) One might perhaps object that the community within which, and for which, the Johannine literature was written is already well on the way to being a sort of sectarian counter-establishment. To some extent no doubt it is: especially in view of the way the fourth gospel speaks about 'the Jews' – as if the opposition to Jesus embraced the whole people, and as if Jesus and his disciples were not themselves Jews – which plainly is quite an ugly expression of sectarian aggression towards that community's Jewish rivals, spilling over into the narrative and distorting it.

But only take this away, so that we are left with the great pre-metaphysical conflict between the two jurisdictions, that of 'this world' and that of God – and there, surely, is the truth.

IV

As the jurisdiction of God stands opposed to the jurisdiction of 'this world', so the pathos of shakenness stands opposed to the pathos of glory.

Of course, the religious art and ritual of the pathos of shakenness may also speak of the glory of God. I do not want to outlaw the word 'glory'! But in this case the glory of God is not a glory mediated, or appropriately imaged, by the this-worldly gloriousness of rulers – or would-be rulers. On the contrary, it is entirely a calling into question of whatever aspects of *their* glory may be mendacious and exploitative.

Compare Martin Luther's twenty-first thesis for the Heidelberg

Disputation of 1518: 'The "theologian of glory" calls the bad good and the good bad. The "theologian of the cross" says what a thing is.'[13]

The 'theology of glory' in this context is, I think, precisely the sort of thinking which represents God's glory in terms of a straightforward continuum from this-worldly glory. It is, as Luther further suggests in the following thesis, 'the wisdom which beholds the invisible things of God as perceived from works': namely, the good works of loyal church-membership, understood as due obeisance to the glory of the church institution, in all its institutional this-worldliness. Or, one might say, it is theology reduced to the level of mere church-ideology. But the cross of Christ, on which a 'king' suffers the death reserved for slaves or other non-citizens, is properly the absolute symbolic overthrow of any such thinking. Herein, it seems to me, there is encapsulated the whole element of pre-political truth in Lutheran doctrine.

What Luther here calls the 'theology of glory' is, in short, simply the theological variant of what, more generally, I am calling 'pathos of glory'. One finds such pathos in the propaganda of great political movements aspiring to win, or to retain governmental power; in the art which the rich and powerful commission; in every sort of aesthetic production which remains essentially ornamental to a world of injustice; and in the self-advertisement of religious movements – large or small, mainstream or sectarian – in so far as their anxiety to attract and keep a maximum number of adherents, the better to maximize their social clout, prevails over any scruples they might have about thereby cheapening their message.

The art of the pathos of shakenness is by no means necessarily better than the art of the pathos of glory in purely aesthetic terms. It may be very crude. And the art of the pathos of glory may be magnificent. Consider, for instance, Dante's *Divine Comedy*. This is, without any question, one of the very greatest works of Christian poetry ever written. And yet it can scarcely be described as an unmitigated expression of the pathos of shakenness. For it lacks the first mark of such pathos, as I have specified it: its *radical* otherness from any simple establishment-mindedness. Granted, Dante was a fierce critic of certain forms of ecclesiastical corruption – and suffered for it. But his faith still remains, very much, that of one particular tendency *within* the Catholic establishment of his day: his epic is designed to reinforce the fear of hell, and the desire for heaven, to which that establishment appealed, not least as an argument for obedience to its demands. The work is beautiful, impassioned, moving, prayerful – indeed, genuinely glorious. And yet, it nevertheless does not – I think – transcend its historic context in quite the way that certain other works of poetry do, which are more deeply shaken.

The core truth of religion in general, I would argue, lies in its according of authority to the pathos of shakenness; the core truth of the Christian gospel, in particular, lies in the unique way it does the same.

Yet this core truth has traditionally almost always been overlaid with elements of ecclesiastical pathos of glory, bound up with a strict discipline of metaphysical and ethical orthodoxy, which is thereby promoted and reinforced. On the one hand, we have the gospel story understood as the grounding for an infinitely restless commitment to honest self-questioning; on the other hand, we have the self-same story enframed by the insistent advocacy of a system of supposedly correct answers – which puts an end to any real thinking, beyond the mere winning of arguments. My project is systematically to try to disentangle these two ultimately opposite modes of intertwined pathos.

V

What chance is there of such a project having any real practical impact on church life?

In fact I think there is some hope. There is hope, basically because of the way in which religious pathos of glory is bound up with the notion of religion as a bulwark against general social chaos. For that is a role from which religion is now, more and more, being set free.

Of course, all religion is about community-building. (This is implicit in the very etymology of the word: its derivation from the Latin *religare*, 'to bind together'.) However, there is a fundamental difference between two alternative binding principles of community. On the one hand, there is community for the sake of mutual entertainment and mutual support in trouble, an environment for friendship; in religious terms, a coming-together for the exchange of insights and the corporate pursuit of truth in action, as an always transcendent ideal. But on the other hand there is community as a back-up to law and order; dedicated to the discouragement of delinquency, and the support of those who would otherwise be prone to it, in keeping to the straight and narrow. The former mode of community is the natural habitat of the pathos of shakenness; the latter, of the pathos of glory – glorifying the upholders and enforcers of law and order, along with everything they represent. And it is the latter which I mean when I speak of religion as a 'bulwark against chaos'.

Now, obviously all societies do require some sort of bulwark against chaos. Nor am I, for one moment, denying the value of the support which religious communities may give to those in special need of social rehabilitation. Only, it is a question of overall priorities with regard to determining what a church, as distinct from any other sort of supportive community, is *primarily* for. And the fact is that the developed capitalism of the present day has actually discovered a new sort of bulwark against general social chaos, which does not have anything to do with religion at all. I mean consumerism: the allure of fashion, in the broadest sense. Law and order rests on a promise of good things reserved for those who do as they ought. Once upon a time religious notions of heaven and hell fulfilled this function; more and more now the promise of a steadily improving material standard of living has taken over. Law and order requires a basic general consensus about moral values. Once it was the job of religion to provide it. But nowadays we are increasingly content to rely on a consensual respect for free market principles, with regard to ideas as well as commodities; and on democratic votes. To the extent that this new ethos prevails, religious observance has ceased to be the necessary part of conventional respectability it once was. This is surely the basic reason why church-attendance in most, if not all, developed capitalist societies has tended over the past several decades to plummet.

I say, thank God! Granted, a liberal free market in ideas does not exactly guarantee deep thinking; and neither does democracy. But at least the result is potentially to liberate religious community-life from the requirements of its old law-and-order role. That role is essentially a service rendered to 'the *basileia* of this world'. At long last, though, the church is now set free to turn more towards its other, altogether more distinctive role, as a community-witness to the requirements of that other *basileia*, the one which Jesus represents – as he stands before Pilate.

Religion as a bulwark against general social chaos is naturally addicted to stressing the unique correctness of its moral law, and of the metaphysics behind it; which it then seeks to invest with pathos of glory. However, in our world this is simply no longer such an urgent need as it once was.

All we have to do is recognize the opportunity, and respond accordingly.

4 'Mythic theology'

Mistrustful as he is of 'the need for pathos' in any form, Benda is not least a fiercely polemical poetry critic.[1] He approves of certain sorts of poetry, the work of Lamartine for instance; but, strictly, only for its entertainment value. He will not allow that poetry should ever have any major role in the shaping of moral attitudes. That, for him, is ultimately a job for philosophy alone.

In this he agrees with Plato; who, in the *Republic*, represents Socrates as arguing for the complete 'banishment' of all the more ambitious forms of poetry from his philosophically-governed utopia.

Let us consider the Platonic argument and its influence.

II

As it happens, the *Republic* contains two separate discussions of poetry: the first in Books 2 and 3, where Plato is considering the general education of the upper classes in a just society; the other almost at the end of the dialogue, in Book 10. Some commentators have been tempted to half-dismiss the latter passage as little more than an incidental appendix to the larger argument of the work as a whole, not meant to be taken all that seriously. That, though, seems to me to be completely wrong.

Granted, the transition to it is rather abrupt and under-explained; and, in terms of argument, it does not add anything very substantial to what has already been said.[2] Yet there surely is a good deal of significance in Plato's decision to return to the topic right *here*. For the passage comes just after Socrates has completed the portrait of his ideal regime, whereupon he immediately concedes that such a regime is most unlikely ever actually to be realized in earth; but that, far rather, it is a 'pattern laid up in heaven', a utopian dream. Very well then, in that case – the reader can scarcely help wondering – what practical consequences might this dream nevertheless have, for those who recognize its ultimate validity, here and now? Implicitly, I think, the closing pages of the *Republic* are very much to be seen as an initial answer to that question.

Two topics are addressed in these pages: poetry and the immortality of the soul. On the one hand, Plato is suggesting, philosophers need to be struggling, in the first instance, to try and gain intellectual hegemony over the domain of religion, with their distinctive understanding of the proper destiny of the soul. But on the other hand, the chief enemy this means that they have to combat is the mainstream tradition of poetry, stemming from Homer. Nothing, in short, from the Platonic point of view, could be more serious.

III

The earlier of the two passages in the *Republic* sets out the case more fully. In the first place, Plato's Socrates here complains, Homer and his followers give a distorted picture of the gods: for philosophy, the divine is nothing other than the perfection of justice, but the poets often portray the gods misbehaving among themselves and acting with the cruellest injustice towards mortals. Second, the poets – portraying Hades as a place of gibbering ghosts – teach people a quite unphilosophical fear of death. And third, they glorify gods and heroes whom they represent as indulging in the most tremendous displays of unregulated pathos: wild laments, uproarious mirth, fierce impulses of lust. These are, from the Platonic point of view, the very worst types of role model.

It is true that, in so far as Plato is also serious about the ideal of the philosopher-ruler, he differs from Benda; who thinks that the true vocation of the *clerc* is entirely 'other-worldly', in the sense of being dissociated from the politics of rule in any form. Nor therefore is Plato altogether opposed to the pathos of glory as such. What he objects to is just Homer's false notion of glory. There will still be some poets left in the Platonic utopia: composing philosophically sound 'hymns to the gods and paeans to good men'[3] – they will in short be the protagonists of an alternative pathos of glory, in the service of the new ruling elite.

Or is this too reductive a reading? The fact is, we just cannot say what Plato would have made of poetry unequivocally expressive of the pathos of shakenness. For he never encountered it.

Inasmuch as his Socratic notion of philosophy is itself such a radically shaken enterprise, perhaps he would, after all, have warmed to it. Maybe he would indeed have been glad to see the philosophically licensed 'hymns to the gods and paeans to good men' referred to in the *Republic* transcend their original grounding in utopian pathos of glory, so as to include works of real shaken, prophetic ambition.

But then again, on the other hand – maybe not.

Counting against this supposition is the specific role allotted to religious worship, more generally, in both the *Republic* and (still more) the *Laws*: which is so very much that of a bulwark against social chaos. In Plato's political vision the primary function of popular religion is, in effect, just to help convert the requirements of philosophy into the form of a sacralized sub-philosophical conventionality; taming the irrational masses. There is no space for any real pathos of shakenness in hymns and paeans meant to be part of *that* process.

Of course, there is much that might well be called 'poetic' in Plato's own writing: above all, his frequent use of myth. But what is the function of these myths? They are, so to speak, moments of relaxation in his dialogues. These dialogues are intended as models of good conversation – and good conversation, after all, requires a certain lightness of touch. Even the most dedicated philosopher needs an occasional intellectual break from pure concepts; from time to time one just has to shrug one's shoulders and turn aside from the all too strenuous business of philosophical dialectic. However, when Plato indulges in myth-making he is no longer trying to *persuade*. Far rather, he is providing a little bit of harmless half-philosophic entertainment, meant to be not so much persuasive as charming. What he decisively outlaws – what he means to ban when he speaks of banishing poetry – is any serious attempt at *persuasion by pathos,* in the way that Homer might be said to be a persuasive advocate of certain values. For him, the only valid form of persuasion is that of pure, pathos-free philosophy.[4]

IV

Actually, the Western philosophic tradition may well be said to have harboured a deep, implicit mistrust of poetry more or less from the outset. Plato simply brings it to the surface.[5] Thus, two hundred years previously, in the early to middle sixth century BCE, Thales of Miletus and his followers Anaximander and Anaximenes were not only the first philosophers; they were also pioneers of prose, as an altogether new species of literary form. Their invocation of the divine *logos* as their inspiration stood in direct opposition to the poets' invocation of the muses. Already at this stage, the elementary difference of philosophy from poetry – that is, the simple difference between philosophy as abstract doctrine, readily adaptable for reproduction in various different academic contexts, and poetry as a set of self-sufficient texts, meant to be recited and taken to heart – was, in itself, a source of rivalry; in that here were two distinct forms of literature competing with one another for sacred authority.

In Plato's thought, it is true, the conflict is especially sharpened by his more general polemic exalting conversational spontaneity over fixed texts of any kind, as the properly primary medium for truth. But, still, the basic issue remains: how to balance between the competing claims of, on the one hand, a discourse which essentially *evokes* and, on the other hand, one which essentially *analyses*. And Benda's self-perception, in this regard, as being a rather conservative upholder of traditional philosophic orthodoxy in general is by no means unjustified. No question about it, he does indeed seem to be drawing on some really quite deep-rooted prejudices.

As an anti-theologian within Christian culture, Benda is in fact an especial admirer not only of Plato, but also of Spinoza and of Kant: two thinkers who set out systematically to excise the element of poetry from biblical religion. So, by way of a follow-up to *La trahison des clercs*, in 1931 he published an essay on the concept of God which is largely Spinozist in character.[6] At other more agnostic moments he invokes Kant, almost as if there were no difference between the two.[7]

Elsewhere, though – in his earliest work, and again (curiously enough) in his later writings from the mid-1940s onwards – he grounds his culture-criticism in a rhetoric of full-blown positivism.[8]

Platonism in all its many guises, the Enlightenment thought of Spinoza and Kant, positivism: what Benda surely approves is just the underlying historic progression, of which these are the three main stages. For, after all, Plato's declaration of war on Homeric poetry did not prevent later generations of *clercs*, especially within Christendom, from attempting some sort of religious compromise between Platonist philosophy and poetry in another form, the poetry of Holy Scripture. Spinoza and Kant, then, represent a decisive rejection of any such compromise – ratcheting the conflict up one stage further. Yet, even so, they still remain in some sort of communication with the compromisers: they still speak affirmatively of 'God', albeit in radically de-poeticized fashion. The effect of positivism is finally to shut down even that residual level of communication. When the positivists speak of religious metaphysics as 'poetry' this has of course become for them an absolutely dismissive verdict. To call it 'poetry' is perhaps kinder than calling it outright 'nonsense'; but, given the positivists' view of poetry, only very marginally so. What else is positivism, in short, if not the old Platonic campaign against unregulated poetry carried to its ultimate all-embracing extreme?

In each case alike, however, I suspect it is the same: just as Benda openly confuses those particular forms of the pathos of glory he most wants to criticize with pathos in general, so too surely, at any rate deep down, do all these others.

The real target of Plato's polemic against Homer is the whole pathos of glory associated with the warrior-ethos of the traditional Greek ruling classes. And, in the same way, the positivists here are very much at one with Spinoza and Kant: in terms of its political origins, their whole project is primarily still intended as a strategy for undermining the pathos of glory associated with the *ancien régime* of Christendom; rubbishing that regime's pretended religious authority.

But none of them draws anything like the basic distinction that I want to draw, between the two species of pathos. And their whole approach is, I think, fundamentally vitiated by that failure.

V

The anti-theologians have sought to extend the ancient philosophical suspicion of poetry into a general mistrust of all pathos, including that of popular religion. True theology, I would suggest, needs to respond by way of an equally general differentiation between the two modes of pathos. That is to say, its proper task is to try to vindicate the pathos of shakenness, as opposed to the pathos of glory, just as much in its most free-spirited poetic form as in its most orthodox popular-religious one.

And yet the trouble is, it is not only the anti-theologians who have inherited, and dogmatically over-generalized, the old Platonic critique of poetry. The same philosophical prejudice seems to be equally deep-rooted *among the theologians themselves.*

Thus consider, for example, the very earliest work of self-styled 'theology' of which we have a few surviving fragments: the encyclopaedic pre-Christian survey of Roman paganism by Marcus Terentius Varro, *Antiquitates rerum humanarum et divinarum.*[9] Varro (116–27 BCE) was by general consent the greatest scholar of his age. His *Antiquitates* appears to have been both a work of meticulous scholarship and a polemical advocacy of religious piety, in all its forms, as an indispensable bulwark of social stability.

But, crucially, Varro was also a Platonist.

He constructs his book on the basis of a distinction that was already traditional in his day, between three types of god; or, more exactly – since the same names may be used for the gods in each category – between three types of 'theology': 'natural', 'civil' and 'mythic'. (Varro himself, it seems, attributed this scheme of things to the *pontifex maximus* Q. Mucius Scaevola, a teacher of the previous generation. Scaevola in his turn may well have derived it from the Stoic philosopher Panaetius of Rhodes, *c.* 180–110 BCE; or perhaps from Panaetius's pupil Posidonius. This, then, was the first properly 'theological' tradition.) 'Natural theology' deals with what philosophy has to tell us about the gods; 'civil theology' is a reflection on the actual religious practices of the general public – in so far as these might be regarded as being of concern to statesmen or political thinkers; 'mythic theology' is a critical commentary on what is mediated to us, religiously, through poetry and theatrical performances. As a theologian, Varro affirms the value of whatever is genuinely pious in each of these contexts. But as a Platonist philosopher, he is nevertheless quite clear that they represent three very different levels of divine truth. Natural theology is for him by far the highest. As for mythic theology, however: dealing with poetry, it can only ever be at best a rather modest salvage operation – seeking out the remote, faint echoes of truth in that which is, intrinsically, most false.

Such was the verdict of those who first conceived a systematic theology, already long before the rise of Christianity. Moreover, I am afraid to say that mainstream orthodox Christian theology has merely tended to perpetuate the same attitude; even to accentuate it.

One can see this very clearly illustrated by Augustine's extensive critique of Varro, in *The City of God*.[10] (That we know anything at all of Varro's work is in fact largely due to Augustine's polemic against it, some four and a half centuries after it was written; no independent text has survived.) Given the inevitable limitations of Varro's pagan perspective, Augustine argues, his basic error is that he is still not Platonist enough: in reality, of the three modes of piety Varro considers, only that which belongs to the domain of natural theology has any actual value whatsoever. The rest is mere dross. And the more seductive the blandishments of the poets in particular, the worse it becomes.

Varro tells us that 'we ought to cultivate the society of the philosophers more than that of the poets'. But this is much too weak a way of putting it, Augustine objects – inasmuch as it continues 'to imply that we should not *utterly shun* the society of the poets'![11] For Augustine, the good Christian theologian should pay heed only to the pagan philosophers; the pagan poets should be consigned to complete oblivion.

Of course, he is not talking about Christian poets. But if pagan poets are so much more objectionable, by virtue of their being poets, than pagan philosophers, then this surely does also imply a corresponding comparative evaluation of Christian poets and Christian philosophers. Augustine is not suggesting that we should shun the society of Christian poets; but, still, the clear implication is that theirs remains a rather minor vocation, by comparison to that of Christian philosopher-theologians.

There is, to be sure, great poetry in Holy Scripture: the poetry of the psalms and the *Song of Songs*; the quite extraordinarily ambitious poetry of the prophets. And is not Augustine himself an admirable appropriator of the poetic truth of Scripture, in his commentaries? He is actually one of the heroes of Paul Avis's recent polemical celebration of the poetic element in Christian tradition: the prime classical representative, for Avis, of a theology envisioning

God as poet.[12] Yet for Augustine – as for classical Christian theology in general – it is not that Scripture is true, in the first instance, *because of* the poetic power with which it articulates the pathos of shakenness. He does not celebrate such pathos in general, but only (in effect) its presence within Scripture; and although he certainly does appreciate that, it is only as a quite secondary reinforcement of the authority which Scripture primarily possesses just by virtue of its canonicity. What ultimately counts for him, in other words, is not any quality which the poetry of Scripture might conceivably have in common with other, non-canonical poetry – or even in the remotest sense, therefore, with pagan poetry.

Neither, therefore, does this poetry provide any precedent for future poetry with similar ambitions. On the road to the City of God poetry is relegated, after all, to a really very modest role. When certain early Christians did, in fact, begin to construct elaborate new poetic mythologies of their own they were immediately condemned as heretical 'Gnostics' for doing so, and expelled from the church. And when others – the Montanists, in the late second and third centuries – sought, without reference to any episcopal sanction, to revive the free poetic spirit of ancient Hebrew prophecy, the same thing happened.[13] Just as in Plato's utopia poetry appears to be reduced to the role of popularizing and embellishing the quite separately arrived-at prosaic insights of the philosophers, so too in the mainstream Catholic church, for which Augustine speaks: the Christian clergy have stepped straight into the censor role envisaged by Plato, for his philosopher-rulers. Such was the armature-logic of the early church's response to persecution: to give too much scope to the free play of the poetic imagination would have unacceptably endangered the strict, theologically policed unity of the church institution, thereby weakening its capacity to survive under pressure. And this armature-logic was then further reinforced by the influence of Platonist metaphysics, to become ingrained Christian instinct.

It is, I think, a fundamentally problematic instinct. For, as a result, theology is seduced into collusion with a species of prejudice which, consistently pursued, must in the end lead to its own downfall: if it survives, it does so only by means of a quite arbitrary, and to that extent untenable, exemption of its own canonical poetry from the general suspicion of all other poetry which it has come to share with hard-line Platonism.

VI

One of the most significant developments in later nineteenth- and twentieth-century philosophy – perhaps *the* most significant development, from a theological point of view – has actually been a great rebellion against Platonism, in precisely this regard.

The Romantic movement had already, it is true, produced various earlier theories of poetic truth, partly preparing the way. But really the two great pioneers here are, first, Nietzsche and then (again) Heidegger. Nietzsche indeed sees himself as turning the whole tradition of Western philosophy upside-down – the main justification for this claim being his decisive philosophical re-evaluation of poetic truth, as such. And Heidegger, from the 1930s onwards, likewise develops his doctrine of truth into a major enterprise of philosophical re-engagement with poetry; especially the poetry of Hölderlin. In this he is also, effectively, carrying forward the Nietzschean revolution, albeit by other means.

For Benda, Nietzsche was therefore one of the prime examples of 'the treason of the *clercs*'.

And yes – when one considers the remarkable popularity of Nietzsche's work (at least certain aspects of it) among the proto-fascist and fully fascist intellectuals of Benda's own day, one may well sympathize with this verdict. While as for Heidegger's notorious political misadventures: true enough, it would be difficult to conceive of any more powerful argument apparently in Benda's favour!

Yet once again, it seems to me that the basic weakness of both the Nietzschean and the Heideggerian approaches is just that neither of these thinkers – any more than their various opponents – has in fact properly distinguished between the pathos of shakenness and the pathos of glory.

VII

Thus, there is I think a profound ambivalence underlying Nietzsche's thought, as regards the very first principles of his 'revaluation of all values'.

To a large extent his governing concern appears to be with the promotion of the most searching sort of intellectual honesty. And in my view everything that is most genuinely challenging in his thought comes down to that. But then at other times it looks much more as though his governing concern was with the maximization of creative originality, or the most vital sort of 'life' in general – which unfortunately produces another altogether less discriminating set of criteria. Nietzsche's concern with intellectual honesty issues in a philosophical poetics dedicated to the most radical pathos of shakenness; his poetic cult of 'life', however, merely serves to blur the distinction between this and the pathos of glory.

For honesty's sake Nietzsche becomes an impassioned poetic celebrant of inner solitariness. One may well question the one-sidedness of the Nietzschean concept of honesty from this point of view, and his evident insensitivity to the demands of honesty in the owning of a *corporate* identity; nevertheless, it is clear that his whole concern here is with honesty. The solitariness his philosophical poetry celebrates is the necessary precondition for a truly uninhibited dissent from the unthinking conventionality of the human herd.

The essential dishonesty of the herd consists in its non-acknowledgement and effective concealment of its 'will to power'. But from the perspective of Nietzschean wisdom 'this world is the will to power – and nothing besides!'[14] In other words: just as natural science interprets physical events in terms of an analysis of interactive energies, so too with the proper philosophical interpretation of ethical and metaphysical ideas. Everything depends on grasping the hidden strategies involved, the interplay of undeclared motives. Most seriously dishonest of all, as Nietzsche sees it, is of course the self-deception of Christian 'slave morality', with its (he thinks) basic transmutation of resentment into ethics as a strategy of revenge. And the shakenness that most matters to him is therefore precisely shakenness out of the spirit of revenge: the shakenness involved in a discipline of truly all-encompassing world-affirmation – in poetic terms, willing without reservation that all that is should also recur eternally. For only so can every last impulse to moralized vengefulness at last be rooted out. Only the most thoroughgoing world-affirmer can be self-accepting enough not to need to lie. That, in briefest outline, is the underlying *honesty*-logic of Nietzsche's argument.

However, his cult of 'life' – in the sense of maximal creative originality – follows quite a different logic. With regard to honesty, Nietzschean wisdom is simply a matter of recognizing the operations of the will to power, where it is concealed; but under the guise of 'life' he also positively celebrates that will. He celebrates it not only at its most honest but also at its most *vital* – for that vitality's sake, in itself. And so he shifts over into celebrating *whatever* effectively transcends the ordinary conventions of the human herd.

This certainly includes the transcendent creativity of a radical honesty, in solitariness and uninhibited dissent. But at the same time it includes other forms of transcendent creativity which have little or nothing to do with honesty: the creativity of great aristocrats and rulers, disdainful of the herd certainly, but just by virtue of their power over it, and not because of its dishonesty.

Straight away, then, the pathos of shakenness blurs into the pathos of glory – and hence all those typical Nietzschean flourishes that so appealed to his fascist readers. He celebrates Napoleon, for instance, as a great 'synthesis of the *inhuman* and *superhuman*'.[15] But what does Napoleon have to do with intellectual honesty? Perhaps that is what Nietzsche means by calling him half-'inhuman'; in what sense, though, is he *also* supposedly half-'superhuman'? Evidently, in the sense that he was a 'great artist of government'.[16] Here we have pure pathos of glory. It is just this sort of aestheticizing attitude to politics which Benda, I think, is most justified in rejecting.

'Plato versus Homer: that', Nietzsche writes, 'is the complete, the genuine antagonism – there the sincerest advocate of the "beyond", the great slanderer of life; here the instinctive deifier, the *golden* nature'.[17] It is clear that Nietzsche himself is unreservedly on Homer's side. He makes no distinction between the pathos of shakenness and the pathos of glory: the fact that Homer's poetry is so overwhelmingly expressive of the latter rather than the former makes no difference to him. For, to his way of thinking, Homer stands for 'life'.

I am in complete agreement with Benda as regards his deep suspicion of this cult of 'life', as the primary source of all values.[18]

VIII

Heidegger, meanwhile, may be said to go beyond Nietzsche pragmatically in two key respects. In the first place, he makes a decisive separation between the Nietzschean polemic against Plato and the Nietzschean polemic against Christianity: taking up the former, bracketing the latter. Second, having himself experimented with the politics of the pathos of glory in a much more practical way than Nietzsche, he then repents of such politics.

In Heidegger's metahistory of Western philosophy, Nietzsche features as the 'last metaphysician'. This judgement has often been rejected as unfair.[19] Is it? I would say, both yes and no. Nietzsche is clearly not a metaphysician in his own sense of the term 'metaphysics'. And it is certainly arguable that Heidegger fails to do adequate justice to the special element of truth inherent in the Nietzschean critique of 'metaphysics'; his interpretation of the Nietzschean doctrines of 'nihilism', 'will to power' and 'eternal return' is extremely one-sided and questionable. But then – the Heideggerian sense of 'metaphysics' is, after all, quite different from the Nietzschean.

For Nietzsche 'metaphysics' appears to mean: dealing with onto-theological doctrines in terms of their overt intellectual content alone; taking them at face value as a source of comfort or moral vindication; and so failing to see their strategic role as expressions of the will to power.

For Heidegger, however, it simply means identifying the highest truth with particular onto-theological *decisions*, such as the decision for or against Christian faith. This is also the sense in which I am using the term.

Heidegger is a post-'metaphysical' thinker inasmuch as he identifies the highest truth not with any particular set of onto-theological decisions but precisely with a certain quality of poetic sensibility – a certain openness to the sublime, to 'Being' – more or less accessible, in principle, to the adherents of all different sorts of onto-theological doctrine. And in Heideggerian terms, the very fact of Nietzsche's sweeping polemical hostility to Christianity automatically renders him a 'metaphysician'.

That is to say, Heidegger is much more responsive than Nietzsche to the rich polyvalence and adaptability of any large-scale tradition like that of Christianity. In view of this, his thinking of 'Being' is premised on a strict bracketing of such 'metaphysical' questions as that of the general truth or untruth of Christian faith, in itself. Hence also his linguistic puritanism, discussed earlier: having bracketed 'metaphysical' debate, he then seeks, so far as possible, to exclude any use of vocabulary traditionally flavoured by it. In comparison to the distinction between true poetic sensibility and its opposite, he treats the distinction between Christian and non-Christian as something quite insignificant; and so the whole energy of his critique is directed against the Platonist mistrust of poetry, without any 'metaphysical' distraction in this sense. He speaks of 'the gods' as Hölderlin speaks of 'the gods': these 'gods' are essentially just so many diverse personifications of the spirit of poetic inspiration. But, as in Hölderlin's work, their relationship to the God of Christianity is left deliberately unclear.

There is an underlying political dimension to this: Nietzsche is much less concerned with the politics of the state than with his struggle against the values of the church; but Heidegger is interested in the possibilities of promoting a revolutionary new form of patriotism, a love of Germany fundamentally focused on its ideal character as 'a nation of thinkers and poets'.

In 1933–4 he dreamt that the Nazi revolution might be turned in this direction. For such purposes, the distinction between Christian and non-Christian was quite secondary. At this point, Heidegger's bid to transcend metaphysics fits directly into a political strategy of solidarity-building which is meant to cut right across all the old metaphysical boundaries. Part of the attraction of Nazism to him was clearly the way in which it was able to draw together churchpeople and unbelievers – Catholics, Protestants, atheists, romantic pagans – into a single overarching movement in which such metaphysical differences had, as it were, been strategically set aside, swallowed up into the new unity of the new 'Germany'. Of course, the intrinsic internationalism of the Catholic church stood opposed to this; and it is true that in the 1930s Heidegger did become quite fiercely anti-Catholic – in that regard. But only ever in that regard. He never had any objection to Catholicism, or any other metaphysical creed, so long as it remained a private affair, essentially peripheral to his trans-metaphysical ideal of 'Germany'.

Meanwhile, however, his subsequent critique of Nietzsche – developed in a sequence of lecture series starting in 1936 – also becomes, as he himself put it, a necessarily oblique 'argument with Nazism'.[20]

In these lecture series Heidegger is articulating, as best he can in the oppressive circumstances of the Third Reich, his recoil from the revolutionary political hopes he had himself entertained in 1933–4. Much of the oddity of his Nietzsche-interpretation in fact clearly derives from this context, and from the way he uses Nietzsche as a symbolic figure, projecting onto Nietzsche everything about the Nazi pathos of glory which had once attracted him but which he now rejects. This 'Nietzsche' – entirely the indiscriminate 'life'-affirmer, with his aggressive glorification of 'the will to power' manifested in great revolutionary deeds of Dionysian free-spiritedness – serves in effect as a representative for Heidegger himself, as he had been in 1933.

It is, crucially, in these lectures that the famous 'turn' in Heidegger's thinking takes place. The 'turn' originates out of his eventual revulsion against the vulgar Nazi pathos of glory; it is, in essence, an attempt to generalize the implications of that revulsion.[21]

And yet the trouble is that, even after the 'turn', he still does not reject the pathos of glory *as such*. For there is no turning here, even after 1945, towards an effective strategy of anti-politics corresponding to its opposite, the pathos of shakenness. He does not start to seek out new corporate loyalties, better expressive of the solidarity of the shaken. That would involve a different sort of immediate historical hope. But he appears, far rather, simply to have renounced all such hope.

What he has abandoned, in short, is not the pathos of glory, but just any immediate ambition to help give it a political embodiment; its conversion into a set of glorious actual promises. So he reconceives the ideal poetic sensibility, in quite a-political terms, as *Gelassenheit*, 'releasement': a wisdom of sheer aloof detachment – evidently, from politics and anti-politics alike.

IX

Of course, Heidegger's dalliance with politics was nothing but a disaster. And yet, at a pre-political – and pre-theological – level, I think he is fundamentally right in the sense of priorities leading him to attempt his move beyond (what he calls) 'metaphysics': his decisive prioritization of a 'post-metaphysical' philosophy's religious vocation both to acknowledge and, so far as possible, to draw upon the unique truth-potential of great poetry. At any rate to this extent, I wholeheartedly agree: we surely do need to get decisively beyond our traditional preoccupation with the supposed correctness or incorrectness of particular onto-theological decisions.

I do not think, though, that this necessarily requires us to follow him in his particular strategy of linguistic puritanism. Heidegger's puritanism certainly helps clarify matters. Yet it does so at the price of breaking off direct communion with church tradition, whose everyday language is such a complex mix of pre-metaphysical meaning with metaphysical over-tones. He sweeps the whole lot away in one grand revolutionary gesture: seeking from now on to speak of ultimate truth neither as unbeliever nor, however, as believer; but in another way. This gesture is very much part and parcel of the same prevailing revolutionary mood that – at quite another level – also issues in his disastrous weakness for the revolutionary rhetoric of the Nazis. Quixotically, Heidegger wanted to convert their revolution into a vehicle for his own. But what moral, then, should we draw from the story? Surely, it is a vivid cautionary tale about the dangers of such a revolutionary impulse – at *any* level. To affirm the truth of the pathos of shakenness is by no means the same thing as to advocate revolution; either politically or in terms of philosophic style. It does not necessarily mean stepping right out of the church's theological tradition, in Heideggerian fashion. One can still remain inside the tradition: strug-gling with the manifold ambiguities of its language, in order to try to open it up. And that, in my view, is the wiser way.

In other words, I agree with Heidegger: it matters far less than is commonly supposed to which particular religious, or irreligious, camp one adheres. What really matters is just that one should be maximally alert to whatever stirrings of poetic truth one may encounter – *from whatever quar-ter*. But I also want to argue, against Heidegger, that everything, in this regard, depends upon our drawing the very sharpest distinction between the pathos of glory and the pathos of shakenness; and that, ideally, we also need to stay as well rooted and engaged within existing theological tradition as we possibly can, in order to pursue this distinction. Because otherwise one risks confusing the difference between 'shakenness' and 'glory' with the very different difference between a (glorious!) revolutionary vanguard and its obscurantist opponents.

In terms of Varro's 'tri-partite theology', all my previous writing has dealt essentially with the interplay between 'natural theology' and 'civil theology'. Here, by contrast, I am engaged in the business of what Varro terms 'mythic theology'. Yet, quite unlike Varro's own form of 'mythic theology', this is intended very much as a systematically post-metaphysical exploration of the pathos of shakenness. It is an investigation of religious truth, fundamentally understood as the *popularization* of such pathos; which therefore begins from great poetry, as the very purest expression of that which is then to be popularized.

Heidegger for his part uses the term 'theology' only to designate a particular sort, or aspect, of metaphysics. But this I think is a much too confining usage. I would prefer to define *true* theology quite simply as:

any form of thought, in so far as it is directed towards the historic self-definition of an authentically faith-based community – where 'authentically faith-based' means one in which the pathos of shakenness can (so to speak) be fully at home.

Hence it becomes the specific task of true 'mythic theology' to try to help provide a proper home – in the actual prayer-life of a substantial community – for the otherwise homeless God of the most shaken poetry, as such.

Part II
Case studies

5   The heritage of Amos

I

To recapitulate: I am writing here as a theologian, committed to church tradition; yet with a particular interest in the reform of popular liturgical practice.

Negatively, the reform I envisage would be an attempt to purge popular liturgy of its traditional admixture of the pathos of glory: whether this be pathos in the service of a secular ideology of rule, or that which serves the immediate self-interest of a ruling elite within the church itself. Or, indeed, both.

At the same time, it would also be a bid to maximize the influence of the pathos of shakenness. I have defined this in terms of three key identifying marks: first, a radical calling into question of establishment-mindedness, in general; second, a restless intensity of concern – the exact opposite to easy agnosticism; and third, an essential generosity of spirit, unconfined by any sort of revolutionary or sectarian regimentation. For my argument is that establishment-mindedness, easy agnosticism and polemical regimentation represent the (anti-Trinitarian) triangular three corners of the fallen '*basileia* of this world'.

What would a liturgy entirely converted from the pathos of glory to the pathos of shakenness actually look like? I do not know. This is an ideal, in principle, only arrivable at by way of a long process of practical experimentation.

However, my aim in what follows is to try to do some of the necessary theoretical spadework in preparation for that experimentation-process; calling on certain works of great poetry, illustrative of the pathos of shakenness at its most profound, for assistance.

And so – where should we begin?

My proposal is that we should begin right at the beginning! Let us start by trying to trace the literary history of such pathos all the way back to its remotest origins. One of the very earliest surviving poetic expressions of something like the pure pathos of shakenness, arguably the earliest of all in fact, is to be found in the book of the Hebrew prophet Amos.

II

The superscription to this book gives us its approximate date:

> [These are] the words of Amos – who was one of the sheep-raisers from
> Tekoa – who had visions concerning Israel in the days of Uzziah the
> king of Judah, and in the days of Jeroboam ben-Joash the king of Israel,
> two years before the earthquake.[1]

The prophecies themselves were probably delivered separately over a period
of several years; 'two years before the earthquake' is most likely when they
were collected together into a single document. We do not know exactly
when the earthquake in question occurred, but we do know when kings
Uzziah and Jeroboam reigned: Uzziah was king of the southern Hebrew
kingdom of Judah from around 792 BCE to around 740 BCE, and Jeroboam
was king of Israel in the north from around the same time, or possibly a bit
later, for some forty-one years. A subsequent reference to Ben-Hadad king
of Damascus, as still being in power, suggests a date some time between 780
and 770 BCE.[2]

To give some sense of inter-cultural synchronicity: we do not know
exactly when Homer lived, but Amos may quite possibly have been a
contemporary of Homer's grandparents. (Not that he has anything in
common with Homer, spiritually.)

Amos was the first of the great Hebrew poet-prophets whose works have
been preserved. This is, in that sense, the first book of the Bible; there are
older fragments in some of the other books, but Amos was the first one
largely written as we now have it. The Bible *opens* with an earthquake!

Tekoa, the town from which he came, lay south of Jerusalem in the kingdom of Judah. His vocation, though, took him north, to denounce the
corruption of the ruling class in the kingdom of Israel.

It was a period when the smaller nations of the region actually enjoyed a
considerable degree of independence from the great imperial powers of
Assyria and Egypt. Some thirty or so years later there began to emerge a
renewed threat from Assyria. But in Amos's day Uzziah and Jeroboam,
apparently operating as allies, were both winning victories and annexing
new territories. There is every reason to suppose that the economy was, on
the whole, prospering. And yet the oracles of Amos speak of imminent
doom, nothing less than the destruction of the whole nation, in punishment
for its sins.

It has been argued by Andersen and Freedman that one can trace a
distinct progression in Amos's prophecy. Thus, there are five symbolic
visions briefly recounted in Chapters 7–9. The first two – a vision of a

locust swarm and a vision of showers of fire – represent threats of all-encompassing retribution from which, following the prophet's intercession, Yahweh/God desists. These, it is suggested, belong to the earliest stage of Amos's mission – in which he still held fast to some hope of corporate repentance and future divine blessing for the repentant Israel, a hope also registered for instance in the oracle of 5: 14–15. Andersen and Freedman further associate this with the drought, famine and plagues reported in 4: 6–11; understood as warnings.[3]

But those warnings were not heeded. So the next three visions – of a plumb-line, of ripe summer fruit, and of an earthquake – proclaim an exasperated, and now irreversible, divine intention to bring about the catastrophe which had previously only been conditionally threatened: 'the end for my people Israel' (8: 2).

Finally there comes a great dramatic showdown, recorded in 7: 10–17, with the high priest Amaziah, in the great shrine of the northern kingdom at Bethel. 'O seer', says Amaziah, 'go, run away to the land of Judah. Eat your food there, and there do your prophesying. But at Bethel never prophesy again, because it is the king's chapel, it is a royal temple.'

Whereupon Amos replies:

> I was no prophet, nor was I trained as a prophet, but I am a cattleman and a dresser of sycamores. And Yahweh took me from following the flock. And Yahweh said to me: 'Go prophesy to my people Israel.' Now hear Yahweh's word! You say,
> 'Don't prophesy against Israel,
>   and don't preach against Isaac's domain!'
> Yahweh, on the contrary, has said the following:
> 'Your wife shall become a prostitute in the city,
>   and your sons and your daughters shall fall by the sword;
>   and your land shall be parcelled out by the measuring line;
>   and you yourself shall die in a polluted land;
>   and Israel shall surely go into exile from its land.'

What happened afterwards is not recorded. But one may well imagine that Amos was arrested and silenced, if not put to death; especially in view of his prophecy of an imminent violent end for King Jeroboam himself (7: 11).[4]

III

The book of Amos may be said to represent the primary 'axial' moment in the history of Hebrew religion.

I use the word 'axial' here the way that Karl Jaspers uses it when he speaks of the 'axial period' of world history.[5] This concept of the 'axial period' is clearly crucial for the future of inter-cultural religious conversation. For now, at the beginning of the third Christian millennium, we are just beginning to witness a great drawing-together of all the major religious traditions of the world into a single all-encompassing conversation-process. It is like a tremendous confluence of rivers. But in order systematically to understand all of what this confluence involves we need to trace each river back to its earliest sources. And by the 'axial period' is meant the whole historic span of those sources.

Not all sacred traditions, however, have this river-like quality. A river presses on towards a distant goal. The great cultural rivers flowing from the axial period are all of them movements of fundamental, ongoing *discontent* with the established order, or customary practices, of the present. The axial period is, essentially, the period of the birth of that fluent discontent.

We surely need some decisive linguistic marker for the resulting transformation. My own proposal is that we should press into service for this purpose the old distinction between 'religion' and 'magic': what the 'axial period' inaugurates, I want to say, is precisely 'religion'. Before the axial period there was – and outside its rivers, there still is – strictly speaking, no religion. There was only, in a broad sense, 'magic'.

Thus: religion (so defined) is built around a concern for salvation, or enlightenment. It is all about a perception of society as being pervasively corrupt, and about aspirations for its thoroughgoing amendment; or, at any rate, the rescuing of as many individuals as possible from it. Prior to the breakthroughs of the axial period – and still to this day in cultures not yet affected by the impulses stemming from those breakthroughs – there was and is none of that. Within the world of magic, sacred ritual does not in any very radical way challenge the prevailing social norms; it is simply an integral part of them. Societies dedicated to magic may indeed become the scene of power struggles, with the devotees of one god pitched against the devotees of another (as in Akhenaten's Egypt, for example). But the struggle is still largely confined to the context of palace intrigue, a channel for the rivalry between competing groups of courtiers, not much more. The rituals of magic serve to articulate, and cater to, the deepest concerns of people who are preoccupied with the demands of sheer survival, the mere pursuit of health and prosperity. Notwithstanding all their extensive differences from one another, what all the great post-axial cultures fundamentally have in common is their opening up to another level of desire, altogether beyond this. And hence their intrinsic restlessness, their perpetual motion, their river-likeness.

There are, then, five main rivers of religious tradition in the world:

1   The river which first emerges into the clear light of day with Amos and the other, subsequent eighth-century BCE Hebrew poet-prophets: Hosea, Isaiah, Micah.

2   The Zoroastrian river, arising out of ancient Persian culture, may be older; even much older. Or it may be younger. The fact is, we simply do not know the dates of Zarathustra.

3   The originally Indian river can be traced back on the one hand to the *Upanishads*, the oldest of which also belong to the eighth century BCE; and on the other hand to Siddharta Gautama, the Buddha, *c.* 563–483 BCE.

4   The originally Greek river is traceable back at least as far as Pythagoras, who lived *c.* 580–504 BCE; although of course its chief formative writings are the dialogues of Plato, 427–347 BCE.

5   The originally Chinese river begins with Confucius, 551–479 BCE, and with the *Tao Te Ching*, which probably dates back to the fourth century BCE.

The primary texts of the axial period itself embody the distinctive genius of each of these traditions in its most elementary form. That is to say: it is, above all, in studying this literature that we are brought face to face with the most far-reachingly decisive contrasts between the five traditions, considered as organic wholes.

Within Hebrew culture the followers of the eighth-century prophets projected their own religious concerns right back onto the remote origins of their people. So they pictured Moses as a great religious leader, driven by a deep religious concern that the Israelites should worship their own God, Yahweh, and none other besides, in token of their absolute cultural otherness from their neighbours. To be honest, it remains quite unclear whether or not there is anything more to this picture than the workings of back-projection; but at all events, the fact is, there is very little evidence of any religion – in the strict sense – at work in Israel during the centuries immediately preceding Amos. In Judges 2: 10, where the historian is linking up his material about later history to the stories of Moses and Joshua, he is obliged to speak rather abruptly of the people, from one generation to another, forgetting what Moses and Joshua are said to have taught. The religious group to which the author of Kings belonged remembered the mid-ninth-century prophets Elijah and Elisha as heroic revivers of what had supposedly thus been forgotten. To what extent, though, was their struggle against the priests of Ba'al Melqart *in actual fact* anything more than a simple, unreligious matter of one aristocratic faction, with a particular affinity for one set of magic rituals, fighting for its privileges over against another, preferring a rival sort of magic? Again, it is hard to say. There is a hint in Amos 2: 12 that the prophet himself felt he had predecessors among the Nazirites: a community of teetotal rigorists, bound together by a set of regulations set out in Numbers 6: 1–21.[6] But all we actually know about the Nazirites are these regulations. We have no evidence as to the thinking behind them: that is, whether they really did have a properly religious vision for the reform of society as a whole, or whether perhaps they merely saw themselves as a little elite set apart with special magic powers.

When it comes to the eighth-century literature, however, there can be no question: what emerges here is a decisively religious challenge to established social norms.

Of all the great axial revolutions, indeed, the Hebrew one is by far the most pathos-laden. Its literature is the most dramatic, the most furious, the most full of grief. But these are very much the sorts of impulse that most of all require a poetic form of expression to convey them. So that, it seems, this is also the axial revolution which more than any other depended on the genius of its poets, beginning with Amos.

It is from that point of view the exact opposite to the Greek axial revolution, mediated by the largely anti-poetic spirit of classical philosophy. And there is a sense in which the whole energy of early Christian theology derived from its systematic attempt to reconcile these two opposites.

In the utterances of the eighth-century Hebrew prophets, as a whole, we encounter poetry, for the first time, pushed to something like the highest pitch of religious intensity – the intensity of a great breakthrough moment.

IV

This is by no means to say that each of these prophecies is an equally pure expression of the pathos of shakenness. They are not.

There is in particular, I think, quite a sharp contrast here between Amos and Hosea.

Yahweh, the God of Israel, had always it seems been a rather solitary god in the pantheon of Palestinian polytheism, lacking any kinship relationship to the other gods. This solitariness was no doubt a crucial factor in facilitating an axial revolution which involved his being conceived quite differently from other gods. For Hosea however, unlike Amos, the separateness of Yahweh from other gods becomes the whole point *in itself*. Thus, what the Yahweh of Amos's prophecy demands above all is 'justice' (*tsedaqah*): an absolute transformation in the relationship between rich and poor. And 'justice' is also the chief demand in the southern-kingdom prophecies of Isaiah and Micah, after Amos. But in Hosea's prophecy the primary issue is rather a cultic one: what Yahweh is demanding is that his people should abandon the worship of other gods.

There is nothing about such cultic reform in the book of Amos. Nor is there anything about 'justice' in the book of Hosea.

Hosea was a prophet of the northern kingdom who flourished probably some decades after Amos. By contrast to Amos's day, this was a period of growing threat from Assyria; which a few years later, in 724–721 BCE, was to culminate in the invasion and final conquest of that kingdom. For many centuries (at least) the Hebrew people, in general, had combined the worship of Yahweh with that of other gods and goddesses: including the national deities of other peoples; the 'Queen of Heaven', particularly important to women; and various deities associated with sacred trees and pillars. Hosea's rejection of this, his campaigning 'Yahweh-aloneism', is perhaps best understood as a sort of emergency-response to the new threat, an attempt morally to fortify Israel's resistance to the Assyrians.[7]

Apart from the Moses-story (which in this particular regard may be little more than the product of post-Hoseanic back-projection) there is no clear evidence of anyone before Hosea ever having been so radically Yahweh-aloneist.[8] As I have said, Elijah's Yahweh-aloneist struggle – a little over a century earlier – had in the first instance simply concerned the cultic practices of the royal court. But Hosea, for his part, is concerned with the cultic practices of the whole people. And by virtue of this, he becomes as it were a sort of Karl Marx figure, above all as an inspiration to the revolutionary Deuteronomist movement which finally came to power in the southern kingdom a little over a century later, in the year 622.

Like Amos, Hosea is a poet of great passion. As the mouthpiece of Yahweh, he denounces Israel's worship of other gods, or Baals, as a form of 'adultery' or 'prostitution'. This is symbolically related to the adulterousness of the prophet's own 'prostitute' wife (1: 2–9; 3: 1–5).[9] The prophet is urged to denounce his 'mother', Israel:

'I am going to court my lovers', she said
'who give me my bread and water,
my wool, my flax, my oil and my drink.'
She would not acknowledge, not she,
that I was the one who was giving her
the corn, the wine, the oil,
and who freely gave her that silver and gold
of which they have made Baals.
(Hosea 2: 5, 8)[10]

Israel, in other words, has been seduced by the promises of magic fertility-cults, to bring prosperity; whereas in reality the nation's whole prosperity depends upon its unity, which ideally requires the strictest possible religious expression from, and reinforcement by, the exclusive worship of Yahweh.

Again, as in the prophecy of Amos, this message is backed up by terrible warnings of impending doom. And no doubt the catastrophe of 724–721 was widely seen as the fulfilment of these warnings, and hence as a decisive vindication of Hosea's prophetic authority.

But note how much better suited this rhetoric is to an actual political movement, aiming at the seizure of governmental power, than is Amos's. The pathos of shakenness in Amos's prophecy is essentially bound up with the sheer *infinitude* of the aspirations he is articulating. Amos has no partic- ular interest in promoting the cult of Yahweh, at the cultic level, as does Hosea. On the contrary. According to Amos, Yahweh says to his people:

> I detest, I loathe your festivals,
>   I have no satisfaction in your solemn gatherings.
> Whatever you sacrifice to me
>   – your burnt offerings and gifts –
>   I cannot accept
>   – your peace offerings and fat cattle –
>   I cannot approve.
> Take your loud songs away from me!
>   I won't listen to your instrumental music.
> But let justice roll on like the ocean,
>   and equity like a perennial stream.
>
>   (Amos 5: 21–4)

Amos's ideal is 'justice'. And 'justice' is infinite, an ideal that can never finally be defined or achieved.

Hosea's ideal, on the other hand, is finite, and perfectly achievable. All that is required in this case is the abandonment of a certain quite specific set of ritual practices, and the preservation of others. Immediately, that provides the necessary programme around which to build a political strat- egy. The concept of Israel's covenant with Yahweh plays a key role in Hosea's thought – a concept which Amos, by contrast, never deploys. Israel's 'adultery' consists in her abandonment of the covenant, sealed at the time of the exodus. But the concept of a covenant provides exactly the sort of format needed for the self-definition of a religious party, intent on setting out its aims and objectives; as the various Yahweh-aloneist revolutionary groups behind the compilation of the books of Exodus, Leviticus, Numbers and Deuteronomy then proceeded to do.

Inasmuch as Yahweh-aloneism was a movement aiming at the revolution- ary seizure of power, the typical pathos of its literature is overwhelmingly pathos of glory. It is the pathos of glory in its most priestly form: an insistence on the proper glory of a separated people; a glorification of pioneering zealots – and of rulers who, in the formula of the Deuteronomic editor of the books of Kings, 'did what was right in the eyes of Yahweh'. The pathos in the poetry of Amos is quite different.

In terms of the three defining marks of the pathos of shakenness, set out earlier: both prophets are equally anti-establishment and impassioned; but when it comes to the third mark – the issue of sectarian or revolutionary regimentation – there could scarcely be a greater contrast. Hosea is a major contributor to the founding of quite a regimented movement; Amos simply is not. It is true, Amos must have had some followers, to preserve his prophecy after his death. Nevertheless, in the larger history of his people, he appears to have been a much more isolated figure than Hosea. Isaiah and Micah were evidently kindred spirits, belonging to the next generation. But there was nothing in Amos's teaching for an actual party to rally round and develop, in the way that the Deuteronomists and others were able to rally round and develop Hosea's Yahweh-aloneism.

As I have said, what we have here is far rather the pure pathos of shakenness; quite uncompromised by the demands of revolutionary agitprop. Amos himself makes it perfectly clear in his response to Amaziah: he prophesies only because he is compelled to – that is, by virtue of his shakenness. He was not born to the task; he was 'a cattleman and dresser of sycamores'. But Yahweh took him from following the flock, and said, 'Go prophesy to my people Israel'. Nor is there any element of political hope, or therefore political calculation involved. For by now his prophetic inspiration tells him that it is already too late. In Chapter 3, verses 3–8, we encounter a curious little sequence of riddles, which appear to be images for Amos's own prophetic vocation:

Do two go together, [he asks]
    unless they have arranged [or it has been arranged for them] to meet?

The 'two' in question, it seems, are prophecy and disaster, brought together by divine decree. Thus:

Does a lion roar in the forest,
    if it has no prey?
Does a young lion thunder from its lair
    unless it has seized [a victim]?
Does a bird alight upon a ground trap,
    if there is no lure for it?
Does a trap spring up from the ground,
    except to make a capture?

The point is: Amos's prophecy is like the lion's roar, or the sound of the trap springing shut. It is too late for the victim. The pathos of shakenness is not always a pathos of despair like this – but such despair is at any rate certainly quite incompatible with any pathos of glory. The pathos of glory feeds off vivid political hopes, for the triumph of one's party.

Amos despairs of ever actually persuading his people. And yet – even though, in his despair, he thinks it will make no difference:

> The lion has roared:
>   who is not frightened?
> My Lord Yahweh has spoken;
>   who could not prophesy?

V

Plainly, Amos's prophecy is not true in quite the way that it purports to be true, itself.

In general, the spirit of the great prophets whose poetry is preserved in the Hebrew scriptures is a profoundly religious spirit, expressed however in a form deriving from the older culture of magic. And the result, it seems to me, is a persistent mismatch between the deeper truth of these prophecies and their actual expression.

For they assume the form of oracles.

'I was no prophet', Amos says to Amaziah. 'I was no *nābî*, nor was I a *ben-nābî*' – which may mean something like an apprentice *nābî*, or else the member of a *nābî*-community. And perhaps the translation should actually be : 'I *am* no *nābî*'. In Hebrew it is ambiguous. At all events, he is protesting that he is not the sort of *nābî* Amaziah supposed him to be. Certainly, he is quite different from any conventional *nābî*. Thanks to the tradition inaugurated by Amos, the word 'prophet' has acquired, for us, a powerfully religious flavour. But in that context the *nābî* was essentially a practitioner of magic: a holy man supposedly gifted with magic insight into the future.

Nevertheless, like a conventional *nābî*, Amos utters oracles. He adopts the familiar form of *nābî*-magic – and converts it into a vehicle for his new, no longer magic, but religious purposes. It is, after all, only natural to begin by adapting what is familiar.

But in doing so here, the trouble is, he appears to be submitting his message to just the same sort of criterion that the practitioners of magic ask to be judged by, in their predictions of the future: did things, in actual fact, turn out as he foretold? And the simple answer has to be that no, they did not. True, in his fifth prophetic vision (Amos 9: 1–4) he speaks (metaphorically?) of a great earthquake; and, as we learn in 1: 1, not long afterwards an earthquake did occur – a moderately impressive coincidence, perhaps. Apart from this, however, it seems that not one of Amos's predictions was fulfilled.

So he predicted imminent military defeat for Israel, with heavy casualties, the sacking of fortresses, the destruction of palaces and sanctuaries, including the one at Bethel, and the sending into exile of the ruling classes; as well as, more specifically, the death of king Jeroboam 'by the sword'. None of these things happened. On the contrary: for several decades immediately thereafter Israel thrived, and Jeroboam lived on to a ripe old age, before finally dying in peace. Nor does it seem that any of the colourful disasters prophesied for the high priest Amaziah and his family ever materialized – for we would surely have been informed if they had. They would have been such remarkable events.

Indeed the Deuteronomistic historian of 2 Kings proceeds to rub the point in, with what looks very much like a polemical attack on the later admirers of Amos. Thus, in Amos 6: 14 it is prophesied that 'the house of Israel' will be overpowered 'from the gateway of Hamath as far as the Wadi Arabah'. The historian picks up this distinctive phrase – which is really rather a sweeping geographical flourish. What happened, he says, was the exact opposite: 'from the gateway of Hamath to the Wadi Arabah' Jeroboam gained territory (2 Kings 14: 25). Amos is not mentioned here by name, but the allusion is nevertheless unmistakable. It seems the prophet Jonah had prophesied against Amos: urging that, notwithstanding the temporary 'bitter affliction' of the people (with the plagues referred to in Amos 4: 6–11?), after all, 'Yahweh had *not* threatened to blot out the name of Israel from under heaven' (2 Kings 14: 26–7). And – as this historian is keen to underline – it was the more optimistic Jonah, not Amos, who was proved right.[11]

One might compare these unfulfilled prophecies of Amos with Micah's equally unfulfilled prophecy of the imminent destruction of the Jerusalem temple (Micah 3: 12). A hundred years after Micah's prophecy the temple was still standing, undamaged. And yet his admirers had a very simple explanation of why this was so. It is explicitly spelled out in Jeremiah 26: 17–19: shocked by Micah's words, it was said, the good king Hezekiah and his people had repented of their sins, and so Yahweh changed his plan. But in Amos's case, by contrast, this sort of argument was impossible. For Amos, at any rate in the later part of his career, made it quite plain that, while Yahweh had indeed pulled back from certain earlier planned disasters, from now on there was to be no turning back. The first two visions of Chapter 7 show Yahweh relenting: faced first with the threat of locusts and then with the threat of fire, the prophet pleads, 'My Lord Yahweh, please forgive, please desist! How can Jacob survive, as he is so small?' – and Yahweh grants his petition. However, when it comes to the third and fourth visions, the period of grace is over. And now Yahweh says: 'The end is coming for my people Israel; I shall never spare them again'.

The catastrophe, irrevocably promised here, did not come; at least not for half a century or so, far longer than anyone could have supposed to be intended. With so much evidence of his failure as a forecaster of the future, one may therefore well wonder why Amos's prophecy was preserved at all. Yet it was. The words of Jonah, whose prediction was proved true, were forgotten; Jonah is remembered only thanks to one fleeting reference in the Deuteronomistic history, and then a much later, not very flattering legend which somehow got attached to his name. But the words of Amos, who was so comprehensively proved wrong, were treasured, presumably by a little group of devotees; written down, copied and kept – at length to take their place as part of the sacred canon. Clearly there were at least some people, right from a very early stage, who did not regard accuracy of prediction as the be-all and end-all of prophetic truth. To say the least!

In a magic culture, what other criterion for the truth of oracles could there be?

None.

But in an emergent religious context a new sort of criterion has just started to appear. Largely devoid as it is of any claim to truth in magic terms, the truth of Amos's prophecy is a purely religious one. And that religious truth surely consists, essentially, in its poetic quality. Or, as I would like to say: its sheer *imaginative invocation of shaking-power.*

By 'shaking-power' here I mean the power of certain experiences to shake one out of one's old unquestioned prejudices, into new thoughtfulness; compelling a fundamental re-evaluation of the whole value-system by which one lives. An individual may be provoked into such a re-evaluation by an experience of severe illness perhaps, or bereavement, anything tending to issue in a heightened sense of his or her own mortality. A community of people, or a cultural group, may likewise be inspired by some great collective experience of misfortune, which disturbs their settled ways. In short, it requires a crisis: either an actual crisis, or if not that, then at least a vividly-imagined potential crisis. The properly religious process is always a process of conversion. And without an urgent sense of crisis, whether personal or public, that process can scarcely get going.

Amos, for his part, simply deploys all the poetic resources at his command to evoke the most urgent possible sense of public crisis, in order that this may shake his hearers out of their moral inertia. He wants 'justice': that is, for the rich and powerful radically to reconsider their treatment of the poor and powerless. And so, as a first step, he seeks to force the powerful rich to imagine themselves defeated and despoiled, rendered suddenly destitute by the triumph of invading armies, led away captive. His aim, at the deepest level, is just to shake them imaginatively out of their comfortable sense of who and what they are; and, in that sense, to make them think. To underline the urgency of so doing, he insists that all these things are in actual fact soon going to happen. But even though this prediction was misguided as a straightforward prediction, the underlying truth of the imaginative exercise, in itself, nevertheless remains.

The book of Amos is thus a great poem of rage – and of 'mourning'. The prophet pronounces woe:

> Woe to you who luxuriate in Zion,
> and [woe] to you who feel secure in Mount Samaria . . .
> [Woe] to you who rush along toward the day of calamity,
>   who draw ever nearer to the reign of lawlessness!
> [Woe] to those who lie on beds of ivory,
>   who sprawl upon their couches;
> and [woe] to those who devour lambs from the flock,
>   and calves from the stall.
> [Woe] to those who improvise on the lyre
>   – like David –
>   who compose for their pleasure on musical instruments!
> [Woe] to those who drink from basins of wine,
>   who anoint themselves with the best oils!
>   They are not distressed at Joseph's crash.
> Now indeed they shall go
>   at the head of those who go into exile,
> they shall depart,
>   these sprawling 'mourners'.
>
>   (Amos 6: 1–7)

The banquet described here turns out at the end to be taking place in the community house of a funerary association: it is a feast for the dead. What the prophet is advocating is a mourning of repentance. But *here* we have a 'mourning' of pure revelry.

Again, the image of the 'sprawling' revellers is also echoed in another passage. A catastrophe is coming, Yahweh declares, when:

> Just as a shepherd rescues from the mouth of a lion
>   two legs or a piece of an ear,
> in the same way shall the Israelites be rescued –
>   those who dwell in Samaria –
>   only the corner of a bed –
>   only a fragment of couch-cushion(?).
>
>   (Amos 3: 12)

These are poignant relics from the wreckage of banqueting halls.

Or, to take another example: Amos imagines a vivid scene, probably of plague in a besieged city, where two men go into a house to bring out the dead. An eerie conversation then ensues, with one man calling out to the other, searching at the far end of the house, 'Have you found anyone alive?' 'No one.' And then the first one says, 'Silence! For we must not invoke Yahweh's name' (Amos 6: 9–10).[12] In the same way that Yahweh rejects any sacrifice offered him, until there is justice, so it seems that in this crisis there can be none of the customary funeral rites; no invocation of Yahweh's name, in any prayer for the dead. In the face of such a disaster the survivors are reduced to stunned silence. No conventional response is any longer possible.

Amos's great discovery, it seems to me, is his transfiguring perception of the way in which such moments of horror may also serve as moments of revelatory truth.

VI

In one way or another it is perhaps always the case that the pathos of shakenness begins with a general sense of danger. The more acute the sense of danger, the more immediately it issues in a heightened awareness of the contingency of the present moral order as a whole – thereby opening up the distant prospect of radically different *better* alternatives, also. Without some accompanying intimation of danger in the present drift of things, the radical reformer's dreams of a better future can scarcely acquire sufficient urgency to be effective.

And certainly one finds a similar sense of danger in Hosea. Whereas, however, Hosea mixes the pathos of shakenness with the pathos of glory, Amos represents the pathos of shakenness in far purer form.

The great Hebrew prophet-poets are all of them, in fact, wrestlers with the implications of urgent communal danger. Whether it be the initial danger of crushing military defeat and the destruction of the nation, as in the oracles of these eighth-century pioneers, or, as is increasingly the case later on, the danger of collective despair after such disasters have actually occurred, in either case the prophets are preoccupied with the potential impact of catastrophe on the ritual life of their community. There are, one might say, three different levels of potential impact here. People may opt for apostasy: symbolically abandoning an identity which no longer seems to offer them anything but humiliation. This is the most superficial sort of response. Or else they may opt for a simple intensification of their custom-ary ritual piety; in effect, as a way of huddling together for mutual comfort. But what the prophets demand is a third way, one involving a decisive qualitative transformation in the whole *ethos* underlying the ritual. The

Yahweh-aloneists polemically uphold this third way, above all, against the first temptation, that of apostasy. Amos, by contrast, upholds it – I would argue, in an altogether more thought-provoking fashion – against the second temptation, that of a merely comforting piety.

Thus, within a magic culture there are (again one might say) two main forms of comforting piety: sacrifice and spells. The practice of sacrifice in this context is designed to achieve a comforting sense of atonement between the individual and society; or rather between the individual and God, inasmuch as God is conceived as the ultimate upholder of society's interests over against those of the individual. It is a device for dealing with one's own anti-social impulses – not by confronting and thoughtfully working through the ethical issues that they raise, but instead by just magicking them away. And so one symbolically projects all such impulses onto a sacrificial victim, who is then ritually thrown out or slaughtered; or at least some token representative of a victim.[13]

The casting of spells, on the other hand, provides a comforting denial of the actual reality of one's powerlessness in the face of uncontrollable events.

Amos, however, shows us Yahweh flatly rejecting the sacrifices which are offered to him:

> Whatever you sacrifice to me
> – your burnt offerings and gifts –
>   I cannot accept
> – your peace offerings and fat cattle –
>   I cannot approve . . .
> But let justice roll on like the ocean,
> and equity like a perennial stream.
>   (Amos 5: 22, 24)

We have in these verses the first intimations of a completely new insight into the intrinsic tension between sacrifice and true justice.[14] At the same time, the images of justice rolling on like the ocean, equity like a perennial stream, may well in fact be meant to echo the magic spells of a rain-making liturgy – in profoundly satirical fashion. For the whole thrust of this call to justice is of course precisely to turn sacred ritual away from a magical yearning to control the uncontrollable, as in a rain-making liturgy; and to reorient it, instead, towards a disciplined acceptance of responsibility, on the part of the rich and powerful, for what they undoubtedly *do* control. So Yahweh rejects both sacrifices and spells.

In a similar way, Amos also mimics what looks very like a conventional call to prayer, only to invert it. 'Come to Bethel', or 'come to Gilgal' – one can well imagine the call to prayer beginning – 'and do your duty to Yahweh'. Bethel and Gilgal were the great pilgrimage shrines, to which people from the whole of Israel would come for annual three-day festivals, of national and individual thanksgiving. But Amos, with bitter irony, converts this call to dutiful obedience into its opposite: in reality, he suggests, under cover of prayer what is being called for is nothing but – *rebellion*. That is, rebellion against Yahweh. So he cries:

> Come to Bethel
>   and *rebel* at Gilgal
>   – *rebel* repeatedly!
> Bring your sacrifices for the morning,
>   your tithes for the third day;
> Burn sacrifices without leaven,
> Thank-offerings – and announce
> Freewill offerings – proclaim.
>   For that's what you love, O Israelites –
>   Oracle of my Lord Yahweh!
>   (Amos 4: 4–5)

'For that's what you love, O Israelites': this love of making sacrifice is evidently set on the same level as the love of luxury and extortionate profiteering of which he speaks in other oracles.

Elsewhere, the prophecy is less sarcastic, altogether blunter:

> For thus Yahweh has said:
>   'O house of Israel,
>   seek me and live!
>   But don't seek [me] at Bethel,
>   and to Gilgal don't come.'
>   (Amos 5: 4–5)

Whereas Hosea's prophecy denounces the ritual worship of other gods, Amos (like a sort of pre-Christian Søren Kierkegaard) urges the true devotees of Yahweh, for Yahweh's sake, at least provisionally and in certain instances to abstain, as a matter of principle, from the ritual worship of Yahweh.[15]

It may well be that these attacks on the worship at Bethel and Gilgal were originally prompted by one quite specific event: namely, the national rejoicing there over the military victories referred to in 6: 13, at Lo-Dabar and Qarnaim.[16] Certainly, Amos deplores that moment of corporate self-congratulation:

> [Woe to] you who are delighted over Lo-Dabar;

[woe to] you who say,
> 'Have we not captured Qarnaim for ourselves by our might?'
>> (Amos 6: 13)

And he prefaces these woes with riddling mockery:

> Do horses run upon the rocks?
> Or does one plough the sea with oxen?
>> But you have turned justice into poison
>>> and the fruit of righteousness into wormwood.
>>>> (Amos 6: 12)

The point of this appears to be a bitter comment on the sense of national glory resulting from those victories. The glory of Israel, he is saying, is nothing but a form of glorious futility. It is like riding one's horses at a gallop onto boulders or sending a team of oxen into the sea to plough it: gloriously flamboyant perhaps, but only in a quite quixotic sense. A glorious defiance of good sense, so to speak. As, indeed, anyone would recognize – who was not blinded by an utter perversity of moral outlook.

Of course, when the people of Israel celebrated their victories they celebrated them as vivid demonstrations of Yahweh's power, and of their own status as Yahweh's chosen people. To this Amos responds in two distinct ways. In the first place, he challenges the narrow ethnocentrism of such an attitude. This is also, no doubt, the polemical significance of the three hymn-fragments that have been inserted into the prophecy at 4: 13, 5: 8–9 and 9: 5–6. These are generally reckoned to be borrowings from another source, spliced into the oracle sequence somewhat at random. But their message nevertheless fits the context perfectly. For on the one hand, they are celebrations of the terrible capacity of Yahweh to act either as creator or as destroyer, and on the other hand, they speak of the sheer cosmic scale of his operations – which far surpass the narrower concerns of any merely ethnic god.

In Chapter 9, verse 7, however, there is a still more direct attack on the conventional ethnocentric pathos of glory:

> Aren't you like Cushites to me, O Israelites? – Oracle of Yahweh – Didn't I bring Israel up from the land of Egypt, the Philistines from Caphtor, and Aram from Qir?

The Cushites were the people of Nubia, or Ethiopia; referred to here, presumably, because they were the remotest people of which Israel had any knowledge.[17] Yet Israel, it seems, has no more reason to boast – *chauvinistically* – of Yahweh's special patronage than even they.[18] Yahweh's providential concern is universal. So not even Israel's chief claim to glory, the exodus story, is allowed to justify the sort of complacency which Amos sees in the celebrations of the capture of Lo-Dabar and Qarnaim.

Then second, in so far as he nevertheless still does (of course) accept the traditional notion of Israel's special chosenness, Amos turns that notion on its head. If chosenness is a blessing at all, he insists, it is the most paradoxical of blessings. It is a blessing wrapped up in what is, to the average sensual human herd-animal, nothing but a curse: a curse of heightened moral responsibility. Thus:

> Hear this word that Yahweh has spoken about you, O Israelites, about the whole family that I brought up from the land of Egypt: 'Only you have I known of all the families of the earth; *therefore* I will punish you for all your iniquities'.
>
> (Amos 3: 1–2)

The opening two chapters of the book form what Andersen and Freedman have called the 'Great Set Speech'. This begins with a series of oracles against Israel's neighbours, denouncing their sins and threatening them with due retribution; just the sort of thing best calculated to delight conventional chauvinist opinion back in Israel itself. But then, with a sudden dramatic reversal, the series culminates in two similar oracles against the two Israelite kingdoms – followed by the pronouncement just cited.

The idea of Israel as Yahweh's chosen people was, it seems, traditionally associated with apocalyptic hopes for a great 'Day of Yahweh' to come, when the incomparable greatness of Yahweh would be vindicated, in a great glow of light, by the most tremendous victories for his chosen people. Amos takes up this idea. For him, the fact is, Yahweh's incomparable greatness is indeed truly incomparable – consisting, as it does, in the most radical otherness from all those other gods, the various deities of the magic world. For *them* to be glorified, certainly, there must be victory for their protégés; but for Yahweh to be glorified, what is required is just the opposite. It is whatever it takes to shake the average sensual human herd-animal out of his or her average human herd-animality. And if that means catastrophe – if the only thing that will actually work is the most drastic sort of shock-therapy, once and for all to uproot the easy conventionality of people's given herd-identities – then so be it.

So he directly attacks the conventional Israelite pathos of glory, here in its core aspiration:

Woe to you who long for Yahweh's Day! What does it mean to *you*? [To you] Yahweh's Day will be darkness rather than light. It will be as though a man were to escape from the lion, only to have the bear meet him; or, having reached his house, to rest his hand on the wall, and have the snake bite him. Is not Yahweh's Day darkness rather than light, pitch darkness without a glimmer of light?

(Amos 5: 18–20)

VII

Not every prophetic articulation of the pathos of shakenness necessarily takes the doom-laden, menacing form that Amos's does, however.

Indeed, if Amos's career represents the first great breakthrough moment for the pathos of shakenness in the history of Hebrew prophecy, then the second is surely that which comes some 230 years later in the work of that anonymous poet whose oracles are preserved in the book of Isaiah, Chapters 40–55, and who is therefore generally known as Deutero-Isaiah. But, in stark contrast to the book of Amos, this collection begins with the words:

Comfort, O comfort my people
   says your God;
Speak tenderly to Jerusalem
   and cry to her,
that she has served her term,
   that her penalty is paid,
that she has received from Yahweh's hand
   double for all her sins.

(Isaiah 40: 1–2)[19]

And its dominant tone, throughout, is one of exuberant hope.

Thus, whereas Amos writes poetry in which an intense pathos of shakenness is intimately intermingled with who knows what other impulses of vindictive rage, Deutero-Isaiah – very differently – writes as a shaken comforter. For, to the people this prophet was addressing, what Amos would have called 'the Day of Yahweh' had come. A generation's span earlier, in the year 587, the southern kingdom of Judah had finally collapsed, just as the northern kingdom had done in 721. The Babylonians, this time, had invaded. They had destroyed the Jerusalem temple, and the whole city with it; driving the ruling classes away into exile. The sacrificial cult, that great focus of national unity denounced by Amos, had ceased.

For a prophet to have gone on speaking, in these circumstances, the way Amos had once spoken to his world, would have been oddly anachronistic at best, if not obscenely so. Deutero-Isaiah was a prophet amongst the exiles; one whose fundamental inspiration consisted in his having been shaken out of the prevailing mood, within that milieu, of shocked resignation and despair.

And yet – there is nevertheless a clear continuity between Deutero-Isaiah and Amos. In particular, Deutero-Isaiah picks up the universalism of the tradition stemming from Amos, to radicalize it. His work represents a second breakthrough moment in the history of Hebrew prophecy, essentially by virtue of the way in which it proclaims *a new infinite demand*.

Amos's work represents the first breakthrough moment by virtue of its articulation of an infinite demand for 'justice'. But in the prophecy of Deutero-Isaiah, for the first time, we are confronted with another no less infinite demand: this time, for *the conversion of the whole world*. Clearly, Deutero-Isaiah is also very much an heir to the whole Yahweh-aloneist tradition. Yet his is a Yahweh-aloneism no longer finitely confined, as was that of Hosea or the later Deuteronomist reformers, to a project of purging Israel's own worship of Yahweh from the encroachments of syncretism. It is, on the contrary, a Yahweh-aloneism now lifted onto a quite new level.

Whereas the earlier Yahweh-aloneists denounce other gods simply as being wrong for Israel, Deutero-Isaiah's prophecy is a response not just to apostasy on the part of his own people but also to the spectacle of native Babylonian ritual, as observed in exile. And it therefore issues in a denunciation of other gods as being wrong for *all* peoples. So, in a series of passages, the prophet represents Yahweh as summoning all the other gods to a trial – in front of a jury made up of every nation in the world.[20] Notwithstanding all their sins, the people of Israel are summoned as witnesses, to address this jury:

> Bring forth the people who are blind, yet have eyes,
>   who are deaf, yet have ears!
> Let all the nations gather together
>   and let the peoples assemble.
>
> (Isaiah 43: 8–9)

The gods are challenged to justify themselves before this jury.

The immediate context is the capture of Babylon by the Persians under Cyrus in 539. And in one of the trial speeches, that of 45: 20–5, those summoned to form the jury are more specifically the 'survivors of the nations'. For now the Babylonians have suffered the same fate as the Israelites before them: they too have been reduced to the plight of 'survivors', following a national catastrophe. In the past they had glorified the magic power of their gods as reflected in the political might of their empire. But from the point of view of the religious devotee of Yahweh this was of course, in any case, a false criterion for assessing what is truly divine. The most radical claim in these speeches is that only Yahweh can '*save*' (45: 20). No other god ranks alongside him in this sense. The 'salvation' in question is clearly not a straightforward military one, for Yahweh had by no means saved his people from defeat in those terms. But rather, I think, it must mean salvation from *the despairing sense of one's own culture's futility*, with which any defeated people is threatened. 'There is no other Rock that I know of' (44: 8), Yahweh boasts; no other reliable refuge from the swirling waters of despair.

The ability of Yahweh to save in *this* sense was, after all, well demonstrated by his people's abiding loyalty to their national traditions, even in exile. From the point of view of those defeated by Cyrus the defeat was also a defeat for their gods: completely unpredictable and baffling. The defeat of Israel, by contrast, had been experienced by at least some of the Israelites as the prophetically predicted act of Yahweh, punishing his people for their sins. It did not undermine the true religious worship of Yahweh, but instead helped purge it of the residues of magic. And Deutero-Isaiah himself – an altogether shrewder (or luckier) forecaster of the future than Amos – had in fact predicted the rise of Cyrus, interpreting it as a scheme of Yahweh's for the future restoration of Israel, under Persian patronage. So that what from the point of view of Babylonian magic thinking seemed simply incomprehensible, and therefore devastating, at the same time looked very much like a mighty vindication of Israelite patience.

It is the apparent coming true of the prediction about Cyrus which is the main actual item of evidence presented to the jury in these speeches.[21] But what is most strikingly new here is not so much the argument in itself. Far more remarkable is the presentation to such a cosmopolitan jury of such a boldly formulated basic proposition: that there is something only known, so far, to the true worshippers of Yahweh – which, however, all other peoples also have an urgent need to learn.

For Deutero-Isaiah, the glory of Yahweh is paradoxically best attested by the *sufferings* of his 'servant'. In this regard, faith in Yahweh was certainly unique. No other sacred doctrine known to the prophet was founded in such a way: on historic memories of affliction, transfigured in retrospect.

And, beyond the relative ephemerality of prophetic predictions fulfilled, it is precisely *that* uniqueness which seems to constitute the real essence of the gospel now to be proclaimed. Or so, at any rate, those other strange texts of his would suggest – the so-called 'servant songs'.

Despite their name, these 'songs' are not really songs. Rather, they belong together as a distinct cluster of four closely interrelated little poems, at:

1   Isaiah 42: 1–4
2   Isaiah 49: 1–6
3   Isaiah 50: 4–9
4   Isaiah 52: 13–53: 12.

Full of mystery, they remain a topic of endless academic dispute.[22]

The controversy revolves, in the first instance, around the elementary-seeming issue of who the particular 'servant' in question was originally supposed to be. Thus: elsewhere, both in the prophetic tradition generally and in Deutero-Isaiah, the 'servant' of Yahweh was most often Israel. And in the second servant song this identification is also quite explicit, as Yahweh declares, 'You are my servant, Israel, in whom I will be glorified' (Isaiah 49: 3). But, on the other hand, the word 'Israel' here may well be a later addition. Moreover, the servant is also described very much as a single individual. It may well be that he is meant to be, in some sense, a purely allegorical personification of the nation as a whole. However, matters are complicated by the fact that in 49: 5–6 he is actually *set over against* the people as whole, inasmuch as Yahweh there says to him:

> It is too light a thing that you should be my servant,
>   to raise up the tribes of Jacob
>   and to restore the survivors of Israel;
> I will give you as a light to the nations,
>   that my salvation may reach to the end of the earth.

Are these words, then, addressed to the allegorical personification of a particular group within the nation, the prophetically inspired elite, representing 'Israel' specifically in its ideal vocation? Or should we rather think of the servant as some actual historic person – elevated perhaps by special merit to a representative role?

In either case, what sort of representative is he? In the first song, he appears to be a man of power. He is not a conventional ruler, it is true, for he spurns the usual pomp of rulership:

> He will not cry or lift up his voice,
>   or make it heard in the street.
>   (Isaiah 42: 2)

Yet he is one who, in the manner of a great leader or like a second Moses, 'is to bring forth justice'. In the third and fourth songs, though, he appears much more like a persecuted prophet. It is in these two songs that we learn of his sufferings: imprisoned, tortured; slapped on the cheeks by his tormentors, having his beard pulled out and being spat upon; but also being horribly disfigured by disease, and therefore shunned; eventually dying, whether of the disease or at the hands of his torturers; and being buried with criminals, even though he was innocent. Here he is no leader, but on the contrary a powerless victim of those in power.

How, then, are we to understand all this? In my view, the only solution is entirely to abandon the conventional question, *who* the servant is meant to be, as a particular individual or corporate person. Instead it is my proposal that we consider these poems far more as programmatic statements about a certain sort of universal vocation. The servant of Yahweh, I think one might say, is nothing other than *a general personification of all those who are religiously shaken.*

This may apply either to a prophet or to a ruler; to an individual, to an elite group, even (in some measure) to a whole nation. But the servant's vocation and his sufferings are, essentially – as I would see it – symbolic of the vocation and the sufferings of shakenness *as such*, in all its very many various forms. Thus, in Deutero-Isaiah we have some of the first stirrings of a properly *self-reflective* pathos of shakenness.[23]

Passionately shaken out of the easy complacencies of his world, Amos battles against them by evoking the vivid spectre of a coming this-worldly hell for the whole of Israel. Deutero-Isaiah does not do that; with regard to the future of Israel he is on the contrary a thoroughgoing prophet of hope. Yet, above all in the fourth of the servant songs, he too has his own vision of this-worldly hell. Unlike Amos, he generalizes its significance by projecting it onto the symbolic figure of the servant; and so abstracts it from history, in the sense that what the servant represents is surely a perennial possibility. Also in sharp contrast to Amos's judgement on Israel, the servant is perceived by the observers who comment on his fate in this song to have suffered excessively, out of all proportion to what he himself deserved.

Nevertheless, there is I think a clear continuity between the two visions. At least by implication, Deutero-Isaiah himself insists upon it; as we see in those other trial speeches, where Yahweh is represented as charging his own people with their pre-exilic sins. In the most striking of these Deutero-Isaiah directly picks up the critical tradition stemming from Amos 5: 21–4:

> I was not the one you called upon, O Jacob,
>   it was not *my* favour you sought, O Israel!
> Your burnt offerings of sheep were not for *me*,
>   it was not *me* whom you honoured with your sacrifices.
> *I* did not make you serve with offerings,
>   or weary you with frankincense.

> You did not buy sweet cane with money for *me*,
> *I* was not satisfied with the fat of your sacrifices.
>
> (Isaiah 43: 22–4)

In the context of Babylonian exile, when for forty years or so there had no longer been any public sacrifices (supposedly) to Yahweh, the only point of such an oracle was to reaffirm the prophet's unswerving loyalty to his predecessors, all the way back to Amos. And besides, what else is the servant if not a symbol for those who have now passed through and endured the very same sort of chastening experience which Amos for his part sees, for the most part, looming in the future; and who have been purged by it? The basic difference is simply one of temporal perspective. It is just that whereas Amos, looking forward to the chastening experience, is absolutely preoccupied with the sinfulness still to be purged away, Deutero-Isaiah's observers – looking back on the servant's past suffering – are far more concerned with what they may have to learn from the heroic example of his endurance.

He died *for us*, these converts declare. That is the aspect of the matter which concerns them:

> He was like one before whom men hide their faces,
> despised – we esteemed him not.
>
> Yet *ours* was the sickness that *he* carried,
> and *ours* the pains *he* bore . . .
> He was pierced on account of our sins,
> crushed on account of our iniquities.
> Chastisement that led to our welfare lay upon him,
> and by means of his stripes there was healing for us.
>
> All we like sheep have gone astray;
> we have turned everyone to his own way,
> but Yahweh laid on him the iniquity of us all.
>
> (Isaiah 53: 3–6)

Here we have imagery drawn from the realm of magic, yet deployed as a metaphor for what is in essence a purely religious truth. 'Yahweh laid on him the iniquity of us all': that is, the servant suffered and died like an animal offered up as a magic sacrificial sin-offering. Clearly, the point of the analogy lies in the way it conveys the transformation of the chorus of observers from mere onlookers into active participants, themselves, in the drama of salvation. Yet what saves them is no mere magic – for the servant is also one who bears religious testimony. And in strict religious terms, his suffering is significant for the salvation of those he addresses simply because of the way his endurance of it serves to endorse his testimony's moral authority. 'He was pierced on account of our sins', the converted observers confess. What, above all, will save them from their sins is surely the inspirational example of a piety with demonstrated ability to endure the shaking power of great affliction; and to *absorb* that power into itself. That is to say, the essential saving power of the servant's testimony consists in the sheer intensity of his shakenness. At the deepest level, I think, the servant has to be understood as a poetic symbol for the whole transformation of shaking power into religious saving power.

But this was exactly what Amos, in his day, was also attempting. And if one is, after all, still looking for particular examples of the general type for which the servant stands, was not Amos in fact the great pioneer of such servants; a great sufferer indeed, suffering both by anticipation, from the horrors he foresaw, and from the lonely fate to which his vocation condemned him?

Certainly, the jubilant tones of Deutero-Isaiah are a far cry from Amos's bitter rage. Yet so the religious pathos of shakenness evolves, as differences of context demand corresponding shifts in poetic form.

6 A shaken sacramentalism
Hölderlin and Blake

I

But what, then, happens to the prophetic spirit – as an inspiration of poetry – in a culture such as ours?

Now that our religious life no longer includes the regular consultation of oracles, the practice which provided the literary format for ancient Hebrew prophecy, clearly that spirit needs new forms.

II

Above all, I think, it migrates into the modern (or postmodern) form of what I would call 'sacramental poetry'.

There is one very remarkable oracle in the prophecy of Amos which already, in a sense, points forwards in this direction. Here the prophet envisages a coming time of *spiritual* famine:

> Behold! The time is coming
>   – Oracle of my Lord Yahweh –
> when I will send famine throughout the earth:
>   not a hunger for food,
>   nor a thirst for water,
>   but a famine of hearing Yahweh's words.
> They shall wander from sea to sea,
>   and from north to east,
> they will run back and forth,
>   seeking the word of Yahweh –
>   but they shall not find it.
>   (Amos 8: 11–12)

'Yahweh's words' in this context cannot be quite the same sort of words as those that Yahweh had delivered to Amos himself – no one could really be imagined 'hungering and thirsting' for his terrible warnings of disaster! But what seems to be in question is another, complementary mode of prophecy: a pathos of shakenness, the shaking power of which resides not so much in the fearful contemplation of catastrophe, as in the loving contemplation of the poetic ideal itself.

'Yahweh's words' are, in this context, the expression of justice: the conjuring up of that ideal, as such. They are infinitely elusive for the simple reason that 'justice' is infinite. It can never fully be attained in the life of any society, there is no end to the struggle it demands. Unlike others, the true lover of 'justice' does not need to be goaded by the contemplation of past or future catastrophes; since, for such a one, even periods which others regard as entirely prosperous are nothing but a time of famine. In short, what Amos is dreaming of here is an eventual end to his own isolation, the emergence of a whole community of kindred spirits, also sharing in the same hunger by which he is driven.

By 'sacramental poetry' I mean a form of shaken religious verse which, self-reflectively, takes as its consistent central theme this infinite hunger by which it is itself inspired; a self-conscious hungering, precisely, for ever greater hunger, as such.

According to the old scholastic definition a sacrament is a sacred sign which is supposed to 'effect what it signifies'. The Eucharist is a symbolic act which 'signifies' – speaks of, defines and interprets – the conferral of divine grace to the church community. Yet it also 'effectively' *is* a conferral of that grace: the act of participation in the symbolism itself becomes a channel through which divine grace operates. And it is the same with sacramental poetry. Such poetry is not only an invocation of God, but in it God is *primarily identified* as the spirit of the very truest and most original poetic inspiration. Moreover, this then becomes the basis for a fierce critique of conventional religion: above all, for its stifling of the free-spirited shaken imaginativeness required for the proper reception, or the proper appreciation, of that inspirational grace. Sacramental poetry in short aspires to be a direct example, so far as possible an infectious display, of the very same grace – the same inspirational hunger – it is also calling for.

When Heidegger celebrates Hölderlin, for instance, this is essentially because Hölderlin is one of the great original pioneers of this sort of poetry. Another, very different – although contemporaneous – example is William Blake.

III

So let us compare these two.

What Hölderlin and Blake have in common is that they are both poets of extraordinary sacramental ambition, responding to the new opportunities for such poetry that had, in their day, been opened up by the great negative impact of the Enlightenment, with its decisive loosening of the old imaginative constraints imposed by traditional Christendom. Otherwise, however, they have almost nothing else in common – indeed, their two bodies of work are so different as to render the comparison between them quite pointless for any other, non-theological literary-critical purpose. But that is precisely what makes it so interesting in specifically theological terms.

For the whole purpose of theology, in this regard, is just to trace the universal first principles of religio-poetic truth, in so far as those principles decisively transcend the limitations of any one particular literary style. Besides what follows from their contemporaneity, here we have two poets with virtually nothing else in common – *except* what is involved in their shared sacramental commitment to the pathos of shakenness. What do I mean by the 'pathos of shakenness'? I defined it earlier in terms of three defining marks: a threefold dynamic of scepticism towards the dominant ways of the world, plus impassioned concern, but also fresh air. An alternative definition, however, would be to say: it is that which these two strange poets – notwithstanding all their obvious differences – nevertheless have in common.

IV

Of the two, Blake was by a few years the older. He was born in 1757. His great religious poetry may be said to begin with *The Marriage of Heaven and Hell*, completed in 1792–3, and he completed his last great epic, *Jerusalem*, around 1815. He died in 1827. Hölderlin was born in 1770 and lived until 1843. But his major poetry spans a period of just six years or so, from 1797 to 1803 – before he was finally incapacitated by schizophrenia.

Neither would have had any awareness of the other. Yet both thus belonged to the same historical epoch: the age of the French Revolution and its immediate consequences. Both were enthusiastic supporters, from a distance, of the Revolution in its early days, prior to the onset of the Terror. (Blake is said, at one stage, to have walked about London provocatively wearing a revolutionary *bonnet rouge* on his head.) Both recoiled from the subsequent violence of the Jacobin regime – yet still got into some political trouble later on. In 1803, following a scuffle with a soldier, Blake was tried for subversion; and, although acquitted, was clearly traumatized by the experience. In 1805 Hölderlin, already very ill, found himself dangerously compromised by his friendship with the radical Sinclair, who was accused of sedition against the Grand Duke of Württemberg.

This was a world characterized by a widespread readiness for unprecedentedly revolutionary religious, or quasi-religious, new beginnings:

ventures of chastened reconstruction, following the arid reductionism of the Enlightenment. The Terror in France, of course, had also been the backdrop to the great sacred-ideological propaganda festivals stage-managed by the painter Jacques-Louis David; solemn observances of the most sinister sentimentality – pure pathos of glory, at its kitschiest. These were supposed to be one such new beginning, appealing to the authority of Rousseau. And the whole impulse of Romantic poetry, in both Britain and Germany, belongs very much to the same context: representing a quite opposite spirit of fundamental cultural reconstruction. At its truest, it is an infinitely more demanding one.[1]

Again, it was a world with a strong tradition of literary critical and philosophical discourse concerning the proper nature of 'the sublime'. Following the translation and revival, by Boileau, of Longinus's classic *Essay on the Sublime* in 1674, a whole series of works on the subject had appeared; culminating in Burke's *Philosophical Enquiry* and Kant's *Critique of Judgement*.[2] But Blake and Hölderlin are surely, by far, the two boldest poet-experimenters of the period, in this mode.

V

In style and tone, however, Blake is really the polar opposite to Hölderlin. In the first place, his work reflects quite a different social context.

'English Blake' (as he called himself) was really London Blake. Apart from the three years he spent at Felpham on the Sussex coast he lived his whole life in the capital.[3] London, in his poetry, is personified as 'a Human awful wonder of God' (*Jerusalem* 34: 29); and becomes an earthly counterpart to the heavenly city, the chief element in the phantasmagoric geography of his last epic.[4] He was an artisan and an autodidact. The son of a hosier, he struggled to make his living as a commercial engraver. His only schooling was in a Drawing School. And he was glad of it: 'There is no use in education', he once remarked, 'It is the great Sin. It is eating of the tree of Knowledge of Good and Evil'.[5] In religious terms, he came from a background of sectarian dissent, traditionally associated with political radicalism.

So he was brought up in intimate familiarity with the Bible, and was at the same time inclined to be acutely mistrustful of the Greek and Latin Classics – which formed so large a part of the conventional bourgeois education he had been spared. In his mature thinking, moreover, this then hardened into a fiercely polemical attitude. On the one hand, in *The Marriage of Heaven and Hell* he describes a dinner party where he enters into the friendliest sort of conversation with the prophets Isaiah and Ezekiel. These, for him, are his true predecessors. But, on the other hand, he denounces 'the Stolen and Perverted Writings of Homer & Ovid; of Plato

& Cicero. which all Men ought to condemn', and which 'are set up by arti-
fice against the Sublime of the Bible'. He is in revolt against 'the silly Greek
and Latin slaves of the Sword'. And 'Rouze up', he cries, 'O Young Men of
the New Age! set your foreheads against the ignorant Hirelings! For we
have Hirelings in the Camp, the Court, & the University. . . . We do not
want either Greek or Roman Models if we are but just & true to our own
Imaginations' (*Milton*, Preface). In short, he associates the classics with the
ruling classes, and rejects them accordingly.[6]

Hölderlin, by contrast, came from small-town Swabia. His was quite a
wealthy bourgeois family, and he received a formal education in which
theological and classical studies went hand in hand. As a student he shared
rooms with Hegel and Schelling at the Tübingen Stift, where all three were
supposedly training to become ministers of the established Lutheran church;
although none of them were ever actually ordained. German intellectual
culture in that period was generally permeated by a fervent love for Greek
antiquity – of which Hölderlin himself was to become the most extravagant
exponent. The landscape of his poetry is a mixture, combining the scenery
he knew from his own quite extensive travels (mostly on foot) through
Germany, Switzerland and France, with dreamy images of Greece. And he
renders Christ into a companion of the Greek gods.

At the same time, these are two poets of very different temperaments; a
difference further reflected in their divergent choice of literary forms.
Blake's whole approach to religious matters is fiercely confrontational. But
Hölderlin is, far rather, a poet of nervously inhibited rage – alternating
between jubilant enthusiasm and choking lamentation. There is a rumbus-
tious humour in Blake's work quite lacking in Hölderlin's, and a recurrent
gleeful vulgarity; informing a general spirit of antinomianism, in particular
with regard to sexual ethics, which is also completely alien to Hölderlin.

Blake is an epic poet who is also both a visual artist and a visionary. He saw
visions regularly. And, of course, much of his work takes shape as a joining
together of poetry and visual art into a collection of intensely auratic, hand-
finished illuminated books. Among the many literary influences on his poetry
are: the books of Isaiah and Ezekiel, again – especially in the light of Robert
Lowth's new understanding of ancient Hebrew poetics; Milton; the recently
translated material from the Icelandic Eddas and from ancient Welsh literature; James Macpherson's fake ancient Gaelic poems attributed to 'Ossian';
Thomas Chatterton's fake mediaeval verse; the Gothic melodramas of the day.
His thinking draws on the visionary doctrines of Swedenborg; the speculations of Paracelsus and Jacob Boehme; the (extremely cranky) syncretic
mythography of such contemporary 'antiquarian' writers as Jacob Bryant,
Thomas Burnet, Edward Davies, Rowland Jones, James Parsons, Henry
Rowlands, William Stukeley and Francis Wilford.

Hölderlin, meanwhile, is a lyric poet who is also a novelist and a (would-be) dramatist. He begins as an admirer of Klopstock and Schiller.[7] But his work is most influenced by the Greeks whom he translated: above all, Sophocles and Pindar. And he belongs to the highly sophisticated intellectual milieu of German idealism. The difference between these two bodies of poetry is not unlike the difference between Blake's visual art and the paintings, say, of Caspar David Friedrich; another contemporary whose work, although less classicist in tone, is nevertheless perhaps the closest visual equivalent to Hölderlin's writing, in its melancholic sublimity.

VI

Blake and Hölderlin: in my view, these are the two truly great modern pioneers of sacramental poetry in the service of the pathos of shakenness.

They follow, in many ways, polar opposite paths. Yet both are extraordinarily ambitious in their shakenness; and, therefore, extraordinarily lonely figures. In neither case does one find any hint of the pathos of glory. The pathos of glory is the bonding sentiment of a coherently organized movement, celebrating the values of its leaders; or of a dominant sociocultural order, celebrating the values of its rulers. But neither Blake nor Hölderlin belonged to any coherent campaigning or evangelistic group.[8] Nor did either ever receive any serious recognition from the cultural establishments of their world. Blake, in his angry isolation, was widely regarded by his acquaintances as 'mad'; that he nevertheless remained sane was no doubt largely due to the fact that he was (in the long run) so happily married, to Catherine. Hölderlin loved another man's wife. She died – whereupon his sanity collapsed, and he never recovered. But the extreme pressure both men lived under was, in a certain sense, the ultimate guarantee of their prophetic integrity: inasmuch as it preserved them (Blake always and Hölderlin at any rate in all his great work) from any temptation to compromise with the pathos of glory.

The Hebrew prophets developed their poetic version of the pathos of shakenness in polemical opposition to the surrounding culture of magic; which they denounced, essentially, for its sheer unshakenness. Blake and Hölderlin, in their sharply contrasting styles, may both be said to develop a poetics of shakenness with an equivalent polemic thrust, directed against the kitsch seductiveness of the Christian ecclesiastical pathos of glory.

Thus Milan Kundera, in his novel *The Unbearable Lightness of Being*, defines 'kitsch', in general, as the aesthetics of a 'categorical agreement with being'; issuing in, as he puts it, an 'absolute denial of shit'.

'Kitsch', that is to say, 'excludes everything from its purview which is essentially unacceptable in human existence'.[9] It is what belongs to an artistic recreation of the world in terms of the purest wish-fulfilment. Such art does not confront us with the disagreeable reality of our own mortality – on the contrary, Kundera also calls it 'a folding screen to curtain off death'.[10] Nor does it in any way disturb our sense of who we are, or what we are called to be. It simply confirms all our prejudices. It is the celebratory beautification of un-shakenness.

Here, in short, we have the whole larger aesthetic environment within which the pathos of glory, generally, is able to flourish; everything the pathos of glory hooks onto, and draws upon, for propaganda purposes. Kundera himself is primarily concerned with the kitsch of totalitarian propaganda, and in particular the Communist version. But it is not hard to identify the sentimentalized Christian equivalents. In this fallen world they are what all the more effective forms of mass-evangelization depend on.

The original revelatory truth of the cross of Christ surely consists in a symbolic laying bare of everything which kitsch, of any sort, seeks to deny or hide away; as we chastened onlookers, witnessing the anguish of the suffering servant, are thereby coaxed into confronting our own corporate reality, in all its unacceptable destructiveness. Yet Christian tradition is very largely a two thousand years' accumulation of sundry devices – ranging from the most narrowly sectarian to the most expansively catholic – for evading, or at least softening, the proper impact of that critical logic, and holding fast to what it is meant to sweep away. At all events, both Blake and Hölderlin, in effect, take Jesus as their primary symbol for salvation from kitsch. But, in order to do so, they are both of them in their different ways driven to experiment with elaborate poetic rescue-strategies, systematically intended to liberate him from the more conventional, kitschy imaginings of the church.

This struggle proceeds, in both cases, at two levels. On the one hand, it is a question of poetic form. On the other hand, it also involves two quite substantive poetic arguments in heterodox Christology. I will come back to those substantive arguments in the following chapters; let us however take the purely formal aspect first.

VII

Both Blake and Hölderlin are poets of the sublime. Their critique is directed against the most sublime sort of kitsch: that is to say, the sort with the greatest pretensions to sacred authority. And they will concede it nothing. So they seek to engage it right at the heart of its own territory.

Thus, in the most general terms, an experience of 'the sublime' may be said to be one which is at the same time both *aesthetically compelling* and yet also, in some way or another, *difficult to grasp*.

First and foremost, the term may refer to certain compellingly vivid and urgent experiences which are difficult to grasp in the sense that they beggar the imagination. The night sky is a sublime spectacle, for instance, when it conjures up thoughts of the unimaginable vastness of the universe. A tremendous storm, viewed in a reflectively contemplative manner from a safe distance, may be sublime; as is the sight of a hydrogen bomb exploding on the horizon; or the prospect of some terribly inhospitable landscape – in so far as such experiences suggest the idea of an unimaginable extremity of suffering. There is something sublime about the pyramids of Giza, say, or the antiquities at Luxor (once one has set aside the distractions of tourism) in that they speak of another culture, so complex and at the same time so alien from our own that we can scarcely imagine how it felt to be a part of it. Certain actions of other people are sublime; namely, when they seem to spring from what is, to us, an unimaginable depth and intensity of spiritual refinement.

But, by analogy, the experience of such challenges to the imagination may also come to serve as a medium of poetic representation for the infinitely compelling yet difficult challenge to our own wills posed in principle by our most sacred ideals. And so, translated into aesthetic form, these ideals themselves may also be termed sublime. Hence, the infinite majesty of God consists in a set of sublime ideals poetically represented by the sublime immensity of the universe considered as a divine creation, the sublime terrors of the most awe-inspiring natural phenomena considered as particular acts of God, the sublime expanse of human history considered as the field of universal divine providence, the sublime achievements of the saints. And *mutatis mutandis* the same poetic process may equally be applied to non-theistic ideals, as well.

In the case of the kitsch sublime, however, the ideals which are being celebrated are purely conventional ones. We are being urged to submit to them without question. Their sublime prestige is actually meant to exempt them from all questioning; it is invoked, very much, to intimidate the potential questioner. Nothing could be more kitsch for example (in Kundera's sense) than the magnificent sublimity of God's concluding speeches in the book of Job, Chapters 38–41: speeches delivered 'out of the whirlwind', to put a quite arbitrary end to all debate.[11]

The anti-kitsch sublime is the opposite, in that its invocation is, on the contrary, a positive affirmation of the questioner. For this is nothing other than the sublime otherness of the *lived* truth, inherent in an authentic individuality, from any mere 'correctness' of doctrinal formulation or group-membership. And so it is the inspirational ideal of an art which – even while continuing to make the very boldest sort of moral claims – nevertheless sets out systematically to parade its own idiosyncrasy, as the product of one particular questioning individual. The poetry of the kitsch sublime draws all its authority from its clichés; the anti-kitsch sublime, by contrast, demands a poetry the true authority of which lies precisely in its systematic subversion of cliché. This is no doubt what Blake, for example, meant by his formula: 'Allegory addressed to the Intellectual powers while it is altogether hidden from the Corporeal Understanding is My Definition of the Most Sublime Poetry'.[12] The 'Corporeal Understanding', here, is just the cliché-loving frame of mind in which we all of us mostly live; or our whole vulnerability to kitsch.

In one of his annotations to the *Works of Sir Joshua Reynolds* Blake speaks of the 'Contempt & Abhorrence' he had always felt for Burke's great *Philosophical Enquiry into the Origins of our Ideas of the Sublime and Beautiful*. He links Burke here with Locke and Bacon, in particular, as three writers who all of them 'mock Inspiration & Vision'.[13] This charge is not further explained. Indeed, in relation to Burke, it might at first sight appear rather strange: for Burke has a thoroughly Gothic taste for the sublime in its darkest, most turbulent and terrifying forms, and this is in fact just the sort of imagery which pervades Blake's own epics. But is not the point precisely that, to Blake, Burke has become a symbol for the potential reduction of the sublime – even in the forms he himself is keenest on – to mere kitsch? At all events, Blake was, to say the least, certainly quite allergic to the conservative pathos of glory tending to be associated with Burkean politics.

There is also another difference between the kitsch and anti-kitsch modes of the sublime. In its absolute repudiation of kitschy cliché, what Blake calls 'the Most Sublime Poetry' is *itself* rendered both compelling and difficult: compelling in the inescapable and fascinating intensity of its moral seriousness – while at the same time intolerably difficult and repugnant to what Blake calls the 'Corporeal Understanding'.

So the actual text as such becomes a sublime object. *This is what makes it sacramental*: an intrinsically sublime expression of hunger for a sublime ideal.

VIII

The emptier and more thwarted the 'Corporeal Understanding', the less distraction there is, away from the pathos of shakenness communicated to the 'Intellectual powers'. Blake's own peculiarly radical strategy for repelling the cliché-lover is a combination of acute iconic disorientation with extensive narrative disintegration.

The image of the 'Vortex' in *Milton* (15: 21–35) for example is presented by him as a formula for 'the nature of eternity'. More specifically, however, it is a vivid description of the sublime impact of his verse, in general, on the visual imagination. The image is intrinsically quite baffling.[14] But it also defines what he is aiming at, in imaginative terms, above all in this epic and in *Jerusalem*: his whole aim, at this level, is to toss his readers into an imaginative vortex. And he surely succeeds. So we are confronted by a sheer overwhelming multitude of diverse swirling figures; or, in places, an overwhelming mass of indigestible detail. And on what scale? Sometimes the talk is of cosmic phenomena; then we switch abruptly to close-up, observing the poet as he stands in his country cottage-garden, or walks the streets of London; then abruptly back again. In *Jerusalem*, moreover, the scenery of the Middle East is bizarrely super-imposed onto that of Britain. Again and again, Blake uses the medium of verse to achieve effects like those found nowadays in the very boldest forms of cinematic animation. It is almost as though the visual images alongside the text were stills from some experimental film.

At the same time, he also increasingly breaks up the narrative flow of his poetry. The disruptions in *The Four Zoas* are, in the first instance, an acci-dental result of rewriting; inasmuch as there are two distinct strata to the work, an earlier and a later one, left juxtaposed. However, in *Milton*, and still more in *Jerusalem*, the discontinuities are clearly more deliberate. The 'Corporeal Understanding' wants unity of narrative plot. Ever more reluctant to entertain it, what Blake offers in *Jerusalem* is, far rather, a sublime unity of vision – mediated through a loose assemblage of overlapping narrative fragments.

Hölderlin, meanwhile, is not composing epic narrative. But the formal sublimity of his later 'hymn'-writing may be said to consist in its fundamen-tal offence to the 'Corporeal Understanding's' conventional expectations of lyric *argument*. For this is a body of verse which, like none other, argues; built around the frequently reiterated conjunctions '*denn*' (for, because), '*doch*' (however), '*aber*' (but), '*nemlich*' (namely), '*darum*' (therefore), '*so*' (thus). These 'hymns' are arguments forced into verse form by the passionate enthu-siasm informing them. Only, their offence derives from their extreme compression: the way the syntax twists and buckles under the strain of fitting so much in, so succinctly.

The style here is, at one level, Pindaric; originating from Hölderlin's own translations of Pindar from the Greek. Yet he infuses it with a completely new religious urgency. And, as in Blake's work, again the effect is of a tremendous pressure of shakenness – fracturing and splitting open its literary containers.

7   Blake
Shakenness in confrontational form

I

In essence, a theological approach to poetry differs from other types of literary criticism in that its primary concern is with the truth, or untruth, of the poet's selective appropriation of religious tradition.

But, again – what is 'truth' here? For the advocates of any form of the pathos of glory, poetic truth is immediately to be defined in terms of the unquestioned value-judgements of their own particular class or sacred institutions. So the pathos of glory is the celebration of a given community's given world-view, simply as given. And the resultant supposedly 'truth-telling' poetry sets out to infuse that world-view with appropriate emotion; amplifying its emotional appeal to, and its emotional demands on, its adherents.

A principled commitment to the pathos of shakenness, on the other hand, springs from the exact opposite approach. For its inspiration lies, precisely, in the most thoughtful possible questioning of *all* such givenness. To my mind, the fullness of poetic truth essentially consists in the very purest and most comprehensive communication of this infinite ideal. Truth-in-shakenness is thus, I have argued, truth at the level of a basic *disposition of the will*: turning away from the simply given, as such, towards fresh reality. However, this underlying disposition may well come to expression in a great variety of different *moods*. The greater the variety actually achieved, the clearer the shakenness as such – in its ultimate transcendence of any single poetic medium, its true catholicity.

Blake's poetry expresses a radical shakenness in one range of moods; Hölderlin's in another. And these two ranges are I think fundamentally complementary to one another.

II

As I have said, Blake's verse has a mood-range determined above all by its sheer *pugnacity*.

His is a poetry of shakenness in the most militant sort of confrontation with unshakenness; its innermost truth consists in its character as an extravagantly confrontational assault on the sacred kitsch of his day. Underlying his whole mythopoeic enterprise is a caustic perception of establishment Christianity as being very largely the worship of the Antichrist.

So he writes epics that are in a sense all about the extreme difficulty, under present conditions, of gaining true access to Jesus, in view of all the obstacles which a corrupt spirituality has interposed. In the last two books of *The Four Zoas* we have several glimpses of Jesus, but only glimpses. At the conclusion to *Milton* Jesus appears in a sudden brief epiphany; and again towards the end of *Jerusalem*. At the beginning of *Jerusalem*, Jesus is claimed as the poet's direct inspiration: 'dictating the words of this mild song'.[1] Yet in all three of these, the epics of Blake's maturity, the chief action consists of a complex interplay between the various different impulses Blake sees at work in the shaping of the Antichrist – as these impulses progress towards eventual redemption or overthrow.

In part, Blake's struggle is against the corruption of Christianity by the poetics of the pathos of glory. And in part it is against the anti-poetics of what he himself calls 'Deism'. His struggle against the pathos of glory is waged primarily in the name of Jesus as a preacher of *forgiveness*; against Deism, it is a celebration of Jesus as the symbolic divine embodiment of 'the Human *Imagination*'.[2]

He attacks the pathos of glory equally in its militaristic and in its sacerdotal forms. At the end of *Jerusalem* the militaristic pathos of glory is named as 'the Covenant of Priam', and as such set over against the true 'Forgiveness of Sins according to the Covenant of Jehovah'.[3] The Covenant of Priam is named after the ancient patriarch of Troy; it represents the Homeric warrior ethos. But Blake's complaint is that establishment Christianity has also sold out to this ethos, thereby becoming a form of 'Religion hidden in War / Namd Moral Virtue'.[4]

And then it intermingles with the sacerdotal pathos of glory, which he perhaps most vividly represents as the fiery 'Wheel of Religion' in the verse part of the address 'To the Christians' at the beginning of *Jerusalem* Chapter 4:

> I stood among my valleys of the south
> And saw a flame of fire, even as a Wheel
> Of fire surrounding all the heavens: it went
> From west to east against the current of
> Creation and devour all things in its loud
> Fury & thundering course round heaven & earth. . . .
> And I asked a Watcher & a Holy-One

Its Name? he answered. It is the Wheel of Religion
I wept & said. Is this the law of Jesus
This terrible devouring sword turning every way
He answerd; Jesus died because he strove
Against the current of this Wheel: its Name
Is Caiaphas, the dark Preacher of Death
Of sin, of sorrow, & of punishment.[5]

                                    (*Jerusalem* 77: 1–6, 12–19)

'I stood among my valleys of the south': against the pretensions of establishment Christianity Blake here lays claim to the scenery of the Bible as his own field of spiritual vision. But in the light of that vision the primal failing of both the Covenant of Priam and the Wheel of Religion, as twin forms of establishment thinking, is in the way they both stand opposed to true 'forgiveness'. For Blake, Jesus is pre-eminently 'the bright Preacher of Life / Creating Nature from this fiery Law / By self-denial & forgiveness of Sin'.[6] The 'Selfhood' to be denied is the self that seeks to dominate, or that colludes with manipulative rule; the 'forgiveness' in question is a fundamental acceptance of free-spirited individual self-expression, encouragement of experimental ways of life, respect for conscientious dissent – even where one disagrees. The pure antithesis to the spirit of Caiaphas, it is a radical calling into question of the supposed sinfulness of so-called 'sins' which are really just offences against herd-morality. And hence it further implies a profound receptiveness to the pathos of shakenness. Jesus, himself the symbolic victim of establishment unforgiveness, is at the same time the true Judge who judges purely on the basis of forgiveness in this sense.

As he makes clear in his last substantial poem, that defiant piece of tomfoolery *The Everlasting Gospel*, Blake does not by any means believe in forgiving the establishment, or in 'loving your enemies' when your enemies are the representatives of establishment religion. ('He who loves his Enemies betrays his Friends / This surely is not what Jesus intends'.[7] At any rate, not in the context of that sort of struggle.) Moreover, he absolutely denies that there is any virtue in humility, where 'humility' is identified with mere submission to the prevailing ways of the world. But he thinks of Jesus as 'Humble to God Haughty to Man'. And he believes in forgiveness as a revolutionary principle.

Such forgiveness however also, he thinks, urgently requires great poetry to promote it: to mock its enemies and encourage its proponents. And the primal failing of what he calls 'Deism' is that it prevents this. Thus, in Blake's usage 'Deism' clearly becomes a very broad category indeed. It is, in the first instance, his general name for the whole tradition of philosophical mistrust of poetry, as a prophetic medium. (In the twentieth century it is everything that Julien Benda admires.)

Sacralized, Deism becomes what he calls 'Natural Religion': by which he means a divinization of Nature *as opposed to* Imagination – although the result is, at once, a denial both of the truly natural and of true religion. In Blake's own world the ancient error of anti-poetry had taken twofold shape. On the one hand, it had become Deism in the conventional sense, the creed of an 'enlightened' establishment culture seeking to harness the newly enhanced prestige of the post-Newtonian natural sciences for secularizing purposes. On the other hand, it seems that for him the category of 'Deism' equally includes any sort of hostility to the pathos of religious enthusiasm; whether it be the hostility of secularizing philosophers or of Anglican bishops, intent on defending their privileges against upstart Nonconformity. And so in his address 'To the Deists', which prefaces *Jerusalem* Chapter 3, he defends monks and Methodists: in the English context, perhaps the two most significant opposing representative types of anti-establishment enthusiasm. Not that either the monastic tradition or Methodism perfectly embodies what he would see as the true gospel spirit of forgiveness. But the point is that only in the context of a hegemonic culture which would cheerfully forgive these enthusiastic dissidents their dissent, and even honour it, might a dissident poetry like his own likewise have a chance of a proper hearing.

For Blake, indeed, the need to vindicate the poetic imagination virtually merges with the need to vindicate gospel-forgiveness. Hence, the Wheel of Religion is not only identified with the archetypally unforgiving spirit of Caiaphas; but is almost in the same breath called 'Natural Religion'.[8] It is said to shrink humanity 'into a little root a fathom long', to roll the sun 'into an orb', the moon 'into a globe': all of which are basic Blakean symbols of diminished imagination.[9] ('What it will be Questioned When the Sun rises do you not see a round Disk of fire somewhat like a Guinea O no no I see an Innumerable company of the Heavenly host crying Holy Holy Holy is the Lord God Almighty.')[10] And, by the same token, in the 'Address to the Deists' Deism is described not only as a diminishment of the religious imagination, which would be a readily intelligible charge; but then – in quite startling fashion – as the very essence of brutal war-mongering unforgiveness, too.[11]

III

As Blake sees it, 'The Modern Church Crucifies Christ with the Head Downwards'.[12]

The true preaching of the gospel of forgiveness, for him, essentially consists in affirming the absolute distinctiveness of each individual's proper vocation – or, to use his own terminology, the proper character of each vocation as a '*Minute Particular*'. Thus, for example, in one of the great speeches of *Jerusalem* Los, the eternal personification of prophetic poetry, addresses his hesitant and angst-ridden other self, his 'Spectre', in these words:

> Go Spectre! Obey my most secret desire:
> Which thou knowest without my speaking: Go to these Fiends of
>   Righteousness
> Tell them to obey their Humanities, & not pretend Holiness;
> When they are murderers: as far as my Hammer and Anvil permit
> Go, tell them that the Worship of God, is honouring his gifts
> In other men: & loving the greatest men best, each according
> To his Genius: which is the Holy Ghost in Man; there is no other
> God, than that God who is the intellectual fountain of Humanity;
> He who envies or calumniates: which is murder & cruelty,
> Murders the Holy-one: Go tell them this & overthrow their cup,
> Their marriage & their baptism, their burial & consecration:
> I have tried to make friends by corporeal gifts but have only
> Made enemies: I never made friends but by spiritual gifts;
> By severe contentions of friendship & the burning fire of thought.
> He who would see the Divinity must see him in his Children
> One first, in friendship & love; then a Divine Family, & in the midst
> Jesus will appear; so he who wishes to see a Vision; a perfect Whole
> Must see it in its Minute Particulars; Organized & not as thou
> O Fiend of Righteousness pretendest; thine is Disorganized
> And snowy cloud: brooder of tempests & destructive War
> You smile with pomp & rigor: you talk of benevolence & virtue!
> I act with benevolence & virtue & get murderd time after time:
> You accumulate Particulars, & murder by analyzing, that you
> May take the aggregate; & you call the aggregate Moral Law:
> And you call that Swelld & bloated Form; a Minute Particular.
> But General Forms have their vitality in particulars: & every
> Particular is a Man; a Divine Member of the Divine Jesus.
>
> (*Jerusalem* 91: 3–30)

Just as Amos and his followers denounced the mere practice of sacrifice, where it was divorced from 'justice', so Blake here – in his more self-reflective, poetically sacramental manner – denounces the Christian sacraments insofar as they are divorced from the 'benevolence & virtue' of true forgiveness.

In what sense does the true appreciation of Minute Particulars require an 'organized' vision? Surely, in the sense that a work of art may be said to be a drawing together of the fruits of individual experience, into an organic form of self-expression. 'Minute Particularity' is, simply, Blake's term for the creative spirit that comes to organic self-expression in the artistic 'spiritual gifts' of the most radical shakenness. The primal perversion of 'the Modern Church', on the other hand, lies in its commitment to a 'disorganized' moral law: an abstractly conceived imposition from above; 'disorganized', not so much in the sense of being incoherent, but by virtue of its manipulative inhibiting of such individual self-expression from below.

The church does indeed make some implicit claim to be appreciative of the Minute Particular, in the lip-service that it pays to God's forgiving love for each single individual. Yet all too often, for Blake, this merely masks the 'Swelld & bloated Form' of moralized, spiritually 'murderous' envy and calumny. Over against which, the whole thrust of Blakean prophecy is to insist on the proper *shaking* power of divine forgiveness.

IV

At one point in the epic narrative of his *Milton* Blake imagines Los descending to him at his home in Lambeth. Los stoops to bind on Blake's sandals, for the journey that will be the poem:

> trembling I stood
> Exceedingly with fear & terror, standing in the Vale
> Of Lambeth: but he kissed me and wishd me health.
> And I became One Man with him arising in my strength:
> Twas too late now to recede. Los had entered into my soul:
> His terrors now possess'd me whole! I arose in fury & strength.
>
> (*Milton* 22: 9–14)

This, then, is Blake's own formula for the essence of his distinctive form of poetic inspiration: a shaken, terrified 'trembling' before the sublime, which nevertheless issues in his rising up 'in fury & strength' to do battle with corruption.

In his Preface to the same work, he looks forward to a 'New Age' when 'the Daughters of Memory shall become the Daughters of Inspiration'. The Daughters of Memory (or the goddess Mnemosyne) are of course the classical muses; and in the first instance this is just another expression of his general preference for the Biblical poetic tradition over the classical. But at the same time he also turns away from 'memory' to 'inspiration' in the sense that he seeks to write epics which decisively transcend the simple retelling of historical or legendary stories. His first attempt at epic was *The French Revolution*, an apocalyptic poeticization of recent history. However, in the two works that followed, *America* and *Europe*, he made the transition; and thereafter the historical material in his writing is strictly confined to more or less veiled allusion, as he constructs myths primarily articulating aspects of eternity.[13]

At least in part, this surely has to be understood as a strategy for evading the pathos of glory. Classical pathos of glory ('the Covenant of Priam', as in the works of Homer and Virgil) produced epic stories in commemoration of the glorious ancestors, representing the idealized self-image of the ruling class. Ecclesiastical pathos of glory ('the Wheel of Religion') focuses on the memory of the church's origins, and on church history as remembered by particular church groups largely for purposes of self-glorification. These are the two forms of the pathos of glory which Blake is most concerned to combat. And his turn from 'memory' to 'inspiration' helps lift his work onto another level from them.

His myth develops in two basic stages. First, in the Lambeth prophecies of the 1790s, he develops a neo-Gnostic creation myth, in which the spirit of false, because unforgiving, theology appears as a fallen cosmic creator-spirit. And then, in his later works, that is joined together with an epic re-envisioning of the Last Judgement, as a multi-faceted unmasking of the Antichrist.

There are several resemblances between Blake's mythology and that of Gnosticism. The Gnostics, after all, were equally confrontational in their rejection of any sort of institutionalized religious establishment. He is fundamentally at one with them in his projection of that confrontation into a vision of cosmic struggle between rival supposedly divine principles; hence the characters of his myth, in their overlapping conflict-riven multiplicity, constitute an eternal community not unlike the Gnostic idea of the '*pleroma*'. He also follows the Jewish Gnosticism of the *Qabbalah* in its anthropomorphic representation of that *pleroma*, as a whole, in the form of the Primal Man, '*adam qadmon*. Thus, Blake's giant 'Albion' – whom he envisages simply prostrated by an exhausting conflict of opposing psychic impulses, and needing to be revived by their reconciliation – is simultaneously the British nation, the international community, everyman, and '*adam qadmon*: that is to say, a constant interplay of metaphors between those four distinct levels of meaning. And the figure of the false creator-god 'Urizen' in his epics is directly analogous to the Gnostic notion of the demiurge. In both cases we are presented with a similar caricature of the 'God' of establishment religion, in general.[14]

Yet Gnosticism is so very largely a case of the 'Daughters of Inspiration' being corrupted into mere protagonists for an other-worldly sectarian pathos of glory: a glorification of the informal sectarian community of 'those who know', and their charismatic teachers. There is none of this in

Blake's work. What opposes the consummate falsehood of fallen Urizen in the Lambeth prophecies is not any sort of sectarian other-worldliness. It is the spirit Blake calls 'Orc'. And Orc is very much a symbol of this-worldly, political rebellion. In the post-Lambeth writings – where Jesus begins to appear on the scene as the saviour-judge of the Last Judgement – all the moral truth of Orc's insurgency is subsumed into him. But Blake's Jesus still remains the this-worldly Orc; only now in a new capacity, and finally triumphant. The Orc of the Lambeth prophecies has nothing to do with the pathos of glory, either: like Jesus in the later epics he represents pure shakenness in itself, not any new post-revolutionary order, nor any revolutionary party-discipline on the way to such an order.[15] Even less does he have anything to do with the Gnostic equivalent.

Moreover, in the Lambeth prophecies fallen cosmic creativity appears not just in one form, as the Gnostics conceived it, but in two. On the one hand there is Urizen, the false supposedly divine source and legitimator of established power at its most unforgiving: desolate, life-denying, imagination-shrivelling – in short, everything anti-poetic. But on the other hand there is also Los, distinct from Urizen inasmuch as he is not so much a law-giver as a spirit of poetic inspiration, 'the Eternal Prophet' – a worker with fire, unlike Urizen who fights against fire – yet in these texts nevertheless very much another fallen figure; in effect, it seems, precisely a general symbol for the poetics of the pathos of glory.

Then in the post-Lambeth writings, the role of Los is transformed. The turning point comes at the end of Night Seven in *The Four Zoas*. Here, for the first time, Los appears – with his female counterpart or 'Emanation' Enitharmon – no longer as a fallen figure, but rather as a contributor to salvation. This is where Blake moves perhaps most positively beyond any Gnostic precedent: at the point where his writing becomes sacramental – as Los becomes his poetic symbol for the religiously truest forms of poetry itself.

The transformation of Los coincides exactly with Blake's shift from the outworkings of his Lambeth mythology to his new post-Lambeth focus on the Last Judgement. Thus, in *The Four Zoas* Night Eight sets the scene; Night Nine, actually entitled 'The Last Judgement', takes shape as a magnificently sustained apocalyptic envisioning of universal salvation, in which even Urizen is restored to innocence. And then, following on from that, the whole action both of *Milton* and of *Jerusalem* is essentially determined by a dialectic of impending apocalypse. *Milton* presents it in terms of a specific localized foreshadowing of the eternal tribunal, as the salvific spirit of Milton descends into Blake's cottage garden at Felpham to confront the monstrous figure of Satan there. *Jerusalem* consists of a repeated summons to judgement – by Los representing all the labour of poetry, by the female figure of Jerusalem representing poetic inspiration, in dialogue with Albion, and by Jerusalem's handmaid Erin who addresses the Daughters of Beulah – alternating with various images of resistance to that summons; until the resistance, at last, abruptly collapses.

For such a confrontational poet as Blake the Last Judgement was clearly a natural theme. He made at least seven different mandala-like paintings of it, full of surging energy. The last one, now lost, was to be his visual *magnum opus* – but the passion he invested in it ended up as self-defeating. A large-scale canvas, he worked at it for some seventeen years, up to his death; overpainting it layer upon layer, darker and darker, until (we are told) it was at last little more than a great expanse of blackness. And he also drafted a belligerent little prose commentary on this work.

But at the same time he completely rejected any conventional notion of the theme. For conventional visions of the Last Judgement have of course so often served merely to express the manipulative self-interest of religious establishments; encapsulating their various metaphysical threats and promises.

To the extent that this is the case, the supposed divine Judge is really none other than that false 'God' whom Blake caricatures in the figure of fallen Urizen, or whom in his more vulgar moments he taunts as 'old Nobodaddy [nobody's daddy] aloft'. In the context of conventional establishment Christianity, fallen Urizen may masquerade as the divine Father of Jesus. Yet Urizen he remains. And everything depends on grasping the absolute difference between the true judgement of 'forgiveness' and the false judgement of fallen Urizen, underneath its various theological disguises.

Essentially at issue here are, thus, two quite opposite attitudes to self-expressive individuality: fallen Urizenic judgement judges individual self-expression according to its conformity or nonconformity, in action, with the will of the establishment; but true, 'forgiving' judgement judges it, far rather, by the degree to which it is or is not *manipulated* by alien interests. 'The Fool shall not enter into Heaven let him be ever so Holy', Blake declares.[16] 'Holy', in this context, appears to mean whatever form of piety meets with establishment approval. 'The Fool', however, is surely his term for anyone who submits to what today we would call manipulation. If the spontaneous inclinations of anyone's conscience should happen to coincide with the will of the establishment, well and good – only, what Blake consistently denounces is just any sort of manipulativeness, to ensure that they do.

And so the Last Judgement envisaged by Blakean myth is not in the first instance a judgement of historic persons; that is, it is not an assessment of souls in terms of their particular achievements or sins, in an historic context. This indeed is the only form of judgement really relevant to the fallen Urizenic point of view, inasmuch as the Urizenic impulse is so very much determined by the historic projects of those in power: glorifying what serves those projects and condemning what impedes them. By contrast, Blake's concern is with the perennial issue of manipulation, as such. He is interested in systematically exploring the full range of different possible degrees and modes of manipulatedness, or resistance to manipulation. The characters brought to judgement in his myth do not belong either to historical actuality or to historical fiction – they are, instead, symbolic personifications of what he calls 'States': eternal, in the sense of trans-historical, existential possibilities.

In short, this judgement of 'States' is basically a step back, behind the historical judgement of particular persons. It is a trans-historic judgement of the various alternative basic mind-sets – manipulative or anti-manipulative – by which historical judgement may let itself be guided.

Blake himself contrasts 'States' with 'Individuals':

> Distinguish therefore States from Individuals in those States.
> States Change: but Individual Identities never change nor cease.
>
> (*Milton* 32: 22–3)

An 'Individual Identity', here, is an unchanging vocation: oneself in the fullness of what one is ideally called to be, free from all manipulative distortion; that deep underlying distinctiveness of every historic person, which the manipulator can never accept or forgive. 'Whenever any Individual Rejects Error & Embraces Truth a Last Judgment passes upon that Individual':[17] for Blake, each Individual is a battleground within which competing states struggle against one another. And his epics are intended as a sublime projection of that struggle.

All the characters in these epics are therefore universal personified states; with just three exceptions. The exceptions are Blake himself, the giant Albion and Jesus.

Blake portrays himself, as a particular individual, on the margins of the action in *Milton* and *Jerusalem*. Albion, one might say, stands for individuality in general: all the unrealized creative potential, both of particular persons and of communities. Jesus is the *eternal summons* to authentic individual self-actualization; the historic individual who the New Testament speaks of as having been effectively swallowed up in this symbolic role. Every other character represents a state, a particular mode of response to that summons. Indeed, even 'Milton' has here become the name of a state, in dialectical relationship to the historic individual Milton.

The basic precondition for Blake's breakthrough to his vision of the Last Judgement was his theoretical development of the concept of states.

V

In fact, the whole structure of Blake's mature mythic scheme directly reflects his theological concerns. This structure is both fourfold and twofold: a fourfold analysis of the various levels of human vulnerability to manipulation; a twofold analysis of the actual alienation of the manipulated, in terms of the social domain involved.

The four levels are represented by the four 'Zoas': Urizen, Luvah, Urthona and Tharmas. Manipulation plays on material or emotional need, with threats and promises. The Zoas in their primary prelapsarian identity – to which they are finally restored – simply personify four levels of basic human neediness. Fallen, in the meantime, they represent the four corresponding forms of manipulativeness.

Only the needy can be manipulated. To the Epicurean philosopher for example this means that true wisdom essentially consists in minimizing one's needs, by living a life of minimal emotional commitment. But this is not Blake's way. On the contrary, he believes in anti-manipulative enlightenment precisely through a dialectic of the most intense passion. Unlike the Epicureans, he is just as much opposed to the thoughtlessness of unimpassioned banality as he is to the thoughtlessness of the manipulated. And so he portrays the Zoas astonished, amazed, trembling, weeping, raging their way through the long shaking process that leads eventually to the liberated, self-accepting self-knowledge that comes with the Last Judgement, where at last they cease to be manipulative.

Their fall is, in each case, a fall into hubris: they set themselves up as false, unforgiving gods. Thus, the false god Urizen of the earlier Lambeth prophecies now becomes one of four. He represents unforgiveness justified and reinforced by manipulative appeal to the supposed cold, clear rationality of 'Moral Law'; which is cold and clear in its essential repudiation of any sort of insurgent enthusiasm – so serving the defensive self-interest of established power.

The primal crime associated with the name of Luvah – represented by Luvah's persuading Urizen to give him charge over the latter's 'Horses of Light' – then seems to stand for an equivalent unforgiveness on the part of the passionate rebel.[18] 'Luvah' is the Zoa-name for Orc. In *The Four Zoas* we see him infected with Urizenic vainglory, and subsequently entering into bitter warfare against Urizen; full of allegorical reference to the wars between Britain and revolutionary France.[19]

'Urthona' is the Zoa-name for Los. Prior to his transformation at the end of *The Four Zoas*, VII, Los is equally hubristic: claiming to act as divine regent for the incapacitated Urizen.[20]

Then in the pathetic figure of fallen Tharmas – proclaiming himself 'God' just after he has been dissolved into a condition of infinite watery chaos, rolling over the body of the sleeping Eternal Man – we see an image of hubristic unforgiveness as the merest moral passivity; deriving, it seems, from a simple loss of any sense of moral solidarity.[21]

Tharmas is the Zoa whose role is least clearly delineated – I think, just because it is the most general role. He is termed 'Parent power'; to him belongs 'the Body of Man'.[22] He seems to represent the most elementary needs of life, from which all others stem. In so far as political oppression is life-denying he is a natural dissident; hence, he becomes 'the Angel of the Tongue', championing free speech.[23] But his fall consists in his defeat. In *Jerusalem* we find him 'slain' by Luvah, in Luvah's 'own city of Paris'; in *The Four Zoas* he flees from Urizen.[24] His tormented relationship with his female emanation, Enion, appears to stand for the vulnerability of the instinct-driven self to the cruder carrot-and-stick tactics of tyranny: Enion turns away from him, he yearns for her – this yearning, I think, in effect symbolically encompasses all the unruly desires of the flesh, on which a manipulative regime may play. The watery chaos filled with 'monsters of the deep' which becomes the fallen Tharmas's natural element represents the soul entirely abandoned to the most immediate impulses of instinct. And the outcome is a politics of more or less reluctant collusion with the oppressor; so that 'the Angel of the Tongue' then degenerates into 'Tharmas . . . the False Tongue' – that is, the lying tongue of the accuser – 'even till Jesus, the image of the Invisible God / Became its prey'.[25]

Urizen and Luvah, by contrast, represent the needs that issue, not merely in reluctant collusion with oppression, but in its positive promotion. For the seduction of oppressive ideology lies in its satisfying both the Urizenic need for a clear-cut rational explanation of things and the Luvahic need for revenge, as an outlet for emotional frustration. In their fallen forms Urizen and Luvah are enemies; yet, at the same time, the falls of both are mutually reinforcing.

'Dark' Urthona, finally – in his fallenness, 'the Spectre of Urthona' – stands for the ordinary human need of the creative artist for social acceptance and ease of life: everything, in short, that tends to divert the artist in particular from the path of outright prophetic testimony against oppression. The first step towards salvation at the end of *The Four Zoas*, VII, occurs in the crucial dialogue there between Los and the Spectre of Urthona which heralds their 'reunion', in the sense of the artist's honestly confessing his human frailties for what they are.[26] (Somewhat along the lines of the archetypal 'confessions' of Jeremiah, perhaps: where the much-persecuted prophet bitterly laments what, in his all-too-human weakness, he experiences as his having been 'seduced' into his vocation by Yahweh, and curses the day of his birth; yet nevertheless still remains as 'seduced' as ever, so that the lament, in the end, simply serves to re-emphasize his unpopular message's God-given authority.)[27] So too, in *Jerusalem* the Spectre persists in his recalcitrance, but is ferociously subdued by Los and compelled to serve as chief labourer in the building of 'Golgonooza', that great city which is the whole of human life transformed by prophetic vision.[28]

In addition, each of the Zoas also has a female Emanation, emotionally torn apart from them in their fall. And it is the systematic contrast between the not-yet-reconciled Spectre, on the one hand, and the separated Emanation on the other hand – as opposing energies within the fallen psyche – which then constitutes Blake's twofold analysis of alienation, in terms of social domain.

Thus, there are in Blake's myth three basic modes of otherness imping-ing on the development of human identity, in that *whatever* otherness is not the saving otherness of Jesus is, on the contrary, a reinforcing *either* of the alienated Spectre *or else* of the alienated Emanation.

Both of these latter modes, I think, essentially need to be seen as representing the erroneous internalization, as one's own, of the will of another, or of many others, where this is actually inimical to one's own true interests, because it destroys authentic imaginative spontaneity. The difference between the two is just that the Spectre is an internalized alien will relating directly to public life, whereas the Emanation belongs in the first instance to private or domestic life, with only a secondary sort of relevance to the public domain.[29] Given the norms of a patriarchal social order, it therefore becomes natural, for the purposes of epic poetry, to picture the Spectre as male, the Emanations as female – even though they are each of them, in principle, inner voices within every human individ-ual, male or female. There are a few scattered references in *Jerusalem* to male Emanations.[30] But for the most part, in so far as an Emanation (or the domestically formed aspect of one's personality) ceases simply to 'emanate', as it should – but 'separates' instead – it becomes for Blake a malign 'Female Will'.[31] While an unreconciled Spectre, by implication, becomes a correspondingly malign male will.

The salvation for which Jesus stands is salvation from both these wills, or forms of manipulation, equally. Albion, it is true, is male; the general representative of humanity's need for salvation. Blake after all is a *public* prophet, looking in the first instance for a public, and hence to him symbolically male, response. Yet he is also quite clear that, in his view, this division of gender roles, the foundation of patriarchy, is itself a fruit of the fall. Indeed, he declares, in this sense 'Sexes must vanish & cease / To be, when Albion arises from his dread repose'.[32] In the meantime, the unreconciled Spectre appears to represent an internalizing of the corrupt pressures of general public opinion; while the separated Emanation repre-sents an internalizing of domestic pressures, deriving from a repressive ethos of guilt-ridden 'Chastity' which systematically falsifies every aspect of family life.

The Four Zoas was originally entitled *Vala*, after the Emanation of Luvah. And, of all the Emanations, Vala also remains the most significantly hubristic. She, above all, is the Emanation who has swelled into a Nature-Goddess.[33] (In the Lambeth prophecy *Europe* Enitharmon, the Emanation of Los, plays this role; but her activities are afterwards increasingly specialized, and confined to the domestic environment of the poet.) The word 'nature' has two meanings for Blake. In the theses entitled 'There is No Natural Religion' it functions as a general designation for reality unimaginatively perceived, by the senses alone.[34] But as he comes to associate it with Vala, it also, more particularly, becomes a name for that which is worshipped in a false religion, whose whole function is manipulatively to transmit habits of submission learnt in domesticity to public life. As the antithesis to the ideal unseparated Emanation 'Jerusalem', Vala further becomes the Goddess of Babylon; hence, the scarlet woman of Revelation 17, upon whose forehead is written 'Mystery, Babylon the Great, the Mother of Harlots and Abomination of the Earth'; and, by further extension, Rahab the harlot of Jericho – celebrated in the book of Joshua (and in Hebrews 11: 31) for betraying her city to the Israelites, but by Blake, in Gnostic fashion, given a polemically reversed significance.[35]

Blake's 'Satan', meanwhile – or the 'Covering Cherub'[36] – is, in the first instance, the sum of all unreconciled Spectres. Insofar as the two terms are distinguished (as in *Milton* 37: 60) 'Satan' designates the spectral attributes of paganism, the 'Covering Cherub' those of biblical religion. But then Vala/Rahab tends to coalesce with Satan.[37] In *The Four Zoas* VIII, for example, cosmic war appears as 'a Vast Hermaphroditic form' from which 'an awful wonder' bursts:

> Satan he was namd
> Son of Perdition terrible his form dishumanizd monstrous
> A male without a female counterpart a howling fiend
> Forlorn of Eden & repugnant to the forms of life
> Yet hiding the shadowy female Vala as in an ark & Curtains
> Abhorrd accursed ever dying an Eternal death
> Being multitudes of tyrant Men in union blasphemous
> Against the divine image.
>
> (*The Four Zoas* 104: 19–30)

Elsewhere, Satan himself is described as a 'Hermaphrodite': the conjunction of spectral fallenness with the fallenness of the separated Emanations; in parody of the ideal androgynous condition of Humanity before the fall.[38]

Fallen Vala/Rahab is his female aspect: as the manipulative rhetoric of what we nowadays call 'family values' enters into political discourse. With her daughter Tirzah, Rahab becomes the symbolic personification of 'Religion hidden in War': that is, the private piety of the 'authoritarian personality', in the sense of the latent sympathizer with totalitarianism.

So Blake multiplies his epic *dramatis personae*, always with the same basic critical concerns in view.

VI

The primary false god in the Lambeth prophecies is fallen Urizen; in the later epics, Satan effectively takes over that role. But there is a significant difference.

Fallen Urizen represents the *anti-sublime*. The Lambeth prophecies are a sublime allegorical portrayal of the anti-sublime; that is their paradox. Urizen's world ('the Ulro', as it comes to be called) is described in terms of the most sublime horror, yet when Urizen falls into a coma what this stands for is in fact a radical stunting of the imaginative capacity to grasp the sublime. Urizenic false religion tends towards the purest Deism, in its original sense.

Satan is indeed partly identified with Urizen.[39] By contrast, however, what he represents is not so much the depoeticizing anti-sublime. It is far rather the *corrupt sublime*. That is, it is the sublime expression of the pathos of glory. This comes out most directly in *Milton*. For here the spectral aspect of Satan is at the same time the poet's 'Shadow'; inasmuch as Blake thinks that the historical Milton was partly enslaved to a spectral sort of theology. And yet Milton is the poet he most admires, as a pioneer of the sublime.[40]

At the climax of *Milton* the two aspects of the poet's inner life, both his false shadow and his true genius, descend together – 'a Cloud & Human Form' – into Blake's garden, by the sea at Felpham. Thus, the Human Form

> collecting all his fibres into impregnable strength
> Descended down a Paved work of all kinds of precious stones
> Out from the eastern sky; descending down into my Cottage
> Garden: clothed in black, severe & silent he descended.
>
> (*Milton* 38: 5–8)

The opposing Cloud is filled with twelve Gods representing paganism, and twenty-seven Heavens representing the various stages of Biblical and church history; as well as forty-eight Starry Regions, which are both the 'Cities of the Levites' and 'Empires of Chaos', or the whole world of priestcraft in its role as an adjunct to warfare. Eventually, though, all these coalesce into the sublime shape of a single sea monster:

> The Spectre of Satan stood upon the roaring sea & beheld
> Milton within his sleeping Humanity! trembling & shuddring
> He stood upon the waves a Twenty-seven-fold mighty Demon
> Gorgeous & beautiful: loud roll his thunders against Milton
> Loud Satan thunderd, loud & dark upon mild Felpham shore
> Not daring to touch one fibre he howld round upon the Sea.
>
> (*Milton* 38: 9–14)

We are no doubt meant to recall here the gorgeous beauty of Satan's appearance as the serpent in Milton's *Paradise Lost*;[41] perhaps too his earlier, whispering approach in that epic to the 'sleeping Humanity' of Eve. But Milton's presence 'within' the sleeping Albion is now a countervailing impulse to wakefulness, in self-defence against the 'twenty-seven-fold' temptations of spuriously sublime church-Christianity – which is thereby compelled to thunder.

Abruptly, the perspective shifts:

> I also stood in Satans bosom & beheld its desolations!
> A ruind Man: a ruind building of God not made with hands.
> Its plains of burning sand, its mountains of marble terrible:
> Its pits & declivities flowing with molten ore & fountains
> Of pitch & nitre; its ruind palaces & cities & mighty works;
> Its furnaces of affliction in which his Angels & Emanations
> Labour with blackend visages among its stupendous ruins
> Arches & pyramids & porches colonades & domes.
>
> (*Milton* 38: 15–22)

This is Blake's demythologization of hell: as the inner state of the 'Selfhood' in each individual; paradoxically understood as an outcome of self-destructive self-identification with the will of the manipulative Other.

Milton addresses Satan:

> Satan! my Spectre! I know my power thee to annihilate
> And be a greater in thy place, & be thy Tabernacle
> A covering for thee to do thy will, till one greater comes
> And smites me as I smote thee & becomes my covering.
>
> (*Milton* 38: 29–32)

But, he declares, he chooses not to. In other words, he will not seek to confront the manipulativeness of established ideology by setting up a new rival sectarianism; since every sectarian ideology, as such, is latently manipulative. Instead he opts for 'Self Annihilation' – in the sense of trying to break the cycle of manipulated manipulativeness, once and for all, in the most radical manner. That, then, is his dramatic challenge. Satan hears it:

> Coming in a cloud, with trumpets & flaming fire
> Saying I am God the judge of all, the living & the dead
> Fall therefore down and worship me, submit thy supreme
> Dictate, to my eternal Will & to my dictate bow
> I hold the Balances of Right & Just & mine the Sword
> Seven Angels bear my Name & in those Seven I appear
> But I alone am God & I alone in Heavn & Earth
> Of all that live dare utter this, others tremble & bow
> Till All Things become One Great Satan, in Holiness
> Oppos'd to Mercy, and the Divine Delusion Jesus be no more.
> *(Milton* 38: 50–39: 2)

But all his raging is in vain. For:

> Suddenly around Milton on my Path, the Starry Seven
> Burnd terrible!
> *(Milton* 39: 3–4)

These are the seven angels from the Book of Revelation. And then:

> my path became a solid fire, as bright
> As the clear Sun & Milton silent came down on my Path.
> And there went forth from the Starry limbs of the Seven: Forms
> Human; with Trumpets innumerable, sounding articulate
> As the Seven spake; and they stood in a mighty Column of Fire
> Surrounding Felphams Vale, reaching to the Mundane Shell,
> Saying
> Awake Albion awake! reclaim thy Reasoning Spectre. Subdue
> Him to the Divine Mercy. Cast him down into the Lake
> Of Los, that ever burneth with fire, ever & ever Amen!
> *(Milton* 39: 4–12)

Even here, it is true, Satan remains closely associated with Urizen: as the '*Reasoning* Spectre', where mere reasoning is set over against true imaginativeness.[42] Only, the emphasis has decisively shifted. Thus note, above all, the correspondences between this epiphany of salvific poetry and the immediately preceding epiphany of Satan: the trumpets, the fire; the seven angels in Satan's entourage as well. The star patterns of the beneficent Starry Seven also recall the stars of the forty-eight Starry Regions associated with Satan. Here, essentially, we have the true sublime engaged in sublime battle with the false sublime; the two sources of inspiration between which, as Blake sees it, the historic Milton had been torn. This is how Blake bears witness to the intrinsic ambivalence of all religious forms.[43]

VII

Blake is at the same time very much at one with the Hebrew prophets – and decisively distanced, again, from any sort of religious sectarianism – in his pressing concern to articulate the corporate vocation of his nation. So the Lambeth prophecies, to begin with, represent a direct negation of the manipulative pathos-of-glory nationalism of the war-mongering British political establishment; celebrating its great enemies the American and French revolutionaries, as manifestations of Orc. And then, post-Lambeth, he also goes on to develop a more positive epic delineation of true Britishness: symbolized by the awakening, or the healing of Albion.

Just as the Hebrew tradition stemming from Amos had identified the true vocation of Israel with an ideal shaken commitment to 'justice', so Blake identifies the true vocation of Britain with an equally shaken ideal commitment to 'forgiveness', in his special sense of that term.

Jerusalem, the city of God, personified as the ideal Emanation of Albion, is the symbol of this vocation. Hence, the epic named after her is more or less randomly bespattered with British place-names, for the most part drawn by Blake from his reading of geography books. The British cathedral cities are personified as a group of not very effective would-be healers of Albion, in partnership with Los. A new group of Spectres now appears, in the shape of the twelve sons of Albion, named after some of Blake's particular personal enemies: spectral forms of British identity. To them there further correspond the twelve daughters of Albion, specifically British forms of female will. And just as Canaan was parcelled out into twelve lots, so too are the counties of Britain, twice: once to the twelve sons of Israel and once to the twelve sons of Albion.[44] The holy mountains of Canaan are given British equivalents. The various districts of London, likewise, lend their names to key features in the landscape of eternity. In general, British names are systematically mixed together with biblical names – to symbolize the continuity of Blake's project with that of the prophets.

In the famous quatrains displaced into the Preface of *Milton*, finally, Blake's imagination carries Jesus, too, into the British landscape:

And did those feet in ancient time,
Walk upon England's mountains green:
And was the holy Lamb of God,
On England's pleasant pastures seen!

And did the Countenance Divine,
Shine forth upon our clouded hills?
And was Jerusalem builded here,
Among these dark Satanic Mills?

To which the Blakean answer is presumably yes, the Saviour is and always has been present, and yes, Jerusalem is and always has been established, wherever – although only to the extent that – anyone truly learns to forgive. The 'dark Satanic Mills' are the great mechanisms of unforgiveness driven by the 'Wheel of Religion'; also represented by the turnings of the zodiac, and operated by Satan as 'the Miller of Eternity', or 'Prince of the Starry Wheels'; the animating spirit of a theology which metaphysically converts the whole benighted universe into a mill for the grinding-down of dissident individuals.[45] And the 'ancient time' in question here is clearly a metaphor for the deepest-seated imaginative capacities of British culture: before – in the sense of being logically prior to – the fall of the British into their own national version of original sin, represented by those mills.[46]

8 Hölderlin
Towards releasement

I

In the poetry of Hebrew prophecy God speaks directly. But in the mainstream culture of late Christendom that no longer happens. So Blake, in this respect at least submitting to the dictates of that mainstream culture, now seeks to convey the shaking-power of divine grace indirectly: by an epic portrayal of the effects of shakenness.

And Hölderlin does the same – only in lyric form.

In Hölderlin's case, however, there is a further difference: Blake's poetry still resembles that of the prophets in that it mediates the pathos of shakenness as a pathos of confrontation, in testimony to a jealous God; but Hölderlin's work, on the contrary, mediates the pathos of shakenness, rather, as a deliberately *non*-confrontational, introverted pathos of mourning and yearning. Gone is the jealousy of the jealous God of biblical tradition. Here, instead, Christ is brought into paradoxical fellowship with the quite *un*-jealous pagan gods of Greek antiquity.

What does this mean?

II

Perhaps the most fundamental theological difference between Blake and Hölderlin is that each takes for granted, in the background, what the other is most of all concerned to accentuate, in the foreground. Thus, whereas Blake's primary concern is to analyse and to denounce the spiritual corruption of establishment Christianity, Hölderlin simply takes it for granted that the world of establishment Christianity is god-forsaken. Blake, on the other hand, seems to take for granted that, as things stand, the true shaken poet's vocation is bound to be marginal and solitary; whereas, in a sense, the whole of Hölderlin's greatest work is nothing but one long anguished struggle to reconcile himself to that inevitability.

During the early years of the French Revolution, whilst he was a student at the Tübingen Stift, Hölderlin wrote a series of 'Hymns to the Ideals of Humanity'. Although he was ostensibly then training to be a Lutheran pastor, these hymns are in fact essentially post-Christian in character. They make no reference to Christ; but are addressed to Immortality, to the Genius of Greece, to the Goddess of Harmony ('Urania'), to the Muse, to Freedom, to Humanity, to Beauty, to Friendship, to Love, to the Genius of Youth, to the Genius of Daring. At the same time, however, they are clearly designed for public use; presumably, in some future equivalent to the new Jacobin sacred festivals. As such, the effect is of a rather etiolated and monotonous pathos of glory. At this early stage in his poetic development Hölderlin certainly seems to have been hoping for something a whole lot more than solitary marginality: he is writing, very much, as one of the would-be guiding spirits of the nascent revolutionary movement, in its theological aspect.

But then, at length, the darker side of the Revolution finally became unmistakable. And Hölderlin was shaken, by this disaster, into a wholesale rethinking of his vocation. Although still far from reconciled with the Christianity of the *ancien régime*, his mature poetry is nevertheless also decisively complicated by a principled renunciation of his earlier political ambitions. He becomes an infinitely more interesting poet as a result, turning away from a revolutionary pathos of glory towards pure pathos of shakenness; from now on, completely removed from any sort of partisan spirit – or, therefore, from any immediate prospect of popularity.

III

Looking back, indeed, Hölderlin actually began to see those old abandoned hopes as having been a form of revolutionary hubris. Hence his special interest, during the period of the later 1790s, in the story of Empedokles, which he made three successive attempts to convert into the topic of a major verse drama.[1] For, as he sees it, this is precisely a classic tale of recoil from hubristic public ambition: a projection of his own recoil.

Empedokles was a native of the Greek colony of Acragas (present-day Agrigento) in Sicily, in the fifth century BCE: a poet who was also a philosopher and man of action; a pioneer in the art of political oratory; in his youth a great athlete; with a reputation, too, as a great healer and worker of miracles. As a poet he wrote religious hymns, a didactic work on medicine, and an epic in three books setting out his philosophical vision of Nature, some fragments of which have survived. He had been a disciple of Pythagoras; but Diogenes Laertius reports that he publicized, to all and sundry, what were meant to be the secret mysteries of Pythagorean doctrine, and was therefore expelled from the Pythagorean Order. Politically, he was a republican and a democrat, a champion of the common people against their overlords. And according to legend he ended his life by throwing himself into the volcanic crater of Mount Etna.

Hölderlin is obsessed with the potential symbolic significance of Empedokles's death. In all three fragmentary versions of the play, Empedokles is represented as a radical politico-religious reformer, tempted to hubris by the adulation of his followers; who, however, struggles to overcome the temptation, and finally opts for death as the most decisive way of once and for all renouncing that adulation.

The three versions differ, most basically, in their presentation of the temptation. In both of the first two Empedokles has in fact already fallen into sin – but is now, as he goes towards his death, repentant. In the first version, his fall is simply represented as resembling that of Tantalus: a matter of self-serving pride. He has pronounced himself a god, in front of all the people.

By contrast, in the second, he is more of a Prometheus, a rebel liberator. His essential crime, as the conservative high priest Hermokrates sees it, lies in his betrayal of divine secrets to the mob. But that way lies anarchy. Such secrets are only safe when confined to the priestly elite; who (as Hermokrates frankly confesses) rule by means of mystification. And in this breach of established order, Empedokles has also alienated the gods. His titanic role as a revolutionary leader has corrupted him; so now he must die, in token of his absolute repentance.

In the third version, on the other hand, Empedokles has not fallen. Here he appears indeed almost as a Christ-like figure. Yet it is his very refusal of hubris which drives him to his death: lest the devotion of his followers be altogether focused, in idolatrous fashion, on his own living presence as a leader – to the detriment of his teachings in themselves.

In whichever of these various forms he is portrayed, though – whether as another Tantalus, another Prometheus or another Christ – Empedokles's death essentially remains for Hölderlin a symbol for true poetic integrity, in the renunciation of premature revolutionary hopes. Clearly, Hölderlin is attracted to the Empedokles story, above all, as a dramatic externalization of his own most fundamental temptation as a poet, and its ultimate overcoming. That is: the temptation represented, most naively, by the Tübingen hymns.

There are, in fact, three basic moments in the dialectic of Hölderlin's thought:

- First, his infinite revolutionary negation of the givenness of the given politico-religious order.
- Then, his qualified negation of that negation – his Empedoklean recoil from the temptations of revolutionary hubris.

- Finally – the main business of his great poetry from around 1799 onwards – his protracted struggle to come to terms with the existential constraints imposed by those first two moments, combined.

The first and second moments are effectively juxtaposed in the very starkest fashion, for instance, in the first of his great hymns from the period (?)1799–1803, 'Wie wenn am Feiertage'.[2] Thus, the first seven and a half verses of this hymn contain his boldest and most explicit welcome to the upheavals of the French Revolution, as a stimulus to poetic creativity. The Revolution is compared here to a thunderstorm, just past; for poetry, it seems, this is 'favourable weather'. Or, again, he compares it to daybreak.

Nature, the poets' tutor, has awoken 'amidst the clang of arms':

> And like the flash of fire in the eye
> Of one who schemes great things, so
> Now the portents, the deeds of the world have lit
> Fresh flames in the souls of the poets.[3]
> ('Wie wenn am Feiertage', lines 28–31)

'The powers of the gods' – the poetic spirit, conceived as so many angels – which had hitherto been oppressed like the poor peasantry, are at long last beginning to be recognized for what they are. 'Shaken by remembrance' of all that has happened, the poets are given the task of bearing prophetic witness to that shakenness:

> we – my fellow poets! – are called to stand
> Bareheaded beneath God's thunder storms,
> To seize the Father's lightning bolt itself
> With our own hand, wrapping in song
> The heavenly gift, to pass it to the people.
> For if we're but pure in heart,
> Like children, and if our hands are guiltless
>
> The Father's bolt, the pure, will never singe us
> And, although convulsed, all anguished with the Almighty's
> Anguish, even so, in the steep downrushing storms
> Of the God's approach, the heart will still hold fast.[4]
> ('Wie wenn am Feiertage', lines 56–66)

This is the sublime Hölderlinian vision of the poet as revolutionary.

Yet then – quite abruptly, the poem disintegrates. As Hölderlin left it, only a few further broken lines remain. And these lines appear to represent a total *volte-face*:

But alas! When of

Alas!

And let me say at once

If I draw near to gaze upon the Heavenly,
They themselves, they throw me down, deep below the living,
Me the false priest, into the dark, that I
Might sing the warning song to those with ears to hear.
There.[5]

('Wie wenn am Feiertage', lines 67–75)

When he speaks of 'the warning song' it may indeed well be that he is thinking, at least in part, quite specifically of his own (not yet abandoned) work on the story of Empedokles.

The image of 'fire from heaven' is one which Hölderlin quite consistently uses to signal the revolutionary moment in his thought. He also associates this with wine, and hence with Dionysus. (As in 'Wie wenn am Feiertage': 'And so it is that now the sons of earth / drink without danger heavenly fire'.)[6] Accordingly, he tends to speak of the opposite, counterbalancing ideal as one of 'sobriety'.

At one level, the contrast is a purely aesthetic one. In his often quoted letter of 4 December 1801 to the dramatist Casimir Ulrich Böhlendorff, for example, he uses the image of 'fire from heaven' to refer, in the most general terms, to the 'warmth' of free-spirited enthusiasm; that is, the inner impulse of any sort of genuine poetic originality. 'Sobriety', as the balancing ideal, is simply understood as 'precision' or 'clarity of presentation': the poet's technical mastery of set forms, traditional disciplines. To the poets of ancient Greece, he argues in this letter, heavenly fire was what came naturally; their great achievement was to cultivate a balancing sobriety. But to the poets of Western modernity, it is the other way round.[7]

Still more fundamental to Hölderlin's thinking as a whole, however, is what one might term the *theological* sobriety of the 'warning song'. For that is what perhaps most decisively sets the scene for the great poetry of his elegies and later hymns. Cut off, once and for all, from the conventional religious culture of his world by his experience of the fire from heaven, he was also then – by this chastened sobriety – cut off from any countervailing dream of revolutionary community. And so he found himself condemned to what was, for him, a terrible inner solitude. That, really, is what it means to him when he goes on, in poems like 'Brod und Wein', 'Germanien', 'Patmos' or 'Mnemosyne', to lament the absence of the gods.

IV

Empedokles throwing himself into the blazing crater of the volcano is, it seems, for Hölderlin a symbolic representation of his own personal option for spiritual solitariness. As such, it is both a tragic and a heroic act. In its tragic aspect it may be seen as an eerie foreshadowing of Hölderlin's own fall into the long living death of his insanity. Yet the prevailing message of the play is that it was, nevertheless, very much the right thing for Empedokles to do.

In its heroic aspect it is a symbolic renunciation of politics. Here Empedokles the detached contemplative philosopher – oriented towards eternity and contemptuous of mere temporal preoccupations – finally condemns and overthrows Empedokles the political activist. Certainly, Hölderlin has none of Blake's absolute antipathy to all philosophy as such.

On the contrary.[8] To put it in Blakean terms: the hubris that chiefly concerns Hölderlin is that of Luvah, not (as in Blake's case) that of Urizen.

V

This is also what renders Hölderlin such an important figure to Heidegger.

Heidegger actually wrote at some considerable length on Hölderlin. His writings included three lecture series at the university of Freiburg – in the winter semester 1934–5 on the hymns 'Germanien' and 'Der Rhein', in the winter semester 1941–2 on the hymn 'Andenken', and in the summer semester of 1942 on the hymn 'Der Ister' – as well as a collection of essays, mostly dating from around the same time-span, *Erläuterungen zu Hölderlins Dichtung*.[9] But in fact his whole thinking, from this period onwards, is profoundly influenced by his reading of Hölderlin.

On the one hand, Heidegger regards Hölderlin as a paradigmatic pioneer of the sort of post-metaphysical rethinking of the holy which he himself now seeks to pursue in philosophical terms.

In Chapter 4 I compared his view of 'metaphysics' with that of Nietzsche. There is a sense in which he seeks to be the philosophical exponent of a Hölderlinian overcoming of metaphysics – as opposed to what Nietzsche is attempting.

Prior to his work on Hölderlin, in *Sein und Zeit* he confronts what he calls 'metaphysics' in the most purely trans-cultural terms. The thinking elaborated here is already premised on a very precise systematic identification of the highest form of existential truth with a maximum of properly appropriated shakenness. (Heidegger himself borrows the Kierkegaardian term '*Angst*'. I prefer 'shakenness', if only to escape the overtones of neurosis associated with *Angst*; but the intended meaning is much the same.) At this stage, however, the trans-cultural universality of the discussion renders it strictly pre-poetic. Thus, the truth in question is defined in terms of the most radical possible working through, by each individual, of all that is, deep down, most disturbing and thought-provoking in the sheer fact of one's own mortality; without reference to any particular culture-specific narrative. And 'meta-physics', then, in this context is quite straightforwardly definable as any sort of thinking with regard to matters of ultimate concern which deploys other criteria, besides that.

But in his later writings Heidegger turns to consider the special potential truth of great poetry as the primary, most direct medium for culturally artic-ulating – and disseminating – the sort of truth which in *Sein und Zeit* he had sought to analyse in its trans-cultural aspect. And to this end he borrows a whole new vocabulary from Hölderlin.

So, like Hölderlin, he starts to speak of 'the gods', 'the God', 'the holy'. By contrast to 'the gods', who represent the various sources of poetic inspi-ration in so far as these are historically contingent, 'the God' here is a term for poetic truth in its perennial essence. 'The holy' – or 'Nature' – serves basically as an alternative, Hölderlin-derived name for what elsewhere he terms 'Being': in effect, the sheer shaking-power of whatever the shaken are shaken by, in its not-yet-interpreted immediacy. Above all, Heidegger values Hölderlin for the extraordinary religious radicality, and the poignant eloquence, of the Hölderlinian evocation of the holy, in this sense.

Yet, on the other hand, Hölderlin is also of crucial importance to him as a specifically *German* poet, helping to define a particular vision of German national identity. In the context of the Third Reich, Heidegger uses his Hölderlin-interpretations as a medium for developing his own distinctive form of German nationalism, by way of an alternative to that of (mainstream) Nazism.

No doubt, the *proper* political sequel to *Sein und Zeit* would have been some systematic exploration of the strategic possibilities for what I have called a 'solidarity of the shaken' in general. That is to say, a solidarity so far as possible grounded in shared shakenness alone – radically mistrust-ful therefore of every sort of propaganda-wielding established power. This actual phrase, 'solidarity of the shaken', was first coined by the Heideggerian Czech philosopher Jan Patočka in the 1970s; he then went on to become one of the co-founders – along with that other notable admirer of Heidegger, Václav Havel – of the dissident human rights movement Charter 77.[10] Heidegger himself, though, had no experience of any such movement in his own world. When Nazism appeared on the scene, it appealed to a set of cultural prejudices he partly shared, with its transcendence of traditional Christian confessionalism and its promise of a third way beyond both Bolshevism and 'Americanism'. But it was also a revolutionary movement with, at its centre, a gaping intellectual void. With prodigious naivety, he thought at first that he might help fill this void, and become a major intellectual co-shaper of the new regime. The very stupidity of the movement was in this sense, I think, its attraction to him: it looked like a blank page. And so it was that in the first days of the Nazi revolution he joined the party and accepted the political post of Rector of the University of Freiburg; which he filled for some ten months, before eventually resigning in February 1934. His writings on Hölderlin (like his Nietzsche lectures) all in fact belong to the long process of his shuddering recoil from that terrible error.

But – as I have said – the trouble is that, for Heidegger, this then becomes a wholesale, quite undiscriminating recoil from the whole domain of politics in any form, even the most shaken. Which, in my view, also profoundly distorts his reading of Hölderlin.

Thus: at the heart of *Sein und Zeit* stands the concept of '*Entschlossenheit*', which the English translators have rendered as 'resoluteness'. This is Heidegger's term for an 'authentic Being-towards-death'.[11] He further defines it as a 'readiness for *Angst*'.[12] It is, one might say, resoluteness in the sense of a resolute staying with shakenness; where shakenness is conceived in the very purest pre-political – as well as pre-poetic – terms; without reference to politics one way or another.

The equivalent concept in his later work, however, is that of '*Gelassenheit*'. This is a term borrowed from the mediaeval mysticism of Meister Eckhart, de-confessionalized; and rendered by the English translators as 'releasement'.[13] Releasement is the equivalent to resoluteness inasmuch as it, too, essentially signifies a staying with shakenness. The difference is that in this case shakenness has come to be conceived far rather in polemically *post*-political terms.

Like 'the essence of truth' in 1930, releasement is described as a matter of 'letting beings be'. It is thinking as a renunciation of willing: a breaking free, first and foremost, from the whole mentality driving the advance of technology, but more generally from all desire for mastery of one's world; a pure contemplativeness, which completely abandons any serious ambition to make an organized intervention in worldly affairs; or a sort of inner emigration, universalized as the highest form of shaken wisdom – not only under conditions of tyranny but, it would appear, everywhere and always. And for Heidegger Hölderlin is very much an heroic representative of this ideal. Hölderlin's turn away from the revolutionary fever of the early 1790s prefigures Heidegger's own turn away from the revolutionary fever of 1933. In Heidegger's reading of him, he therefore comes to stand for a true pride in Germany, as a land of thinkers and poets, decisively set apart from the corrupting influence of political agitation.

Just as vulgar Nazism sought to render Adolf Hitler into the symbolic personification of German destiny, so Heidegger in 1934 sets out to identify true Germanness with the very different symbolic figure of Hölderlin. Henceforth, he urges, if we want to know what it means to be authentically German we will have to refer, in the first instance, to this poetic legacy. It is Hölderlin, and no other, who has to be acknowledged as the true founder of a new Germany! However paradoxical such a claim might seem, that is what would now provide the basis for '"politics" in the highest and ownmost sense' of the word; which is no longer really politics in any conventional sense at all, but rather the exact opposite.[14] If there is indeed to be a revolution, he now contends, it should precisely be one which installs the spirit of Hölderlin as the leading spirit within German culture as a whole; that is to say, the spirit of releasement – as rendered into sacramental poetry.

Over against the exuberant rage and wild promises of Nazi propaganda, Heidegger thus exalts a poetry whose *Grundstimmung* or fundamental tone is, as he puts it, one of 'hallowed grief', over the flight of the ancient gods. Although in view of the prevailing pressure of censorship the antithesis here had to remain veiled and implicit, it is certainly quite radical.

And yet – note the consequences. Inasmuch as Heidegger is now rejecting the vulgar Nazi pathos of glory, not for being pathos of glory *as such*, but simply for being (in the conventional sense) political, he still has not arrived at what I would regard as the key definitive counter-concept, the pathos of shakenness. He has no clear concept of the pathos of shakenness *in itself*, as the proper substance of poetic truth; for he is so obse___d with the particular *form* it assumes in Hölderlin's poetry that th___ all he sees.

One can well understand why Heidegger should have felt su__urden on empathy with Hölderlin – but the result surely is that he l can ever, in Hölderlin's work far greater than any single literary en__ are indeed to all fairness, be expected to bear. _he Hölderlinian

Against Heidegger, I would want to argue th__ery much in con- grasp the undoubted element of profound _press the pathos of vision, then Hölderlin really does have t__th is primarily in th__ junction with other poets, such as Bla__ form. And only so c shakenness in quite different forms. B __ *substance* of that pathos; only sec__ this be clarified.[15]

VI

What is more, I think that there is also another major weakness in the Heideggerian reading: the way Heidegger allows his focus on Hölderlin's Germanness so very largely to obscure the true significance of Hölderlin's eccentric Christianity.[16] Which is a shame – especially since Hölderlin's poetic response to Christ actually involves much of his most interesting exploration of (what Heidegger calls) releasement.

For the fact is that, as a young cosmopolitan sympathizer with the French revolutionaries, Hölderlin in his earliest writings appears altogether to reject both Germany and Christianity, together; simply idealizing ancient Greece as the symbolic antithesis to both.[17] But his turn away from the Revolution immediately brings with it a twofold process of re-evaluation in this regard.

As I have said, in the later rewriting of *Der Tod des Empedokles* he increasingly portrays Empedokles as a Christ-like redeemer. A new character is introduced into the third version: Manes, an Egyptian sage, Empedokles's old teacher. And there is a scene where Manes, in discussion with Empedokles, sets out – as an abstract possibility – what a true redeemer's death might be like. It sounds very much like a foreshadowing of the death of Jesus. However, Manes asks, would the death that Empedokles now proposes be of that sort? In this scene he is very sceptical.

Yet, according to Hölderlin's sketch for the ending of the play, in the final scene, after Empedokles had in fact died, it was planned that Manes would confess that, yes, he was now convinced of Empedokles's divine vocation. So that Empedokles begins to appear as a forerunner of Christ.

And then, in the great elegies and hymns that followed, Christ himself begins to figure directly. He appears here as 'the last' of the gods.

How can this be?

It is, on the face of it, such a bizarre suggestion! In the hymn 'Der Einzige' ('The Unique One') Hölderlin names Christ as 'the brother' of Herakles and Dionysus ('Evius') – but, in the very next breath, also confesses to a certain 'shame' thus associating him with those 'worldly men'.[18]

Nevertheless, again in the same poem he speaks of searching through the commune of the gods, in the hope of finding in their midst the one he loves. And having apparently failed in his quest, he cries out:

> My
> O you, my good lord!
> Why did you
> Away? And
> I enquired am
> The heroes and ... ients,

The gods, why were you still
Hidden? And now it grieves
My soul, you old immortals, to find
You too (it seems) so clamorous
That serving either
I must forgo the other.

    Yet well I know, I am the one
To blame! For I cling
Too tight to you, O Christ![19]
        ('Der Einzige', lines 36–50)

So it would seem that, while he confesses to a sense of shame at placing Christ in the company of the Greek gods, at the same time he is also ashamed of that shame itself. The apparent either/or choice between them is, after all, nothing but illusion. This whole poem is said to be, deep down, an expression of excessively *clinging* love for Christ:

    My love however clings to one
Alone. Indeed, it's true
This time my song's been too impulsive,
A sin of self-indulgence –
For which I'll make amends
In songs that are to come.
Always a proper balance
Eludes me.[20]
        ('Der Einzige', lines 66–73)

We have here the clearest possible indication that, as Hölderlin himself sees it, his association of Christ with these other gods is no mere poetic conceit. On the contrary, it is a matter of conscience.

    In my view, it has essentially to be seen as just another logical corollary of the basic Empedoklean turn in his thinking. Thus: his repudiation of the confrontational partisan politics associated with the French Revolution is at the same time a repudiation of confrontational and partisan politics in general. He wants to appeal to the true authority of Christ, in the first instance against the sacred kitsch of conventional Christianity, and then against every other form of soullessness in modern life as a whole – but it must be in the most non-confrontational and non-partisan way possible. He does not want to argue either for or against any particular church or any particular sect as such. His is a purely poetical vision.

This surely is the sense in which his 'Christ' belongs with the Greek gods. They have no worshipping community; no community that might ever become confrontationally partisan on their behalf. Once they did. But no longer. And having lost their worshipping communities, they now live on in poetry alone. In that sense, they have as it were been purified.

This is not Hölderlin's own formulation. But nevertheless I think it quite accurately represents the underlying logic of his procedure.

Of course, since Christ still does have his worshipping communities very much alive, there is endless danger of the Christ-invoking poet's getting mixed up in the confrontational partisan conflict of those communities; whether for or against them. Hölderlin's strategy, however, is basically designed to avoid this. It is all about staying on another level.

Faced with the provocations of corrupt and doctrinaire establishment Christianity on the one hand, or of corrupt and doctrinaire irreligion on the other, this is not always easy. When Hölderlin speaks of 'clinging too tight' to Christ he is surely thinking of his own continuing temptation to lapse back into a much more confrontational and partisan critique – and to do so, now, in Christ's name.

There is indeed a rather curious passage in 'Patmos' which I think also encapsulates the same anxiety, only in another form.[21] Hölderlin here has just completed his most definitive reworking of the gospel story; when suddenly his musings on the past receive a quite startling, pugnacious interruption:

> But if someone, spurring himself on
> As we talked sadly on the road, should catch me off my guard
> With an attack, and tempt me, slave that I am, to make
> A graven image of the God –
> Visible in anger once I saw
> The Lord of Heaven, not that I should be something, but
> To learn . . .[22]
>
> ('Patmos', lines 167–73)

This attacker is presumably some polemical advocate – or polemical enemy – of existing organized religion who lures the poet, by way of response, into a much more dogmatically cut and dried expression of his own point of view than he would wish. Two figures talking sadly together on the road: the scene is immediately reminiscent of the story in Luke 24: 13–35, where the two disciples, walking to Emmaus, look back over the events leading up to the death of Jesus – and cannot understand what it all means. But the sort of misunderstanding, in relation to the gospel, which matters most to Hölderlin is precisely that which issues in impatient polemical aggression; where one invokes the wrath of God, not just in order to learn, but so as 'to be something' oneself. This for him, it seems, is the very essence of idolatry. And, alas, it is infectious.

He sets Christ in the company of the other gods – who are now in fact deprived of any living communities within which, or in the name of which their worshippers might aspire to gain power and 'to be something' – essentially, I think, by way of a remedy against such idolatry.

VII

There is no partisan confrontationalism in Hölderlin's poetry; but instead its world-historical *Grundstimmung* is one of 'hallowed grief'. The essential parameters of that 'hallowed grief' are set out, in a sense, most definitively in the two great elegies, 'Heimkunft' ('Homecoming') and 'Brod und Wein' ('Bread and Wine').[23]

In 'Heimkunft' the 'hallowed grief' is in fact rather pushed into the background; for this is not primarily a poem concerned with matters of world history.[24] Here Hölderlin is concerned, far rather, in purely private terms with his own vocation as poet. It is a poem of exultation in that vocation. The homecoming in question is, it appears, essentially twofold: he is both describing a literal homecoming, out of Switzerland, into Swabia – and at the same time bringing about a spiritual homecoming, into the presence of 'the God'. That is, the God of his own tumultuous poetic inspiration.

But there is nevertheless a distinct counter-current of world-historical anxiety present in this poem. It is already there in the simple fact that the God is symbolically envisaged as being at home, not in the poet's homeland, but on the contrary back in the mountains he is travelling away from. He is glad to be returning to his people, yet the fact is, their cultural world is one which is quite alien to the proper demands of the highest poetic truth. As he sits in the boat crossing Lake Constance he offers up an anxious prayer:

> Much, too, I prayed for the fatherland's sake, lest unbidden
> The Spirit should suddenly come and we were destroyed.[25]
> ('Heimkunft', lines 39–40)

In this prayer, once again, he expresses his chastened fear of revolutionary excess. And then, at the end of the poem, as he looks forward to the festive meal marking his return to the family home, further troubling questions surge to the fore:

> When we bless the meal, in whose name should it be, and when we
> Take rest at night, tell me, what prayerful thanks are due?
> Is it right to name the Most High? No god approves what's unseemly,

>   And our hearts scarcely have space to provide him a home.
> All too often words fail us; lacking names for the holy,
>   Even if stirred, does that mean that we'd better not speak?[26]
>
>   ('Heimkunft', lines 97–102)

'Heimkunft' is, on the surface, a celebration of being at home. Yet these questions remain – as the reason why, after all, the true poet can never be altogether at home. For – so the poem concludes – 'whether he like it or not' these are cares which the poet must always 'carry in his soul', whilst 'the others' do not.[27] The poem's cheerfulness simply depends on the poet's having come to accept that this is not their vocation.

'The God' is sublimely present in 'Heimkunft', up in the mountains; but only as a datum of the poet's own private experience. In 'Brod und Wein' on the other hand, a poem with much more public concerns, there is no such presence at all. Here, on the contrary, the God ('Father Aether') appears as the chief of the many gods – who have all now *abandoned* humanity.[28]

Thus, 'Brod und Wein' is both a commemoration of what once was – when, in the mythic past, the gods did grace the earth – and an expression of yearning for their return. These gods belong both to another time and to another place: that is their special mode of sublimity. So the poem summons us, in imagination, to Greece:

> Come! Come to the isthmus! Where the vast expanse of the sea roars
>   Round Parnassus, and at Delphi bright snow trims the rocks.
> To Mount Olympus, come! To the heights of Cithaeron,
>   To the pines' shade, the grape-covered slopes, the source of loud
> Thebe and Ismenos, down in the country of Cadmus!
>   The God for whom we now wait hails from there, and points back.
>
> Blessed Greece! You house of the heavenly, where they all dwell
>   So is it true then, what once in our youth we were told?
> Festive hall! With the sea for its floor! Whose tables are mountains!
>   Founded in time immemorial, truly unique![29]
>
>   ('Brod und Wein', lines 49–58)

Hölderlin had never been to Greece. The landscape here is an entirely imagined one. In fact, it seems to function precisely as a symbol for the whole world of the poetic imagination as such. It is, in symbolic terms, the urgently self-affirmative self-projection of Hölderlin's own very inmost self-expressive creativity. This is framed in world-historical myth, the better to articulate a prophetic demand for cultural transformation, in which the most free-spirited sort of poetic self-expression, generally, may come to be accorded the highest religious honours; but it is projected backwards into a lost golden age owing to his fundamental preference for lament, rather than confrontational rage against the current powers that be.

The setting for this poem is the middle of the night. The poet is alone, awake whilst the city around him sleeps. And he experiences the entire present age of history as an age of night. He looks back over the day that is past: the luminous day of Greek antiquity. This is envisaged as a time when mortals and immortals mingled freely. But, alas:

> We've come too late. For, though the gods still live on,
> It's up in the other world they are, over our heads.
> There they've not ceased. And yet, such is their gentle forbearance,
> It seems they no longer care to be bothered with us.
> For we're delicate vessels, we mortals, easily shattered,
> And their presence is pressure we can seldom sustain.
> Ever after, life is a dream.[30]
>
> ('Brod und Wein', lines 109–15)

The benightedness of the present age essentially consists in the lack of proper religious recognition for poetic truth. Hölderlin registers the problem almost with despair:

> In the meantime . . . often I think that
> It might be better to sleep than to be so bereft,
> So endlessly waiting, and what's there to say or to do?
> I don't know. What use is a poet born out of date?[31]
>
> ('Brod und Wein', lines 119–22)

What use indeed? The whole poem, in a sense, leads up to and revolves around this elementary question.

And in the final two strophes he gives his answer. He refers to the bread and wine of the Christian Eucharist. The highest form of poetry – so he suggests – has the same function as the Eucharist: to convert material drawn from everyday experience into a sacrament of world-historical remembrance. Except, of course, that the remembrance with which he himself is concerned is not just the remembrance of Biblical or church history. And Christ, as the 'wine god', is effectively identified here with Dionysus.

This Christ is the last of the gods. He is the god whose advent signalled the Father's withdrawal: the bringer of comfort, whose essential role it is to equip us to endure the privations of world-historical night. He is the reconciler of night and day, the harrower of hell. And the hell that he harrows is Plato's cave. It is this world. Thus:

the Son of the Highest descends – the Syrian –
    Bearing his torch, down, into the shadowy depths.
Those blessed with wisdom perceive it; imprisoned souls flicker
    To life with a smile, eyes thaw in response to the light.
The titan, asleep in the arms of the earth, dreams gentler dreams,
    And even that mean brute Cerberus drinks, and finds peace.[32]
                        ('Brod und Wein', lines 157–62)

For Hölderlin true poetry, now, is nothing other than Christ's torchlight for the harrowing of hell.

VIII

Hölderlin's invocation of the departed Greek gods is meant to underline the radicality of his abiding negation of Christian kitsch: as he rejects both its hubristic dogmatism and the complacent conventionality which that dogmatism helps protect, its apparent closure to any truly fresh poetic impulse. But when on the other hand he speaks of Christ, this is his dialectical negation of that negation; a counter-balancing movement of hope, for a new beginning. It is in the same spirit that he also counter-balances his enthusiasm for the imagined landscape of Greece with a mythopoeic celebration of those 'demi-gods', the great rivers of his own homeland. The Rhine, the Danube, Christ: these are his primary symbols for all that, even now, still helps render possible a sacramental project like his own.

Then in 'Patmos' he turns to reconsider the gospel story of Christ's departure from the world.[33] This poem is, in the first instance, a celebration of the apostle John. Hölderlin therefore begins his account by alluding to the way in which the gospel of John describes the last supper: as Jesus sits with his disciples, sharing 'the mystery of the vine', and discourses at length about the significance of his imminent death:

                for he never
Tired, all that time, of seeking
To expound goodness and, where needed, to soothe
The turbulent rage of the world.
For all shall be well. Whereupon – he died. Much might
Be said about this. And they saw him, his friends, right at the last
Raising his eyes in triumph, most joyful,

    Yet they were sad.[34]
                        ('Patmos', lines 84–91)

'Much might be said about this': well yes, and over the years one or two things have indeed been said about it. But with these abrupt words, drawing attention to everything he himself is *not* in fact saying, it is as though Hölderlin were ostentatiously wiping the slate clean, erasing all the historic accretions of pious kitsch.

'Yet they were sad': in Hölderlin's retelling of the story, this is not just the sadness of immediate bereavement. In direct antithesis to the kitsch triumphalism with which the church has usually tended to celebrate the great missionary efforts of the apostolic period, from the Acts of the Apostles onwards, here the apostles are symbolically described as being wrenched away in anguish from their homeland and their friends, sent away over the mountains as it were into exile, their community dissolved.

Pentecost is pictured with menacing rolls of thunder, the apostles huddled pensively together. They are described in sinister terms as 'the heroes of death'. Thus, what they are heading into is all darkness. And not only for them personally: they are just the first to register, with heroic fortitude, the new darkness of the age as a whole.

> For now the Royal One extinguished
> The sun's day and snapped
> Asunder the straight-beaming
> Sceptre, with sovereign will, suffering,
> Yet patient, until the right time
> Should come again.[35]
> ('Patmos', lines 108–13)

There follows an image of the Ascension: Christ, hastening away, glances back one last time – and to the apostles it is as if they have been 'seized by the hair'. In that glance there is a terrible compulsion, born from their yearning that he should stay. Again, the traditional imagery of the Ascension undergoes a fierce mutation. The golden beams of light shining from the ascending Christ are transformed into golden ropes, binding those left behind, as prisoners to their obsession. The apostles have become symbols of Hölderlin's own obsessiveness. Or the obsessiveness driving dissident religious poetry, in dark times, generally.

Which brings us, at last, to a larger overview of subsequent Christian history; and so to the central question and answer of this poem:

> But when he goes and dies,
> To whom beauty most of all
> Adhered, so that it was
> A wonder even for the hosts of heaven to behold,

And when, henceforth for ever an enigma
To each other, those once bonded
By remembrance have it seems forgotten
To communicate, when it's not the sand
Only, or the willows, but also the temples
The wind whips away,
When the demi-god and his friends
Are dishonoured, and the Highest
Himself averts his face
From a world in which
No immortal any longer now appears, in the skies or
On the green earth, what is this?

It is the sower's cast, when he scoops up
The wheat with his shovel
And flings it out, clear, swinging it over the threshing-floor.[36]

('Patmos', lines 136–54)

In short, the whole history of Christendom is for Hölderlin essentially to be seen as one great winnowing process.

It has in his view been a purgative dark night of the European soul.

IX

The hope deriving from this vision of things is at its most vibrant in 'Friedensfeier' ('Celebration of Peace').[37] It would actually appear that the immediate occasion for 'Friedensfeier' was Napoleon's signing of the Peace of Lunéville in 1802; but the new peace inaugurated by that event is transfigured here, in Hölderlin's excited imagination, to become the harbinger of a whole new golden age. And the poem represents this by the image of a great feast.

The key issue however in 'Friedensfeier', from a Christological point of view, is clearly the identification of the chief guest: the so-called 'prince of the feast'. Indeed, this 'prince' is just about as enigmatic a figure as 'the servant of Yahweh' in the 'servant songs' of Deutero-Isaiah. The poet hails him as a 'divine' being; a stranger from a foreign land, yet eager to overcome that foreignness and be a friend to those who greet him; known to all; the hero of 'millennial' struggles, now at last triumphant. But who is he?

As a matter of fact, I think he is precisely 'the servant of Yahweh' again, in a new guise: that is to say, a symbolic personification of the shaken prophetic spirit, in general, to which all shaken poetry as such bears witness.

Some commentators have supposed that he is simply Napoleon. But then why the mystification? Others have suggested that he is the personification of Peace. And yes, maybe that is right – if one takes the term 'peace' in the very broadest sense of *shalom*, as signifying infinitely more than a mere immediate end to political conflict. Friedrich Beissner's proposal, on the other hand, is that we should see the prince as representing 'the Genius of the German People'; which fits well with Hölderlin's concern in other works to redefine the ultimate vocation of the German-speaking world, as a potential home to the shaken spirit. Only, why in that case is the Germanness of the prince not more clearly emphasized?

Or is he Christ?

This is perhaps the most teasing question of all. Christ is, at any rate, also invited to the feast. But is that subsequent, unambiguous invitation to Christ essentially – as other commentators have argued – just a repetition and amplification of the initial invitation to the prince? Or are they two separate figures? And if so, how are they related?

If I am right, then what we are presented with in 'Friedensfeier' is really the interaction between two faces of the most profound shakenness; two faces which are at one level identical, yet at another level also distinct. On the one hand, the prince represents shakenness mediated through the heroism of a solitary, because persistently 'foreign', free-spiritedness, expressed in prophetic form. Elsewhere in the poem, such prophetic free-spiritedness in general is also called the 'Spirit of the World'. Christ, on the other hand, represents that same spirit, precisely in so far as it has been appropriated into, and altogether more widely disseminated through, the popular religion of Christendom.

At one point Hölderlin represents himself calling Christ 'zum Fürsten des Festes'.[38] Which is ambiguous, since it can mean either that Christ is being *presented* to the prince of the feast – or else, on the contrary, that he is being invited *to be* the prince. Either way, however, the peace being celebrated in 'Friedensfeier' surely includes, right at its very heart, a fundamental reconciliation between the competing demands of solitary free-spiritedness and popular religion.

This is, in short, a poem of urgent desire for a popular religious culture at long last fully capable of appropriating the poetic products of the most thoroughgoing inner solitude. That is what the feast (as I would understand it) most fundamentally symbolizes. And Hölderlin's whole polemical concern is to insist on the proper radicality of the transformation involved:

> Many are the lessons
> That we've learnt together since the dawn which made of us
> A conversation; soon, though, we shall be a song.[39]
>
> ('Friedensfeier', lines 91–3)

X

But what renders his work most poignant, it seems to me, is its recurrent quality of *shaken despair*.

There is nothing self-indulgent about this. On the contrary, he is continually deploring his despair, battling against it; and the poignancy derives very much from that struggle. Thus, take for example the short hymn 'Mnemosyne'. One of the very last works he managed to complete before his final breakdown, 'Mnemosyne' is a wonderfully compressed little mosaic of a poem:

> Ripe, dipped in fire, and well cooked are
> The fruits, in this their earthy time of trial, and it's a law
> That everything, snake-like, wriggles in,
> Prophetic, dreaming on
> The hazy hills of heaven. And we've
> So much to pack and carry,
> Like a shoulder-load
> Of kindling wood. But the paths are
> Evil. Like wild stallions,
> In other words, the hobbled elements
> And ancient laws of the earth
> Resist all discipline. Always
> There's this yearning to press infinitely on. But we've so much to pack
> And carry. Such a need for loyalty.
> Forwards, though, and backwards we had rather
> Not look. Let ourselves rock and be lulled
> As if in a skiff on the sea.

> But I beg, tell me, how? Sunshine
> We see on the ground and a scattering of dust
> And, locally, the shadows of forests, and on roof-tops
> Blossoming smoke, a peaceable sight
> By ancient battlements; indeed,
> They can help, these signs of the day, heal
> The soul of one who's in tortured dispute with heaven.
> For snow, which betokens
> Like the fresh lilies
> All things noble in spirit, shines
> Half-melted on the green
> Alpine meadow, as, speaking of the cross, once
> Set up to honour those who died

Along the way, a wanderer
Climbs, in anger, with his friend
To peer into
The distance, but what is this?

    Under the fig-tree dead
My Achilles is lost to me,
And Ajax lies
By the grottoes of the sea,
By brooks, not far from the Scamander.
With a sound in his temples like
The constant wind that buffets unmoved
Salamis, his home, far away
Great Ajax died.
Patroclus, by contrast, was in the king's armour. And there died
Many others also. But on Cithaeron lay
Eleutherae, city of Mnemosyne. From her too,
When God had laid his cloak aside, the Evening Power then severed
A lock of hair. Hence, notwithstanding
That the Heavenly Ones abhor all forms of wild and
Self-destructive passion, it can't be helped; such is
The erring grief I feel.[40]

                                            ('Mnemosyne')

    Literally, the Heavenly Ones are said to disapprove of anyone who fails to 'pull themselves together, [so] sparing their souls'. Which echoes the first strophe, with its talk of an infinite yearning, and the comparison with wild stallions resisting any attempt to tame them: the 'hobbled elements and ancient laws of the earth' are evidently, again, a metaphor for all the wild and self-destructive passion that is sublimated into this prophetic verse.

    The first strophe begins with a series of basic sacramental images for the general enterprise of such poetry. These poems are fruit. And they are dreams – dreamt on 'the hills of heaven'. The hills are perhaps clouds, marking the juncture of heaven and earth. (Hence my addition of the adjective 'hazy', which is admittedly not there in the German.) As in a dream, all manner of different memories and passions enter into the work of the imagination: often poisonous, like snakes, associated with temptation; not least, the temptation acknowledged at the hymn's end.

    And yet, to be the kind of poet that Hölderlin is – to be properly 'loyal', as he puts it, to that vocation – involves a decisive exposure to all the potential shaking-power of one's life-experience. As so often with Hölderlin, the basic image for that shaking-power is fire. The fruit which is shaken poetry is 'dipped in', and 'cooked' ripe by the fire of the sun: it is 'tested' by that exposure, to find out how much intensity of prophetic inspiration it can endure. To assume the responsibility which informs this sort of poetry is like carrying a load of logs on one's shoulders. The word 'Scheitern' may mean firewood, or ship-wreckage – or, by extension, failure: it represents a lifetime's experience all chopped or broken up; ready to be ignited. Thus, already here the prophetic poet's vocation, in itself, is defined in terms vividly redolent of the temptation to despair. The temptation is, it seems, intrinsic to the vocation.

Then he pulls back: evoking the alternative possibility of another sort of poetry; what Blake would call the poetry of 'Beulah'. This would be a poetry of simple pleasure in 'the signs of the day', the sheer beauty of nature and the words which evoke it; deriving from an ecstatic self-forgetfulness, fixed fast in the present moment; and offering a tranquil moment of respite, for one who otherwise – like Jeremiah – is continually driven to lament his higher calling.

Whether such 'Beulah'-poetry is to be rejected as a mistaken flight from responsibility, or allowed to be a valid concomitant to the poetry of shaken-ness, is left an open question. But, in any case, how is it to be sustained?

The possibility is in fact no sooner evoked than it is abandoned. Whereupon we are presented with a quite opposite image of the poet, now in the company of a friend (Sinclair?), raging – at this time Hölderlin was, indeed, already more than half-insane – as he climbs an Alpine path.

Whereas the poetry of 'Beulah' looks neither backwards nor forwards, the wanderer in the mountains 'peers into the distance'; specifically, towards the long-lost past of the Greek golden age. But that age is represented, here, entirely in terms of heroic death. First, we are reminded of the great deaths in the *Iliad*; with a particular emphasis on the suicide of Ajax, compulsively driven as by an inner gale, like the poet himself. And then we see the death of the whole culture: represented by Mnemosyne, the goddess of memory and mother of the muses. She has died. The severing of a lock of hair was part of the Greek funeral rites; and the allusion to her sacred city, 'lying' on mount Cithaeron, is also significant, in that it had in fact long been an altogether abandoned city, nothing but ruins. The death of Memory signifies the breakage of all effective public contact with the great truths of the Classic past. It is in that sense the death of freedom – as the name of the goddess's city, in Greek, evokes freedom. And hence it is the death of hope.

God has laid his cloak aside: the cloak is a symbol for everything that shields us from the true shaking-power of reality, and so renders ordinary everyday life possible. With its removal the blazing divine fire of the sun, referred to at the beginning of the poem, becomes overwhelming, deadly.

Christ, hitherto for Hölderlin always the primary symbol of sustaining hope for the shaken, is in this poem finally reduced to a sheer inert woodenness: in the form of a wayside crucifix, up in the mountains, commemorating the dead. (Very much as in a Caspar David Friedrich painting.) And so the poet's sanity, unsustained, collapses.

Everything, in the end, has gone wrong.

9 'After Auschwitz'
The case of Nelly Sachs

I

There remains, finally, just one further example I want to consider; in illustration of yet another form of poetic shakenness. Namely: that which is a wrestling with inescapable corporate trauma.

II

Thus, the intrinsic truth of the pathos of shakenness, I have wanted to argue, consists in its quality as a revelatory response to the moral bankruptcy of 'the *basileia* of this world'. But, although 'the *basileia* of this world' is always in truth morally bankrupt, that bankruptcy is by no means always obvious. Only in the most extreme circumstances is it revealed for all to see.

Herein lies the special theological significance of the great nightmares of history. Such as, in the twentieth century of course above all, the unique horror bound up with the memories of genocidal totalitarianism.

For here – in Nazi Germany or the Stalinist Soviet Union – was a situation in which ordinary establishment-mindedness verged, at times even very directly, into collusion with mass-murder; in which the cultivation of a cool agnosticism had become a quite absurdly superficial irrelevancy to the actual horror of what was happening; in which the confining narrowness of sectarian loyalties was intolerably highlighted, by being set alongside such a vast community of shared suffering.

'*After Auschwitz no more poetry*'. Theodor Adorno's formula is, in the first instance, a thrust at all those like Heidegger who after the war still sought to preserve a high-minded ideal of Germany as 'a nation of thinkers and poets'; or any other post-Auschwitz vision which, as in Heidegger's case, exalts the potential truth-bearing qualities of sublime poetry while at the same time failing imaginatively to address the full reality of that nightmare.

No more poetry? No more pathos of glory, certainly.

No more theology, either, in any sort of collusion with the pathos of glory – as Adorno also put it, 'after Auschwitz there is no word tinged from on high, not even a theological one, that has any right unless it underwent a transformation'.[1] Yet as regards poetry he himself subsequently withdrew the remark, at any rate to this extent: that, after all, 'perennial suffering has as much right to expression as a tortured man has to scream'.[2] And clearly there is a particular authority inherent in those works of shaken poetry which spring most directly from the horror, and most immediately wrestle with it.

Writings, that is to say, like those of Nelly Sachs.

Although her work is still remarkably little known outside Germany, Nelly Sachs is in fact, I think, perhaps the greatest – at any rate the *theologically* most significant – religious poet of the last century.

III

Sachs was indeed herself very much an admirer of Hölderlin; just as she was also an admirer of his contemporaries, Novalis and Brentano, for instance. However, her work registers the shock of a sensibility shaped by such influences brought face to face with the fantastic violence of modern barbarism.

Her first book of poetry was published in 1947: *In den Wohnungen des Todes* (*In the Habitations of Death*). This was a collection of work, dedicated to the memory of 'my dead brothers and sisters', written over the previous four years. She was fifty-five at the time, and living in Stockholm, having as a Jew been forced to flee from Berlin.

Actually, she had had the narrowest of escapes. By the time that her, and her mother's, entry visas to Sweden eventually arrived in May 1940 they had already received their concentration-camp summons. Flights to Stockholm were about to be discontinued, but on the advice of a friendly Gestapo agent they caught the very last one – he warned them that if they took the train instead they would almost certainly be turned back at the border. Only days later there was enacted a comprehensive ban on emigration.[3]

She had always been a person richly gifted with the intense inner solitariness and vulnerability of the potential shaken poet.[4] In Berlin, prior to the Nazi period, she had lived what can only be called a rather sheltered life as the only daughter of a wealthy businessman; no preparation at all for the horrors that were to ensue. At the age of seventeen she fell unhappily in love with a man who could never be hers. To her dying day she kept his identity a secret, and this remained the great love of her life. Eventually, he perished in one of the death camps; her grief over the death of her whole world had its focus in her grief for him. Alone with her mother in exile, she turned to poetry as, for her, the only possible means of psychological survival. She had written before, but only now in this crisis did she begin to find her true voice. It was the shocking news of the death camps which quite suddenly transformed her from a minor poet, with little or no contact with the literary mainstream, into a great one.

Her work appears to have been an almost compulsive response to the anguish of her situation; to begin with, largely regardless of any prospect of publication. As she herself expressed it, she was not the adherent of any particular literary school. But:

> the terrible experiences, by which I myself was brought to the very brink of death and darkness – they were my teachers. If I had not been able to write I would not have survived. Death was my teacher . . . my metaphors are my wounds. Only so is my work to be understood.[5]

All her work is of this character, from *In den Wohnungen des Todes* onwards, right up to her death in 1970.

In the end, the pressures giving rise to her work partly overwhelmed her. Beginning in the late 1950s she at length began to receive some public recognition, which culminated in the award of the Nobel Prize for literature in 1966. Yet at the same time her mental health started to give way. She began to suffer prolonged bouts of acute paranoia, and spent a considerable portion of 1960–3 in a psychiatric hospital. Her poetry represents the sane and lucid voice of a tormented soul, broken by the nightmare which had inspired her.

IV

Sachs's main work falls into two categories. Some of it is experimental verse drama: a series of pieces, like contemporary mystery plays, in which she tries out various combinations of poetry with music and mime, or dance.[6] The rest consists of short, more or less explosive lyric compositions.

Ehrhard Bahr protests against Hans Magnus Enzensberger's remark that all of Sachs's writings, from the 1940s onwards, ought to be seen as successive contributions to a single book; one also needs to appreciate the very significant evolution, he insists, right up to the end, in both her thinking and her style.[7] But there is at least this much truth in Enzensberger's remark: the real power of her work lies far more in the cumulative impact it has as a whole than in any individual poems. The poems continually echo one another, drawing much of their meaning from the echoes. And the logic of their evolution is very much her pursuit of a single pilgrimage.

When she was awarded the Nobel Prize, jointly with the Israeli poet Samuel Joseph Agnon, the citation spoke of 'her outstanding lyrical and dramatic works, which interpret the fate of Israel with such emotional force'.

And yet she came from a family completely assimilated to the surrounding

Gentile culture; without any religious or other given ties to Jewish tradition. She had been brought up to be a patriotic German, with no sense at all of having anything in common with the impoverished Yiddish-speaking Jews of Eastern Europe. In the world of her upbringing Jewishness had been little more than a rather insignificant embarrassment. It was only the Hitler regime that rendered her seriously Jewish.

In the 1930s she had indeed become an active participant in the Cultural Association of Berlin Jews. This was an organization acceptable to the Nazi regime, in line with their insistence that Jewish artists and writers should henceforth concern themselves exclusively with proper 'Jewish' themes, which ought to be quite separate from the major themes of properly 'German' art and literature. She participated in the Cultural Association as the only public space available, but she certainly never reconciled herself to this spirit of cultural apartheid. And even later on, although the starting point of her major work is the tragedy of the Jewish people, at the same time she still continued to regard herself very much as a German poet. In this regard the Nobel Prize citation is perhaps somewhat misleading. She writes both as a Jew and as a German – or, rather, always as a poet of humanity.

Certainly, she appears to have been quite mistrustful of any tendency to interpret the catastrophe of European Jewry in terms of a defiantly Zionist pathos of glory. A number of her earliest friends and promoters in Sweden were themselves Zionists: the composer Moses Pergament, the literary critic Walter Berendsohn, the journalist and film-director Erwin Leiser. And when in the later 1950s Sachs's work began to become better known one of the immediate results of this was in fact to bring to the surface the latent conflict between her world-view and theirs. Especially painful problems arose with regard to Pergament's work in converting her verse drama *Eli* into an opera. This drama represents one of her very earliest responses to the news of the death camps.[8] Like André Schwarz-Bart's novel *The Last of the Just*, it is an attempt to deal with the catastrophe in terms of the old Hasidic legends of the *lamed vavnik*, the hidden 'just men' on whose existence the very survival of the world depends: the central character, the young cobbler Michael, is one of these 'just men', in a time of great cruelty. As Sachs herself originally conceived it, this 'mystery play about the suffering of Israel' was essentially a yearning prayer for repentance and reconciliation. But Pergament's opera version was such that one Swedish reviewer saw it rather as expressing a passionate thirst for revenge. Sachs was horrified. The crisis coincided with her descent into paranoia, and no doubt to some extent contributed to it; her previously very close friendship with the composer collapsed.[9]

The very last thing she wanted was to be associated with the politics of revenge.[10] In radical contradiction to such politics, hers is indeed essentially a poetry of releasement – in the truest sense.

And hence the particular vision of God informing her poetry. Of course this is the God of Israel; yet not at all as envisaged by the prophets. Quite unlike the prophets, she does not on the whole envisage God as *judge*.[11] Against such a catastrophic background one can, after all, scarcely conceive of any invocation of God as judge that would not immediately tend to resonate with moralized vengefulness. Therefore she, so to speak, resolutely brackets the theme. The God she invokes is not the God of prophecy, but the God of mysticism; in effect beyond the nightmares of history, the object of an infinite shaken desire. Bengt Holmqvist identifies as the 'key-word', continually recurring in Sachs's poetry and most fundamentally identifying its distinctive spirit, the word *Sehnsucht*, 'longing'.[12] Hers is a poetry of home-sick longing for God – in the midst of a worldly exile which also becomes a metaphor for the mystical exile of the soul.

In general, she shows no fear of grand rhetoric. But it is as though her whole project were to redeem the more monumental possibilities of language from the corruptions of false pathos and propaganda. She is in this regard a direct heir to Hölderlin: there is certainly something quite Hölderlinian in her characteristic combination of exalted anguish with an extreme compressed restlessness of thought and imagery, always teetering on the brink of silence. (Many of her poems, for instance, especially her later ones, end in a hyphen: itself a gesture of insatiable longing, for the inexpressible.)

Her poetic pilgimage begins with a series of monumentally rhetorical poems written in direct response to the catastrophe of her people. *In den Wohnungen des Todes* includes a cycle of 'prayers', each like a candle lit on Yom Kippur, for 'the dead bridegroom', the man she had loved; a cycle of 'epitaphs written in the air' for other particular victims; and a cycle of 'choruses after midnight' commenting on the event from various perspectives. Here we have the lamentations of 'abandoned objects'; of the rescued; of the wanderers; of the orphans; of the dead; of the shadows; of the stones; of the stars; of 'invisible things'; of the clouds; of the trees; of the comforters who can no longer comfort; of the unborn; of the holy land.

The opening poem supplies the collection with its title:

O the chimneys
On the artfully contrived habitations of death
As Israel's flesh went up in smoke
Through the air –
A star received it, like a sweep
It went black,
Or was it a sunbeam?

O the chimneys!
Freedom roads for Jeremiah and Job's dust –
Who contrived you and built, stone on stone,
For fugitives the path of smoke?

O the habitations of death,
Invitingly prepared
For the master of the house, the guest turned host –
O you fingers,
Laying down the threshold
Like a blade, to sever death from life –

O you chimneys,
O you fingers,
And Israel's flesh in smoke through the air![13]
(*In den Wohnungen des Todes*)

It is of course death itself which is transformed from guest to host, and the 'inviting preparation' of the place is the disguising of gas chambers as showers. The fingers pointing down are perhaps those of the SS officers at the entry ramp to Auschwitz, directing newcomers to their fate. The chimneys themselves become, by juxtaposition, other fingers; fingers, now, pointing upwards – towards what? Towards Jeremiah's and Job's God; here in the minimal role of giver of death-as-release. The implicit paradox is bitter enough. But from this point onwards Sachs's work as a whole becomes a systematic sublimation of her own immediate longing for death-as-release, into an acutely chastened spirituality of releasement-in-survival.

As for the star that turns black: stars are a recurrent element in her imagery. Her invocation of them, right from the outset, seems essentially to reflect her desperate longing for a larger perspective, beyond the crippling proximity of her grief. That is, her longing for the releasement that comes from a more distanced vision.

Horror mingles here with an irrepressible naivety of creative longing, as in certain paintings of Chagall's. So too in another poem, for example, she turns from the imagery of smoke to that of dust and sand:

But who then emptied the sand from your shoes
After you'd been summoned up to die?
All that accumulated sand
From Israel's wanderings?
Burning Sinai sand,
Sand mixed with nightingale throats,

Sand mixed with butterfly wings,
Sand mixed with snake-dust yearnings,
Sand mixed with all that was shed from the wisdom of Solomon,
Sand mixed with the bitterness in the mystery of wormwood –

O you fingers
Which emptied the sand from the shoes of the dead,
Tomorrow you too will be dust
In the shoes of others to come![14]

(*In den Wohnungen des Todes*)

On the one hand, in this poem, she is thinking of the great piles of shoes left behind in the death camps; on the other hand, via the memory of the exodus, the perspective abruptly enlarges, to embrace first the whole history of Israel, in all its beautiful creativity, and then the entire world-historical future. This is another way of doing what she also does with star-imagery: it has the same distancing effect. Both alike are ways of pursuing the same quest for releasement; not the release of amnesia – but the releasement that comes from being lifted imaginatively out, beyond.

Sachs was a close friend of that other great survivor-poet of the Holocaust, Paul Celan. Both are equally exploring the sublime of releasement; the work of both alike is, at one level, essentially a systematic attempt to point to, and enact, the extraordinary difficulty of authentic releasement-enabling communication in such circumstances – without in any way, as it were, profaning the memories to be worked through. However, Celan's poetry is for the most part quite ostentatiously silent about God. So he writes a 'psalm' in praise, not of God, but of 'no one'; or he summons up the almond-shaped nimbus which signifies divinity in certain images of ancient or mediaeval Christian iconography, yet the almond is full of 'nothingness'.[15] And in a poem dedicated to Sachs, commemorating a conversation with her in 1960, the issue arises quite directly: 'The talk was of your God', he writes, 'I spoke / against him'.[16] At least in part, no doubt what Celan is rejecting is any hint of a collusion with theodicy, in response to what had happened.

And yet there is really no theodicy in Sachs's vision, either. For what is theodicy? It is the theoretical underpinning of a sacralized pathos of glory, an attempt to defend the promises which naturally go with such pathos. Unlike the pathos of glory, the pathos of shakenness does not belong to any strategy of seduction that would require the sort of promises which theodicy defends. And since the only apparent *power* of God in Sachs's mystical vision is the power at work in human longing, her distinctive vision leaves no scope, at all, either for theodicy or, therefore, for metaphysical rebellion against God.[17] When she speaks of God, she does so, simply, out of that same basic impulse to releasement – from the sheer crippling immediacy of trauma – which pervades her whole work.

V

Sachs's poetry pursues a dialectic of, in her own phrase, 'flight and transformation'. Thus, it is both the record of her own particular emotional experience as a fugitive, and at the same time a struggle to transform that experience – through the recording of it – into an opening towards, so far as possible, universal spiritual truth. *Flucht und Verwandlung* (*Flight and Transformation*) is actually the title of her fourth collection, published in 1959. The poem which she chose to read out at the Nobel Prize award-ceremony comes from that collection, and is a typical example of her tightly compressed handling of imagery around this basic theme:

> For the fugitive,
> what wealth of welcome
> on the way –
>
> Enveloped
> in the cloth of winds
> feet in the prayer of sand
> which never reaches its amen
> for it must pass
> by way of fin to wing
> and then beyond –
>
> The sick butterfly
> is soon reacquainted with the sea –
> This stone
> with the insect inscribed
> has given itself into my hand –
>
> Deprived of home
> I hold the transformations of the world –[18]
> > (*Flucht und Verwandlung*)

Much of the meaning of Sachs's poems, in general, derives from the system of echoes she has established; with each one catching echoes from the others. And so it is here. The figure of the wanderer, ironically clothed in her exposure to the elements, and blown hither and thither through the sandy desert, recalls the wanderings of the Biblical Israel, linked to the poet's own exile. The movement from 'sand' to 'fin' to 'wing' symbolizes the ascending transformations of the human spirit; whilst the butterfly, by virtue of its development from egg to larva to chrysalis and beyond, is an ancient Orphic symbol of the same. Sand, in her lexicon, is associated partly with Israel's wandering through the desert, but partly also with 'dust', as a token of the vanity bound up with human transience. ('For dust thou art, and unto dust shalt thou return', Genesis 3: 19.) The way of transcendence becomes, for her, a 'journey into the dust-less'.[19] The fish, with its fin, represents one aspect of this journey: namely, the initial moment of being shaken out of the spiritual inertia of contentment; that moment, indeed, at it most extreme – as an experience of sheer dumb affliction. In her brief memoir of her life under Nazi rule, she describes an incident in which members of the Nazi SA, accompanied by their womenfolk, burst into her and her mother's flat and, before their eyes, proceeded to ransack it. The shock of which had left her literally speechless: 'for five days . . . my voice was gone to the fishes'.[20] And the image of the fish, wherever it recurs in her writing, echoes that idiomatic expression. Hence, the evolutionary transformation of 'fin' into 'wing' symbolizes the very essence of her poetic project, as a recovery of fitting speech.

The wing evokes the butterfly, 'sick' with bearing the burden of historic nightmare; while healing comes from the butterfly's rediscovery of 'the sea'. This is another significantly ambivalent image in Sachs's work as a whole: associated, as it is, in equal measure both with death and with divinity. She was much influenced by her reading of the thirteenth-century Kabbalist classic, the *Zohar*; and there the 'primordial sea' appears as an image of divine fullness, back into which each human soul is called to flow. 'What wealth of welcome on the way'; literally, 'what great reception'. Already on the way – before death, yet by virtue of a dying-to-the-world – the fugitive is 'received', by divine grace, into transcendence. Flight is transformed into inner transformation. It is on this basis that her poetry seeks to become an enduring verbal monument to the fugitive's experience; preserving it, in her metaphor, as a piece of amber bearing the ancient imprint of a fly.

The collecting of such fossils was, as it happens, an especially popular occupation among the bourgeoisie of early twentieth-century Berlin, the world in which Sachs was brought up. And the insect is also, for her, a poignant image of powerlessness. Compare for instance the opening words of her memoir: 'Time under dictatorship. Who dictates? All do! Except for those laid flat on their backs, like a beetle in the face of death'.[21] Yet there can be no greater poetic contribution to what she calls 'the transformations of the world', from cruelty to true humanity, than the due commemoration of such suffering.

There is of course a whole tradition of spirituality stemming from the *Zohar* which deals with the Jewish experience of national homelessness by assimilating it to a cosmic vision of divine homelessness. In the *Zohar* itself, to begin with, the fall of Adam is interpreted as further entailing the exile of the Shekhinah, God's female alter ego in earthly manifestation. Then among the descendants of those expelled from Spain, in sixteenth-century Palestine, the Safed school led by Isaac Luria actually envisaged a whole vista of successive divine exiles: positing, behind the exile of Shekhinah, the prior exile of the many divine sparks, following upon the 'Breaking of the Vessels' which was the origin of all evil; and, behind the 'Breaking of the Vessels', the still more primordial self-imposed exile of God from a part of himself, the 'tsimtsum' or withdrawal-aspect intrinsic to the very act of creation. Sachs's thought has none of the discursively metaphysical quality of such speculations. And yet, in her oblique and entirely poetic way, she too is doing something analogous.

She appears to have first discovered the *Zohar* in 1950 – with great enthusiasm. And thereafter, the author of the *Zohar*, Moses de Leon, became for her the primary symbolic representative of true poetry in general; as in the little cycle of poems celebrating his work, which she wrote in 1952.[22]

Not that her religious inspiration was by any means exclusively Jewish in character. On the contrary, her original encounter with mystical spirituality was rather through the Christian tradition, as mediated to her by the Romantics. And her theological loyalties were always essentially trans-confessional – so that in her verse Christ rubs shoulders with Elijah, as twin symbols of redemption.[23] The Baal Shem Tov, likewise, with St Francis.[24]

VI

There are, one might say, two basic imperatives driving Sachs's work.

The first is just the straightforward need of loyalty to the memory of the dead: to honour those the Nazis had sought to consign to oblivion, with some sort of commemorative poetic monument. To be sure, this involves a continual re-opening of wounds. And yet, for her, it is a duty. As she expresses it in one of the poems of her third collection, *Und niemand weiß weiter* (*And No One Knows How To Go On*):

> With wild honey
> mourners of old
> sought to nourish
> the embalmed sleep
> of the grave
> and migrant pulses
> poured date wine
> into the honeycomb
> of mysteries.

In the black crystal of night
the stiffened wasp
of danced out time
lay tight enclosed –

But you,
but you,
how shall I nourish you?

Love leaps over
every dusty milestone,
like the chopped-up sun
in pain
intent on its own downfall.

With my downfall
I will nourish you – [25]

Her poetry is, to begin with, a movement of flight, out of the 'black crystal of night'. This phrase ('der schwarze Kristall der Nacht') immediately evokes the great Nazi rampage of Kristallnacht; the stiffened wasp is an image for the forces of persecution, now belittled in defeat, rendered powerless. Set over against the 'black crystal' and its wasp, on the other hand, is 'the honeycomb of mysteries': one might say, the pathos of shakenness in all its works. Pathos of shakenness, pathos of mourning – the image of the honeycomb emerges, in dream-like fashion, out of the image of an ancient barrow-grave. (Again, the antiquity of this image provides the distancing-effect she is always after.) The curious abstractness of the phrase 'migrant pulses' serves to link together the idea of bees, tracking back and forth in search of nectar, with the idea of ancient mourners, yearning for death as a homecoming. The point surely is: the sweetness of Sachs's poetry, in general, derives from her own sublated death-wish, her urgent sun-set love for the dead.

Yet, at the same time, the second imperative is the requirement that one should only remember in such a way as to help, once and for all, break the cycle of violence.

Thus, it is not just that she seeks to express something *more* than vengeful Jewish rage against the Germans. But, far rather, what she is looking for is precisely the very purest *antithesis* to any such spirit of vengefulness, whatever the circumstances. Her flight from the 'black crystal of night' becomes a flight from the whole dynamics of revenge – within which of course the Nazis themselves were also trapped. And the transformation she yearns for is first and foremost, I think, the most radical possible releasement from that temptation.

Hence, indeed, her continual impulse to universalize her experience. This applies both to the horror and to her countervailing hope: the horror she is responding to is not only the particular horror of what has happened to the Jews of Europe, it is the universal horror of persecution as such; whilst the hope that she clings to is a hope not just for Jews but for all fugitives, everywhere – in both the literal and the metaphorical sense.

Her prayer is 'That the Persecuted Should Not Become Persecutors': this is in fact the actual title of a poem she was moved to write in September 1948, on hearing the news that the United Nations representative in Jerusalem, Count Folke Bernadotte, had been assassinated. And here we have a very clear example of her universalizing of the horror she herself had been exposed to. So, in her memoir of life in the Third Reich, *Life Under Threat*, she describes hearing the footsteps of the SA men coming to pillage her flat:

> There came footsteps. Strong footsteps. Footsteps in which the Law had settled down and made itself at home. Footsteps became kicks against the door. 'Open up right away', they said, the time belongs to us![26]

But in the poem these footsteps are universalized. They have now become the steps of a sinister dance; a dance of nothing less than cosmic proportions:

> Footsteps –
> In what echoing grottoes
> are you preserved,
> who once alerted the ear
> to death's approach?
>
> Footsteps –
> no longer the oracular warning of death
> in the inspection of entrails, flight of birds,
> Mars sweating blood –
> only footsteps –
>
> Footsteps –
> primeval game of executioner and victim,
> persecutor and persecuted,
> hunter and hunted –
>
> Footsteps
> rendering time ravenous,

the hour lupine,
swallowing the fugitive's flight
in blood.

Footsteps
marking time in shrieks and sighs,
outflow of blood until it clots,
the death's sweat mounting hour by hour –

Footsteps of the executioners
over footsteps of the victims,
seconds ticking round in the earth's cycle,
what hideous black moon is it, pulling you?

Where does your squeak fit
into the music of the spheres?[27]
                              (*Sternverdunkelung*)

As for her countervailing hope, on the other hand, this is for instance decisively severed from the particularity of any particular historic identity – whether confessional-religious, cultural or political – in the following poem from *Und niemand weiß weiter*:

How many seas soaked into the sand,
how much sand prayed hard into stone,
how much time wept away in the sea shells' melody,
how much of being abandoned to death
in the pearly eyes of the fish,
how many morning trumpets in coral,
how many star-patterns in crystal,
how much burgeoning glee in the gull's throat,
how many threads of homesick desire
criss-crossing the night-net of the stars,
how much fertile soil
for the root of the word:
You –
behind all the crashing-down screens
of the mysteries
You – [28]

Here we have yet another array of her typically elemental imagery. Already in itself, that elemental quality consistently tends to shift the focus of attention away, beyond the immediate particularity of the historical context. But in this case these are also precisely images for the accumulated legacy of history as a whole. What else, indeed, are the screens that are crashing down if not everything that has gone into the historical construction of the poet's identity? She seeks to commemorate the dead in a manner which breaks free from history, inasmuch as history is a continual cycle of grievance and revenge. Her poetic project is, in this sense, essentially iconoclastic: it is a direct attempt to contribute to the crashing-down of the screens ('die Gitter', perhaps better 'the fences' or 'the prison bars') in the hope of thereby breaking through to the universal truth of what Martin Buber called the pure 'I–thou' relationship – as opposed to the depersonalized 'I–it' dynamics of vindictive ideology.[29]

Sachs's poetry deals with the anguish of her exile by continually trying to envisage it *sub specie aeternitatis*. Cramped and confined by the pressures of her situation, in a noisy little Stockholm flat (its noisiness became increasingly oppressive to her as her mental health deteriorated) she seeks to create another space for her imagination, full of vast stellar distances and great vistas over time. And this yearning for distance then coalesces with her ethical impulse towards a universalizing vision. Another very striking example is provided by the opening poem of *Flucht und Verwandlung*, where both tendencies combine into a surreal eschatology:

Whoever
dies here last
will carry the seed of the sun
between their lips
whilst the night thunders
with their last wrestlings.

All the dreams
that coursing blood evokes
will shoot in zig-zag bolts
from twisted shoulders
to pierce and nail the flesh of heaven
with the mystery of torment.

Since Noah's ark pursued its path
down
through the starry heights
whoever dies here last
will have the shoes on their feet
filled with water

and through it a fish
its back-fin taut as a sail with longing for home
will tow the black-spattered age
to rest everlasting.[30]

Here, an apocalyptic context is conjured up where one would normally expect some vision of the last judgement. And yet the conventional judgement-scene is supplanted, first, by a phantasmagoric scene of crucifixion; then by a celestial Noah's ark, representing the refugee's haven; and finally by some mixed imagery of fishy affliction and pilgrim yearning.

Note especially however, in this poem, how (as also in Blake's work) the latent element of moralized vengefulness in conventional eschatology has been expunged.

VII

Sachs's poetry as a whole is a pilgrimage towards releasement. And even as she began to sink amidst the waves of mental illness, that poetic journey nevertheless continued forward. One mark of this is her shift away from the buttonholing rhetoric of much of her earlier work, towards a no less intense, and yet at the same time more detached manner.

Take for example two poems with related thematic material, one from *Sternverdunkelung* in the late 1940s, the other from *Glühende Rätsel* (*Glowing Riddles*) published in 1966. The earlier poem is flamboyantly addressed to the 'peoples of the earth':

Peoples of the earth,
you who wrap yourselves around with the power
of the unknown stars like rolls of thread,
you who sew only to unpick again,
you who climb your Babel towers
like beehive-builders
patrolling the sweetness
to sting and be stung –

Peoples of the earth,
do not destroy the universe of words,
do not sever with the knives of hatred
the voice, which is coeval with the breath of life.

Peoples of the earth,

O let no one plan death, who speaks of flourishing –
and let no one mean blood, who says cradle –

Peoples of the earth,
do not dig up words from their roots,
leave them to spin the horizon
round to the true heaven,
and like a mask behind which gapes the night
let them in their hidden aspect
give birth to constellations.[31]

(Sternverdunkelung)

The later poem expresses the same concerns, and also picks up the image
of the beehive again. But it does so in an altogether less rhetorical way:

These millennia
breathing in and out
for ever circling round some angry catchword
out of the beehive of the sun
second after stinging second
virulent attackers
secret torturers

Never a breathing space as in Ur
where a childish people tugged white ribbons
to play sleep-ball with the moon –

Along the street the woman
runs at breakneck speed
seeking medicine for the sick child

Vowels and consonants
cry out in every language:
Help![32]

(Glühende Rätsel)

The difference is just that, whereas the first poem is simply a direct crying-
out, in the second Sachs takes a step back, sketches in a world-historical
context and then *observes* poetry crying out. It is in that sense a distinctly
more detached version of the same.

The direct plea, 'let no one mean blood, who says cradle' is transmuted
into the image of poetry as the woman running to get help for her sick child;

for what else does this child represent, if not human culture, dangerously sick under the oppression of propaganda-lies, or 'angry catchwords'? The image of the tower of Babel is replaced by the image of Ur, the city from which Abraham originally set out to inaugurate the history of Israel. In her dramatic works *Abram im Salz* (*Abram Battling with the Waves*) and *Nachtwache* (*Nightwatch*) Sachs goes back to the old legends about Abram/Abraham's childhood in Ur, under the tyrannical rule of Nimrod.[33] In these works Ur serves her very much as a primeval symbol of totalitarianism. And the innocence of the 'childish people' of Ur in the present poem is presumably, again, the false innocence of a people who have opted (both frivolously and manipulatively) for an attitude of sleepy resignation to tyranny, as represented by the idolatry of moon-worship. The implicit point of the contrast, thus, lies in the prophetic advantage accruing to the especial 'breathlessness' of Israel's experience of history, out in the heat of the day – with Israel here symbolically representing the spirit of shaken poetry 'in every language'. The first poem is an agitated, shaken piece of rhetoric; the second, a detached affirmation of the pathos of shakenness, in its world-historical vocation.

VIII

It is of course only natural, with regard to any historical experience of oppression, for the victims and their heirs to remember the past much more vividly, and in a much more engaged fashion, than the oppressor-group and their heirs. (In contemporary Britain, for example, one has only to compare the different ways in which black and white communities remember the transatlantic slave trade; or the different ways in which, especially, the Irish and the British remember the history of their dealings with one another.) And in order to prevent historic trauma from turning poisonous and propagating further violence, two things are surely needed. The first is that the heirs of the oppressors should, after all, begin to take the moral realities of the past a bit more seriously – and, moreover, that they should do so even without the aid of violent reminders from the heirs of the victims. But then the second is that, for their part, the heirs of the victims should also find release from history: in the sense of, so far as possible, renouncing their inherited sense of intrinsic corporate innocence, as an all too easy moral luxury.

Broadly speaking, the basic substantive contrast between the religious traditions of Middle Eastern origin – Judaism, Christianity, Islam – and the religious traditions of the Far East, especially those of Buddhism, may be said to come down to the difference between two quite opposite orientations to historic memory. Thus, the former traditions all identify salvation quite closely with historic hopes, for future justice upon earth and the overthrow of oppression; and they look back to the past at least to some extent in that light, as providing paradigms for political, or anti-political, resistance. So salvation comes to be essentially bound up with certain communal loyalties, and with the history of struggle shaping them. But Buddhist spirituality, by contrast, relates in principle far more loosely to its communal loyalties. It identifies salvation – or, to be more exact, enlightenment – with non-attachment, not least, precisely to any history-shaped identity. Therefore, I think, it may very well be argued that whereas the distinctive truths of originally Middle Eastern religion are of particular urgency to the heirs of oppressors, as a stimulus to historic honesty, what, conversely, the heirs of the oppressed as such most need, by way of releasement from destructive memory, is a good corrective dose of Buddhist truth.

At all events this is, in effect, just what Sachs's moral vision represents.

It is true that, in terms of actual imagery, she mostly still continues to operate within the given ambit of Jewish or Christian tradition. But, even so, it seems to me that her underlying project does have a distinct flavour of what pre-eminently belongs to the spirituality of Buddhism. Indeed she herself also hints at this, in the following little poem from *Glühende Rätsel* where she invokes the memory of the great fourteenth-century Tibetan Buddhist reformer, Tsong Khapa:

Leave without a backward glance –
sweep the last quaking-grass from your eyes
When Tsong Khapa left his master
he never turned around to look
Departure dwelt in every stride
Time was a bonfire blazing from his shoulders –

The one left behind called out:
'Throw his hut down into the abyss –'
And the hut hovered over the abyss
shot through with five-coloured light –
And he stepped unceremoniously out
into the dissolving space which is pure spirit
And his house was a house no longer
Only light – [34]

There, in a nutshell, is the history-transcendent aspect of her ideal.

In her own case, to be sure, it was not a spiritual master she had to leave behind. But it was the sheer brutal shock of exile itself, in its destructive quality as sheer trauma; it having been that shock which originally provided her with her true apprenticeship in such poetry. Her own 'hut' was her poetry. To begin with, it had been altogether a matter of looking back and taking leave – how could it have been otherwise? She had been so violently thrown down into 'the quaking-grass'. But now, at last, no longer.

IX

The opening lines of *Glühende Rätsel* provide a more personal statement:

> Tonight
> as I was on a dark side-street
> turning the corner
> my shadow laid itself
> over my arm
> This tired out garment
> wanted to be carried
> And I heard the nothing-colour say:
> *You've made it through!*[35]

'The nothing-colour' is a phrase which also appears in her unpublished *Letters from the Night*, written after her mother's death in 1950: there, it is an expanse of white – understood as a representation of 'where the divine dwells'.[36] Elsewhere in her work white is primarily associated with death, or with the overwhelming of speech by great suffering.[37] Again, in the *Zohar* the first and highest of the 'sefiroth', or emanations of God, Kether Elyon, is described as being colourless; although, in this case, also 'neither white nor black'.[38] But in Sachs's poem the point is perhaps best expressed in Buddhist terms. What speaks here is, surely, the wisdom of nirvana.

The pitiable childish shadow, demanding to be carried, is (I think) an image of the illusory 'self', constituted by its attachments. And the very fact that it appears now as a shadow or a 'garment', set apart from the one who is 'beyond', is already in itself a token of that 'beyondness'. Again, the dark side-street is no doubt meant to have sinister connotations of flight; whilst the night has much the same symbolic significance as St John of the Cross's purgatively transformative 'dark night of the soul'.

These lines thus capture Sachs's own final experience of releasement from her past. With the irony of the bitterest despair in 'O die Schornsteine' she had spoken of the chimneys of the death camp crematoria as 'freedom roads for Jeremiah and Job's dust'. Here, twenty years later, she glimpses the end of another sort of 'freedom road': the 'freedom road' that she herself had been building, with her poetry.

Part III

Conclusion

10 Incredulity and liturgy

I

The truth of God, the truth of the soul: these are not truths of correct belief. They are, far rather, names for a certain depth of poetic truth. The truth that answers to the deepest faith.

Yet, at the same time, proper faith in that truth no doubt also depends upon the most radical *incredulity*. That is, incredulity towards all that falls short of such depth.

Indeed, I would argue that poetic truth at the deepest level calls for something like an incredulity-*auction* in this sense. I am using the term 'incredulity' here strictly as a term of approbation. In which case, it seems to me that it comes in two basic forms: first, incredulity towards metaphysics; and, second, incredulity towards the claims of the pathos of glory.

Again: by 'metaphysics' in this context I mean any discourse on such topics as the existence and nature of God or of the soul, in so far as it has become divorced from the pathos of shakenness by being set apart from the immediacy of poetic utterance generally. Metaphysics is no doubt a necessity for any religious community. It is what religious communities need to bond them spiritually together at times when they lack a sufficient impulse of fresh poetic inspiration to do so; or when such impulses of fresh poetic inspiration as there are remain too maverick. And poetic truth, moreover, surely requires the continued existence of coherent religious communities, in order, as far as possible, to preserve a stockpile of potentially resonant religious vocabulary for its use – a vocabulary still steeped in prayer, which thereby retains something of the accumulated power this sort of truth demands, for its raw material.

Only, of course, the trouble is that metaphysical thinking constantly tends to assert its own self-sufficiency. And so it reduces the truth of faith to the formulations of a closely regulated orthodoxy; which then unfortunately serves positively to inhibit, or even suppress, fresh poetic creativity; holding it fast within narrow limits and downgrading its potential significance. To this extent, no matter how necessary metaphysical thinking may be, poetic truth clearly does demand a fundamental incredulity towards it.

Note, though: inasmuch as this is an incredulity towards metaphysics in general, it also decisively outbids the incredulity of any ordinary form of *atheism*. For what ordinary atheism counterposes to theistic metaphysics is just another rival form of God-less metaphysics. (Or else, perhaps, a form of positivism – which, however, differs from atheist metaphysics only in the sense of being that much the *more* set apart from the immediacy of poetic utterance.) And neither do I believe in the ordinary atheist's account of atheism, as the pure product of a passion for truth. It may well be that such atheists are driven by a real passion for truth; but, even so, I very much doubt whether this is really why they do not believe in God. I am far more inclined to suppose that ordinary atheism is the outcome of that passion being mixed with a certain myopia: a fundamental failure – simply – to see the full potential of the poetic, in its proper religious role, as an imaginative medium for the demands of honesty.

No, the most serious intellectual challenge to traditional religion is not atheism – but it comes from thinkers like Nietzsche or Heidegger, who criticize traditional religion precisely *for its poetic impoverishment*. Or, one might say, *for not in the end being religious enough*. Thus Nietzsche is no atheist, in any ordinary sense: he is on the contrary a devotee of the poetry-god Dionysus. And neither is Heidegger an atheist: he is a devotee of the Hölderlinian gods. These are thinkers driven by a basic incredulity towards all metaphysics, both ecclesiastical and anti-ecclesiastical alike; in pursuit of the very deepest poetic truth.

And yet, I have argued, in another way both Nietzsche and Heidegger are also, themselves, all too credulous.

For, after all, they still believe in certain forms of the pathos of glory. This is what finally impels them out of the Christian tradition. Incredulity towards metaphysics, alone, would by no means require *that*.

But they are, at the same time, also looking for a rival community to the church; one that would in their eyes be more worthy of a post-metaphysically-inspired pathos of glory. In Nietzsche's case it would be a tiny elite of radically anti-Christian 'free spirits'. In Heidegger's, it would be a much larger community, to some extent still overlapping with the churches but with quite a different centre of gravity: a community of Germans, intent on cultivating a pride in Germany essentially as a 'nation of thinkers and poets'. Either way, though, the pathos being promoted is at least in part a pathos of glory; that is, pathos in the service of coercive power, glamorizing and sanctifying it. Nietzsche fantasizes about the mighty future deeds of his elite, once they have seized power. Heidegger does not fantasize; when offered the chance, he actually attempts to construct an appropriate power base for his cause, within a larger revolutionary movement. But in both cases, I think, the underlying error is the same – and it is still not clearly seen by Heidegger even after his hopes had foundered.

The true exercise of coercive power does not need to be glamorized or sanctified by any form of pathos; all that is required is a straightforward and respectful acknowledgement of its necessity, where it really is necessary, without any further trimmings. Anything that goes further will always risk, incidentally, glamorizing or sanctifying mere mindless ambition. And therefore, I would argue, it is not only the still-metaphysical, or merely positivist, incredulity of atheism which needs to be outbid. The same also applies to the altogether more radical incredulity of these particular post-metaphysicians.

II

There is however just one thing that the thoughtful mind *cannot* not believe in, at this level; just one thing which one cannot *thoughtfully* not believe in. And that is the truth mediated by the pathos of shakenness: the truth of sheer thoughtfulness, as such.

One may or may not *see* it. But not to see it is by no means the same as deliberately to call in question any of its claims. For how, after all, could truth ever come from thinking less, or with less depth of concern?

At this point, then, the auction stops. The only issues remaining are what, in actual practice, it means to disentangle the intrinsic truth of such pathos from its incidental accompaniments; and how best to transmit it.

III

I am writing as a Christian theologian, looking to the current needs and opportunities of Christian theology. Yet the poets I have been discussing are none of them orthodox Christians. Blake regarded himself as a Christian, but clearly had no interest in being orthodox. Hölderlin remained a sort of Christian; only, filled with a quite unorthodox nostalgia for Greek paganism. Sachs is a less ambitiously original myth-maker than either Blake or Hölderlin, hence theologically less eccentric. However, her relationship to Christianity was never more than that of a sympathetic outsider.

So why these? The answer is: precisely in order to illustrate what seems to me to be the ultimate lack of space for the authentic expression of the pathos of shakenness in mainstream church tradition, as it now is, in any of its forms.

Thus, the whole underlying theme of my argument has been the basic contrast, or opposition, between two very different types of opposition. On the one hand, there is the metaphysical opposition between orthodox doctrine, correctly formulated, and whatever either deviates from orthodoxy or else falls short of its most convincing formulation. But then, on the other hand, there is the opposition between the two modes of pathos.

Debate at the level of the first opposition concerns what we should think, in the sense of what answers we should give to metaphysical questions. At issue in the second opposition, though, is the elementary, trans-metaphysical question of what, in the very deepest sense, it really means to *think* at all. In this latter case, therefore, the goal is not so much a set of final answers – it is, far rather, an ideal honesty. The pathos of glory glorifies the ultimately dishonest values of 'the *basileia* of this world': whether as a celebration of conventional establishment-mindedness; a glamorizing of elegant agnostic ease; or a polemical advocacy of sectarian or revolutionary regimentation. The pathos of shakenness, belonging to 'the *basileia* not of this world', is the honest opposite, in each particular. And my essential argument has simply been that – *for the purposes of salvation* – the first of these two oppositions, the metaphysical one, matters a good deal less than mainstream church tradition has tended to suppose. Whereas the second, on the contrary, matters far more.

Nor is this argument just an idle bit of theory.

It not only has theoretical implications, for the reading of shaken poetry. I think it also has quite practical implications, for the reconstruction of the church's liturgy. For what has been the basic rationale traditionally at work in shaping our liturgical calendar?

Judging from the results: for the most part, an absolutely primary importance has been accorded to the church's supposed role as the carrier-community for correct metaphysical doctrine. In view of which, the first priority for the designers of the church's liturgy has been the growth and prosperity of their community, by whatever means considered most effective for that purpose, virtually regardless of any other consideration.

In so far as the carrier-community for metaphysical correctness is most likely to grow and prosper with the aid of a liturgy saturated with self-serving pathos of glory, well then, according to this logic, so be it. With the result that a liturgical year has developed which is, one might almost say, one long parade of all the reasons which the institutional church thinks it has to boast about itself. Much of our liturgy has, in effect, become a sort of salesman's pitch for the this-worldly church-institution, sublated into prayer. The sins we confess tend only to be those we commit as individuals; not those of the church as a corporate entity. But redemption is, all too often, more or less identified in practice with uncritically loyal church-membership.

IV

'What is truth?'

At the most *primordial* level, I have argued – at the level where it is still a pre-theoretic solicitation of the will – it is an impulse primarily rendered articulate in the interplay between fine art, at its best, and public liturgy, at its best.

Therefore I come back to the question first posed at the end of Part One, the beginning of Part Two: suppose, as regards liturgy, we were systematically to revise our priorities – so that henceforth we no longer placed quite so much emphasis on the church's role as carrier-community of metaphysical correctness, but focused instead, far more, on its vocation to bear poetic testimony to 'the *basileia* not of this world' as such – what would follow?

Previously, I left the question hanging. But now, by way of a pointer forwards, I would at any rate like just to sketch out the rough beginnings of a possible answer.

Liturgy is, by its nature, a populist art. For it to bear poetic testimony to 'the *basileia* not of this world' means that it has to try and facilitate the very deepest shaken participation in the shaking truth of revelation, for the greatest possible number. In which case, there are two basic criteria for success: first, a maximum *fidelity* to that shaking truth, in all its original purity; and second, a maximum popularizing *conductivity* for it. These are, so to speak, the two poles between which all theology, deep down, is constantly pulled back and forth.

The tension is analogous to that which obtains with regard to any major project of opinion-changing reform within a democracy. Liturgical conductivity depends on the size of the community involved – the larger the better; on its accumulation of traditional loyalties – the greater the better; and on the historic resonances of its narrative – the richer the better. But one recruits and, over the long term, retains members most easily by cheapening the demands of faith. The easy way to achieve a liturgy of maximum conductivity is to abandon the pathos of shakenness altogether, and go for transmitting the pathos of glory instead. It is far easier to stay faithful to the pathos of shakenness if one simply gives up on the pursuit of conductivity. And yet, what earthly use is any liturgy unless people actually want to participate?

I think it is a matter of quite gradually nudging things forward. It is true that for the purposes of liturgical conductivity people need to feel spiritually at home, in a familiar imaginative landscape mapped out by well-known key reference points. Hence the value of having a fixed canon of scripture, and at least some age-old customary patterns of prayer. The preservation of conductivity requires that any change be gradual. Yet the shaking power of revelation itself cannot, in principle, be confined either by any particular canonical world-view, or by any particular set of sacred customs. In short, what is surely needed is a systematic strategy for opening little windows in liturgical tradition, wherever possible, to whatever depths of revelation may lie beyond it.

And so here are two immediate proposals, with this in view. The first is intended as a way of confronting ecclesiastical pathos of glory head on; the second is for the celebration of shaken creativity in general.

A Christian Day of Atonement?

Good liturgy, in the first place, is not a form of propaganda. It is the exact opposite, a medicine against propaganda; a meditation on all that propaganda-kitsch conceals.

To be sure, there is certainly no lack of opportunities for such meditation in our traditional calendar: at Easter, Christmas, Pentecost; in Holy Week; throughout Lent and Advent. But in actual practice, the fact is, ecclesiastical pathos of glory has crept in almost everywhere: privatizing our sense of sin; institutionalizing our vision of redemption; in general, stifling the demands of pure anti-propaganda thoughtfulness by subordinating them to those of communal self-interest. So much so that, in the end, it seems to me the only real remedy would be to introduce an altogether new observance, uncompromised by past habits, as a corrective, specifically designed to highlight the issue: a new celebration of honesty; an occasion for the church to focus in all frankness on its corporate failings, past and present – as measured by the most exacting standards of 'the *basileia* not of this world'.

The greatest festival of the Jewish liturgical calendar, Yom Kippur or the Day of Atonement, originated very much as an attempt at the liturgical appropriation of the prophetic spirit. I have argued that the heritage of Hebrew prophecy, overall, is crucially ambivalent: mixing together, as it does, the two tendencies primordially represented by Amos and Hosea. In so far, though, as Yom Kippur is that most paradoxical and demanding of projects, a bid to develop liturgy acceptable even to the God of Amos – that is just the kind of thing I mean.

The God of Amos is such a fierce repudiator of all hitherto existing liturgy, for its disconnectedness from 'justice', its pathos of glory. To the extent that Yom Kippur is intended as a direct response to this challenge, I would argue that we Christians also need to introduce, experiment with, and develop something like our own annual equivalent. If only as a partial counterbalance to our ongoing, year-long celebrations of the church's glorious origins and glorious saints, I think it would be good for us to devote at least one day a year, also, to the poetically shaken, repentant liturgical commemoration of such things as: the history of Christian anti-Semitism; the church's historic role as a persecutor of cultural minorities of all sorts; its collusion with slavery and racism generally; the traditional oppressiveness of Christian patriarchy; the whole miserable record of Christian war-mongering; ecclesiastical obscurantism down the centuries. Quietly and soberly asking ourselves how all this was possible – and what is therefore ideally required, in order that nothing of the same sort should ever again be repeated.

Shaken artists' days?

But then, second, do we not equally need to celebrate the memory of all the great individual pioneers, in the poetic articulation of the pathos of shakenness?

Granted, many of the church's greatest saints already come into that category. However there are others too, like those whom I have been considering – shaken creative artists, indeed, of every type – who, sometimes just by virtue of their shakenness, remain more marginal to orthodox church-tradition. And so, alongside saints' days, might we not – in a similar spirit of gratitude – likewise commemorate them, with dedicated days, as well? Such commemorations would, admittedly, tend to differ from saints' days in that they would have to deal with texts (and other works) often standing in a rather complex dialectical relationship to holy scripture. Yet, after all – what better way could one ever hope to find, than this, to help reinvigorate our response to the deep poetic truths of holy scripture itself?[1]

'I still have many things to say to you', Jesus says to his disciples (John 16: 12–13), 'but you cannot bear them now. When the Spirit of truth comes, then that Spirit will lead you into the fullness of truth'.

Come, Holy Spirit!

11 *Envoi*

In the name
        of namelessness –

searching for names

        to name
                that sparkling
                        at first imperceptible

                        as if *ex nihilo*

                                advent
                                of insight

                which
                again and again
                        as once in Galilee
                                slips straight back away
                                        into the darkness

                                        of the gawping crowd

                or to name *that peace*
                        which the world
                                cannot give

                        which however
                                is no peace –

so now

because
    truth is orphaned

       (in nomine Patris)

  and exiled

  divided
  and scattered

  confined within babble-towered bedlam
  yet itching
    to be
       out along the pebble pathways
          of the desert

       or clambering the mountain top
          beyond the clouds

          beyond the cultures

          beyond their manifold
             thunderous
                rival
                   banalities

          where there is only one
            parentage

  which is

  the voice
    of
    conscience

       in knowledge of whom
          standeth our eternal life
       whose service
          is perfect freedom –

and then again
because

truth wears a thorny crown
of twisted words

(*et Filii*)

and
round the Word

there circle storms
of whispered flattery
and muttered threat

violence in smiling masquerade

fervent unforgiveness
glamour
kitsch

where every shouted slogan
is a hammer blow

so that

the broken voice
of
the imagination

cries for aid

*Eli, Eli
lama sabachthani?* –

and
because

truth builds with wind and fire

(*et Spiriti Sancti*)

which is

the steady voice

of
honest reason

   calling
     (*behold how good*
     and joyful
     a thing it is)

   for collaboration

   to open up the book of the past
     unhindered by shame

   and to open up the book of the future
     unhindered by fear –

accordingly
I pray

   for that advent's fulfilment

     in that
     prophetic peace –

(perhaps

perhaps
at last!)

In the name
   of namelessness –

I pray –

Appendix 1
Albion versus Leviathan

I

One possible definition of religious truth, I have suggested, is that it is the popularization of the pathos of shakenness. At all events, that is the definition which provides the basis for the sort of 'mythic theology' I am exploring here. Immediately, however, there is an obvious tension in this: the purer the articulation of the pathos of shakenness in great poetry, the less readily popularizable it tends to be; the more it is popularized – through public ritual and all that goes to give meaning to such ritual – the more it is inevitably endangered, by the encroaching power of kitsch.

And on either side of this tension there are two very different disciplines of thought. On the one hand, there is the discipline of shaken poetry. On the other hand, there is the discipline of systematic, or unpoetic, philosophy. After all, the old Platonist prejudice against poetry is not merely fortuitous. The whole vocation of systematic philosophy is surely to do the very opposite to what poetry best does. The great strength of poetry as a medium for shakenness is precisely the intrinsic potential shaking-power of its pathos; its prophetic capacity to jolt and provoke, disturbing the ordinary apathy which allows a corrupt established order to maintain itself by sheer mindless inertia. But the great potential strength of systematic philosophy on the other hand, as a medium for shakenness, surely lies in its special quality as a *negotiating-process*, on the way to the working-out of a rational consensus.[1] It is in this aspect, one might say, the special art of negotiating away the immediate apparent contradictoriness of the diverse shaken visions constituting the world of what Blake would call the Minute Particulars.

II

The more vigorous the poetic shaking-power involved, the more difficult the philosophic negotiating-process. But also the more necessary.

Blake, for his part, represents the poetic side of this opposition pushed to its most uncompromising extreme. This is his genius – yet at the same time, I think, also the basic limitation of his vision. Thus: compare, for example, his poetic giant 'Albion' with that other very notable English giant, the philosophical 'Leviathan' of Thomas Hobbes.

III

Like Albion, Leviathan is a giant elaboration of the ancient metaphor of 'the body politic'. There he stands in the copper-plate engraving that adorns the title page of the original 1651 English edition of Hobbes's masterpiece: looming over the horizon above a city, with a crown on his head, a sword in his right hand, a crozier in his left; dressed, it seems, in chain mail – but the chain mail consists of numerous little people, all gazing upwards into his face. Just as Blake represents pure shaken poetry, so Hobbes represents pure shaken philosophy. In that sense, there could scarcely be a greater difference. He is a thinker who identifies the very essence of the sacred, in peculiarly radical fashion, with the consensual outcome of the most elementary sort of negotiating-process, namely the 'social contract'.

Hobbes is indeed arguably just as much a shaken thinker as Blake, just as fierce a critic of unthinking conventional prejudice, albeit in the opposite mode.[2] That is what makes the contrast here so striking – as an indication of what is, in my view, the most fundamental one-sidedness of the Blakean vision.

Not that Blake ever actually comments on Hobbes. He denounces Bacon, Newton and Locke: the modern English thinkers perhaps most admired by the intellectual establishment of his day. They are his target just because of their prestige and respectability. But Hobbes was never taken up by the establishment in the way that they were. For, even though he upholds the ideal of a maximally secure and effective political establishment, as such, Hobbes does so in a manner which distinctly alarmed the actual establishment itself. The very name he adopts for his political ideal serves to convey the strong element of mischief in his intellectual make-up: Leviathan is originally the Hebrew name of a mythical sea-monster, described in Job 40–1. And in the Middle Ages this monster had become identified with Satan (in association with the idea of God catching Satan like a fish, with Christ as the bait and the cross as the fish hook).[3] In Hobbes's scheme, on the other hand, Leviathan is the commonwealth – regarded as a 'Mortall God'.[4] He cites Job 41: 33 (in the Authorized Version), 'Upon earth there is not his like', reverentially; evidently taking special (almost Blakean!) delight in this symbolic reversal of the mediaeval notion.[5] It is not for nothing that he gained for himself a certain reputation for intellectual devilishness, or secret atheism. He was certainly anything but a straightforward establishment ideologue.

No less than Blake, in fact, Hobbes too is first and foremost a radical critic of manipulative sacred ideology. Only, whereas Blake is preoccupied with the threat of such ideology when it is allied with social contract-enforcing government, Hobbes on the contrary is obsessed with its threat when it is allied with social contract-dissolving insurgency. For that was what he witnessed in the build-up to the Civil War: the great shaking experience to which his shaken philosophy is responding.

In Blake's mythology Albion lies sick. His sickness represents the prevailing manipulativeness of the ruling class; above all, as this is backed up by claims of religious sanction. (Orc symbolizes a fallen rebelliousness – but even here the primary reference is to a rebelliousness which has now come to power, as in post-revolutionary France.) Blake seeks to provide the richest and most resonant possible poetic vocabulary for the denunciation of the manipulativeness of rulers, and it is from such poetry that Albion draws his life.

But, by contrast, the sickness threatening Leviathan comes from the manipulativeness of 'sedition'; leading to the death that is civil war.[6] Again, the worst of all for Hobbes is where such sedition pretends to godliness – as in the case of the Presbyterian opposition movement of his own day. Leviathan (sea monster, giant artificial man and mortal God, all in one) draws his life from the social contract. That is to say: from an agreement among neighbours to live together in peace, not on the basis of any shared ideals that might be distorted into manipulativeness, but solely on the quite unmanipulative basis of an appeal to each individual's own immediate self-interest. For Hobbes this most basic, pre-moral source of sociability is also in principle the most sacred, for the simple reason that – unlike any other sacred ideal – it can never, by its very nature, be rendered manipulative.

The result is a complete theological opposition. Hobbes, notwithstanding his longstanding reputation as a closet atheist, is in fact arguably the greatest of specifically Anglican theologians as such: in that he, more than any other, has provided a truly interesting argument to the effect that Anglicanism is, or could at any rate become, the very highest form of Christianity – by virtue of the way it reconciles secular and sacred authority, drawing both together into the ideal unity of healthy Leviathan. Whereas Blake remains amongst the most radically anti-Anglican of Dissenters.

But this opposition is by no means due to either of them being an actual ideological accomplice of the particular form of manipulativeness denounced by the other. It is simply that, while Blake the prophetic poet focuses on forgiveness as the imagination-liberating opposite of oppression by the powerful, Hobbes – the philosopher, concerned with rational consensus-building – focuses on the social contract, as the proper non-manipulative basis for social peace. Nothing nowadays, it is true, could be more dated than

Hobbes's actual theological vision: now that developed capitalism is, more and more, abandoning religion as a moral bulwark against anarchy, to replace it with consumerism instead. Yet, even though secularized, the underlying necessary complementarity of Albion and Leviathan surely remains.

IV

Pure shaken prophetic poetry versus pure shaken negotiative philosophy: what interests me, in short, for my particular theological purposes is the sense in which Blake and Hobbes may actually be seen as representing the two opposite extremes of a certain spiritual continuum; both, in the end, more or less equally extravagant in their contradictory one-sidednesses.

Even though Blake does not include Hobbes in his regular catalogue of spiritual opponents, it is indeed quite clear what his verdict on Hobbes would be. Hobbes's reverence for Euclidean geometry, as the ideal model for philosophical reasoning in general, is surely a classic expression of the spirit of fallen Urizen, the way Blake conceives it. While as for Leviathan: in his primary sea-monster aspect, it would no doubt be hard for Blake to resist directly identifying him with the serpentine form of Satan, the Covering Cherub. The trouble is that for Blake *all* forms of systematic philosophy are in effect fallen-Urizenic. He makes no distinction between systematic philosophy as corrupted into a mere ideological apologetics for establishment manipulativeness on the one hand, and, on the other hand, systematic philosophy in its authentic shaken role, as represented by Hobbes; he has no positive poetic symbolism at all for the proper mediatory, consensus-building vocation of philosophy. Because he simply does not see it.

Instead, he envisages just two alternatives for the shaken spirit: topographically symbolized by the contrast between 'Eden' and 'Beulah'. These two mythic locations, in the first place, represent two different aspects of his own poetry. Thus, his poetry is partly inspired by 'the Daughters of Beulah', the muses invoked at the beginning of *Milton*; and partly by 'the Sons of Eden', the prophetic emissaries of the Saviour, who is said to dictate the words of *Jerusalem*.[7] The Sons of Eden are direct participants in the 'the great Wars of Eternity'.[8] But Beulah, by contrast, is 'a place where Contrarieties are equally True . . . Where no dispute can come'.[9] The poetry of Eden is driven, prophetic; written for the sake of bearing testimony to others. Beulah-poetry is written for the poet's own pleasure, out of a purely inner conversation with oneself. The only 'Contrarieties' it deals with are thus complementary aspects of the given world-view within which it operates.

For Blake, the highest truth is that which belongs to the poetry of Eden. In so far as he also indulges in the consolations of Beulah, this is only by way of necessary refreshment, to re-equip himself for what lies beyond. In its primary sense, as the dwelling place of the consolatory muses, Beulah stands for a certain mode of poetic inspiration; secondarily, it becomes a general symbol for every sort of spiritual consolation. As such, it is a dream-world: 'A Soft Moony Universe feminine lovely / Pure mild & Gentle given in Mercy to those who sleep / Eternally'; a pastoral idyll, permeated with every sort of easy-going sensual pleasure.[10] The twenty-seven false churches of Judaeo-Christian history are, for Blake, 'the Monstrous Churches of Beulah', in that their dreams of heaven have all been Beulah dreams and so, to that extent, a with-drawal from the inevitably conflict-ridden political task of actually building Jerusalem, city of Edenic liberty, here on earth.[11] And yet, in the politically darkest times Jerusalem, who is sister to the muses, may take refuge with them, in inner emigration – 'gently snatch'd away: and hid in Beulah'.[12] It is a place created to provide 'a mild & pleasant Rest' for the Sons of Eden, when they are wearied in their warfare.[13]

Nowhere, however, does he recognize the need for any other species of spiritual discipline to balance the harshly confrontational poetry of Eden, besides that of Beulah. He has no imagery for a place of properly *philosophical* retreat. That whole domain remains, for him, an absolute *terra incognita*; nor does he leave any vacant space for it anywhere on his imaginative map.

V

Certainly I agree with Blake to the extent that he is simply upholding the intrinsic truth of shaken poetry against the traditional prejudices of the philosophers. But then, at the same time, I also want to argue – against Blake – that that impassioned mode of truth needs to be integrated into a larger solidarity ideal; in open partnership with the more detached truth of shaken philosophy.

For what matters, to my mind, is the solidarity of the shaken *in general*. This is a solidarity which may, and ideally needs to, come to expression in all manner of different styles; poetic or philosophical. Properly understood, though, it seems to me that the truth is in the solidarity, not the style. Good mythic theology, I think, is fundamentally a discipline of reconciling the truth of shaken poetry with that of shaken philosophy, in the service of the solidarity of the shaken.

Blake's verse draws its strength from a feral spirituality; akin to that of Amos. The prophet compares Yahweh to a lion:

> The lion has roared;
> who is not frightened?

My Lord Yahweh has spoken;
who could not prophesy?
                    (Amos 3: 8)[14]

In Blake's case, of course, it is a tiger:

Tyger Tyger, burning bright,
In the forests of the night;
What immortal hand or eye,
Could frame thy fearful symmetry?

In what distant deeps or skies.
Burnt the fire of thine eyes?
On what wings dare he aspire?
What the hand, dare seize the fire?

And what the shoulder, & what art,
Could twist the sinews of thy heart?
And when thy heart began to beat,
What dread hand? & what dread feet?

What the hammer? what the chain,
In what furnace was thy brain?
What the anvil? what dread grasp,
Dare its deadly terrors clasp![15]

The point of these questions is surely that the creation of the tiger is an image for the prevailing inspiration of Blake's own creativity: this poetry is essentially a manifestation of God in tiger-creative mood. And no doubt it is too much to ask of such poetry that it should also be appreciative of other approaches. For when did tigers ever negotiate?

Only, I think, it therefore becomes the sympathetic theologian's task to negotiate on his behalf; not in any way seeking to deny his one-sidedness, for it is undeniable – yet nevertheless struggling to ensure that, even in spite of it, his prophetic voice should still be quite clearly heard as such.

Appendix 2
Salvation history and romanticism

I

Blake's theology is, essentially, a critique of 'unforgiveness'. By which he means something like: the instinctive repressiveness of the established order; its systematic hostility to any sort of ethical or religious experimentation, and failure to recognize the necessity of shaken dissent, as a basic prerequisite for true cultural creativity. Hölderlin by contrast does not speak of 'forgiveness', because he does not focus as Blake does on the theme of divine judgement. And yet, deep down, his ideal does nevertheless seem to be quite closely akin to this.

Again, his philhellenism is entirely un-Blakean. However, in a sense the whole point of his curious treatment of Christ, as a companion of the Greek gods, is precisely to gesture towards the ideal of a renewed Christianity, finally instilled with something like the Blakean spirit of forgiveness. For what matters here, above all, is the complete lack of doctrinaire rigidity in the religion of ancient Greece.

The special power of Hölderlin's work, on the other hand, consists in its fragile subjectivity, as he agonizes over his own spiritual solitude in a culture whose popular and official religiosity still remains so utterly alien to his ideal. Blake, an equally isolated figure, seems almost to revel in his isolation; even as he dreams his dream of redeemed community, a rebuilt Jerusalem in England's green and pleasant land. But Hölderlin is tormented by isolation. His image of ancient Greece is a mythopoeic projection of his counter-factual dream of a culture within which free-spirited, shaken poetry would be fully integrated. When he speaks of Christ, it is always as both a throwback and a forerunner, symbolically representing his ardent hope for the future coming of another such culture. At times, as in 'Friedensfeier' that hope is represented as an imminent real possibility; elsewhere, and most finally of all in 'Mnemosyne', he descends towards despair. His whole work oscillates between these two poles.

What would it actually take, though, for this dream of Hölderlin's to be, in any real degree, fulfilled?

In his early youth, as I have already mentioned, Hölderlin had in fact developed a close friendship with Hegel: first of all in the period 1788–93 when they were fellow-students at the Tübingen Stift, and even shared a room together; then also in 1797–8 when they were near neighbours in Frankfurt. And there is I think a very interesting relationship to be traced, especially, between the challenge raised by Hölderlin's later poetry and the dialectical strategies of Hegel's later philosophical theology.

II

Indeed, it seems that during those two years at Frankfurt Hegel was quite considerably influenced by Hölderlin. Of the two, at that time Hölderlin was much the more up to date with the very latest philosophical developments: he had been in Jena and attended the lectures of Fichte; and was already struggling, in his own philosophical thinking, to get 'beyond' the Fichtean radicalization of Kant. Hegel arrived in Frankfurt still a more or less straightforward Kantian. It may well have been the influence of Hölderlin (and that of Sinclair, who was also party to their conversations there) which first prompted Hegel to start questioning the Kantian world-view.

For Kant and Fichte, of course, the philosophical truth of God needs to be decisively set apart from any traditional Christian notion of revelation in history. God is, from their point of view, simply the legislator of the 'moral law', understood in completely ahistoric – and unpoetic – terms as an eternally valid set of abstract first principles. As Hölderlin saw it, Kant was 'the Moses of our nation, leading it out of its Egyptian slumbers into the free, solitary desert of his speculation'.[1] The purgative discipline of Kantian reductionism was a necessary first stage on the journey, he thought, but the true promised land nevertheless lay beyond. For what he, Sinclair and Hegel were now after was precisely a *renewed* sense of divine revelation in history, not yet glimpsed by Kant or Fichte, tracing the work of God as made manifest in the inspirations of a shaken self-expressive poetic creativity, on the part of both individuals and whole cultures: divine creativity properly reconciled with, and so freely channelled through, the creativity of mortals – to magnificent effect for instance in ancient Greece, but with altogether more ambivalence in Christendom.

This is very much the governing concern of Hegel's Frankfurt writings.[2] And so too, his whole later philosophy from then onwards is, at its core, essentially just a systematic amplification of that original turning away from Kant, which he accomplished in the company of Hölderlin.

III

What is more, Hegel's later philosophical Christology also has quite significant points of contact with Blake's thought. (Not that either would ever
have been at all aware of the other, but even so.) Thus, take for instance his
discussion of 'evil and its forgiveness' in the *Phenomenology of Spirit*.

In order to understand this passage, one has to set it in context. It comes
at the end of a long chapter, simply entitled 'Spirit', which contains a very
general survey of cultural conflict, between opposing sorts of ethos.

The conflict set out in Sophocles' play *Antigone* is discussed: that is, a
situation of dramatic confrontation between the ethos of loyalty to the state
and that of loyalty to the family. So are the triangular moral conflicts
between the ethos of the aristocracy, the ethos of the merchant classes and
the demands of the state; both in the feudal world and also in the context
of absolute monarchy. But then we arrive at something else. Under the heading of 'faith and pure insight' Hegel turns to consider the perennial conflict
between established religion and its shaken critics.

He defines 'pure insight' as: that state of mind for which 'the Notion is
alone the actual'.[3] Let us decode this. 'The actual' is here a term for that
which truly matters, as divine reality. And the 'Notion' in question is the
notion of 'Spirit'; it is the movement towards a proper recognition of 'Spirit'
for what it is. 'Spirit', however, is essentially Hegel's general name for the
energy of authentic shakenness: the infinite undoing of every sort of merely
complacent and unthinking mental stasis; that which the whole of the
Phenomenology of Spirit is meant to illustrate, at every different level of
experience. 'Pure insight', in other words, is nothing other than an absolute
identification of divine reality with the pathos of shakenness, as such. It is
thus, one might say, precisely that basic level of theological insight which
Hegel himself shares with both Hölderlin and Blake.

'Pure insight', Hegel argues, is the real truth of faith.[4] Other forms of
faith may serve as a vehicle for Spirit – but only imperfectly, mixing the
impulses of Spirit with other impulses, in the muddled medium of conventional religious picture-thinking. True faith, prior to 'pure insight', is, as he
puts it, 'the tranquil pure *consciousness* of Spirit as *essence*'; that is, the
proper essence of the sacred. However, 'pure insight' is 'the *self*-conscious-
ness of Spirit as essence'. It is a form of faith which is both shaken and, at
the same time, fully aware that that quality of shakenness, in itself, is what
counts as its claim to truth.

In its first appearance, though, 'pure insight' is 'not yet *realized*': it remains
very much an unfinished project.[5] And this is the problem by which
Hölderlin, especially, is so agonized. For he, like Blake, represents 'pure
insight' still at the stage of being the insight of one single, solitary individual.[6]

Yet, by its very nature, it is an affirmation regarding the true vocation of *every* individual.[7] And so Hegel now sets himself to consider how a more general recognition of this may eventually be brought about.

First he considers the essentially anti-poetic sort of strategy represented by the Enlightenment; which both Hölderlin and Blake reject. What Hegel in this context calls 'the Enlightenment' is a campaign of, in the first instance, self-consciously shaken thought, against pseudo-religious 'superstition' and its associated politics, which subsequently however degenerates into the impurity of mere ideological warfare. Thus, in the heat of the struggle, the combatants cease to discriminate. Their critique tends to become a mere all-out onslaught on all pre-existing forms of organized faith, implicitly including even those which themselves come closest to the authentic thoughtfulness of 'pure insight'. The 'enlightened' have altogether lost sight of the countervailing elements of valid shaken-ness within the faith-traditions whose corruption they caricature.[8] And, as a result, their attack leaves nothing standing. The only sort of faith that they will now allow is one which has been effectively emptied of all real imaginative content: a purely abstract rationalism, with little or no poetic power remaining.[9]

Hegel illustrates the logic of this sort of strategy by allusion to the French *philosophes*, the Jacobin dictatorship, the Kantian/Fichtean doctrine of 'religion within the limits of pure reason alone'. But then – having peered down these various blind alleys – he turns back. Once again, he returns to the original problem. If the strategy of the Enlightenment will not do, for the popularization of 'pure insight' – what will?

The need is for a poetically far richer religious strategy. And it is with this goal in view that in the following chapter he will embark on a systematic sketch of the historic evolution of religion in general. Before he does so, though, he wants to try and spell out, just a little further, what the primary existential dynamic must be for a proper religiousness of 'pure insight'. His discussion of 'evil and its forgiveness' has essentially to be understood as an attempt to do that.

Thus, just like Blake, Hegel is primarily concerned with the forgiveness of dissent – and, above all, the dissent that issues from 'pure insight'. His argu-ment, as it were, pursues a dialogue between two opposing points of view.[10] On the one hand, there is the dissident. On the other hand, there is one who challenges the dissident. The dissident is challenged to justify his or her dissent, and responds by appealing to the inner dictates of conscience; however, the challenger (the 'universal consciousness', representing the prevailing moral consensus) is deeply mistrustful of this, accusing the dissi-dent (in the challenger's eyes, the 'evil consciousness') of all manner of mixed motive, and hence hypocrisy. Very well, the dissident responds – but, in that case, what are *your* motives? It is true, 'pure insight' is always mixed up with other, less pure motives; this the dissident frankly acknowledges. Yet to wait for *perfectly* pure motives would mean never acting at all. (The condition which Hegel contemptuously refers to as that of the 'beautiful soul'.) And what else is a rigidly unbending criticism of the dissident's 'hypocrisy', without any reciprocal confession of mixed motives on the part of the challenger – if not absolute hypocrisy itself?

A true, poetically vibrant religious culture of 'pure insight' would at the same time be one which consistently promoted a generous spirit of 'forgiveness' towards the creatively shaken, conscientious dissident, as such. Indeed, it must be – since it is the essential insight of 'pure insight' that God is Spirit, and the whole point of that designation is that Spirit is always *first and foremost* the shaking power by which the conscientious dissident is creatively shaken, out of the prevailing thoughtlessness of automatic conformity.

What is more, by situating his discussion of 'forgiveness' right here, at the very threshold of his systematic consideration of religion, Hegel is also making this his absolutely primary criterion for the assessment of religious truth or falsehood in general.[11] Just as, *mutatis mutandis*, Blake also does.

IV

And so what does Hegel, as a philosopher, add to the 'pure insight' he shares with these poets? Above all, I think he adds two things:

1   a systematic strategy for drawing the *whole* conceptual legacy of orthodox Christian theological tradition, so far as possible, into effective harmony with 'pure insight'
2   a vital first step towards a systematic theory of aesthetic truth generally, and poetic truth in particular, with his fundamental distinction between the three modes of 'symbolic', 'classical' and 'romantic' art.

V

Hegel's strategy for interweaving 'pure insight' into the mainstream legacy of Christian theology takes shape, essentially, as an argument regarding the *necessity* of the Incarnation.

Cur Deus homo? He is in effect the first Christian thinker since Anselm, in 1098, who takes up Anselm's elementary question, why the salvation of humanity should necessarily require God's becoming incarnate, rather than any other means, and who attempts to provide an alternative answer to Anselm's. Unfortunately, he nowhere brings the whole of this argument decisively together – instead, the various parts of it are strewn through his work, at various levels. But let me briefly try to reconstruct it; beginning from where, as just noted, he is in most direct agreement with Blake.[12]

As with Blake, his central theological concern is that religion should be imbued with a political spirit of forgiveness: the absolute antithesis to any sort of political manipulativeness, in the broadest sense; or, therefore, manipulatedness. And his philosophical term for that elementary state of fallenness which essentially consists in being vulnerable to manipulation, in general, is '*unhappy consciousness*'.

This is, in other words, that condition of inner mental servitude whose torments and eventual overcoming is also the basic theme of the Blakean epics. It is in principle a universal phenomenon, present in every culture without exception.[13] But on the other hand it becomes most articulate, receives its most explicit symbolic expression, in a monotheistic context; as is represented by the hubristic claims of Urizen, Tharmas and Luvah in Blake's myth – each of them, in their fallenness, at various times claiming to be the one true God.

The unhappiness of the 'unhappy consciousness' may indeed be masked. It may very often sincerely feel itself to be full of the most passionate joy: in the prescribed rejoicing of certain sorts of piety, for example. And yet deep down, for Hegel as for Blake, it is nevertheless 'unhappy' in that it is an *inwardly divided* state of mind; a condition of the soul riven, as it were, between two opposing selves, one the unforgiving oppressor of the other. The oppressed self is the shaken self, the potential questioner and free thinker. The oppressor self is the frightened conformist, ever anxious to fit in and to please. What renders the 'unhappy consciousness' objectively unhappy is just the triumph of the oppressor self. And the point is: the conflict between these two selves is at its poetic clearest when the frightened but internally triumphant oppressor self projects its oppressiveness onto the one true God, purporting to represent God and so to participate in divine authority.

The more extravagant the kitsch-sublime absolute otherness of the 'God' invoked by the 'unhappy consciousness', the more formidable is the effect; the more absolute the unforgiveness. In the thinking of Deutero-Isaiah we have already observed a profoundly shaken progress towards monotheism. Yet monotheism is in this respect a radically ambivalent phenomenon. For Hegel, the deep truth of the Incarnation consists in its symbolic differentiation of true, shaken monotheism from that other, false monotheism which is the supreme poetic expression of the 'unhappy consciousness'.

Thus: whereas the monotheism of the 'unhappy consciousness' serves to crush the oppressed shaken self by effectively envisaging God as a projection of the unforgiving oppressor self, the dogma of the Incarnation on the contrary precisely *identifies* the one God with the symbolic representative of all shaken selves, a crucified dissident. There could not possibly be a more complete symbolic reversal. This, as Hegel sees it, is why the Incarnation is necessary for salvation. Or rather, this is how the Incarnation, by being 'necessary', serves to define that particular mode or level of 'salvation' which is the deepest truth of Christian faith: what Christian faith, understood in Hegelian terms, saves us from is just the 'unhappy consciousness' and all its works.

Nothing, though, is as slippery as religious truth. Religion, by representing and transmitting this truth in the pre-philosophic form of picture-thinking, immediately renders it ambiguous. In itself, the truth of the gospel, as a symbolic overcoming of the 'unhappy consciousness', is a universal truth; that is, a truth also expressible, at least to some extent, in all sorts of other cultural forms, and not only in terms of explicit Christian faith. But picture-thinking, by its very nature, particularizes. The 'unhappy consciousness' is a universal phenomenon: a universal devaluation of all human individuality, as such, inasmuch as it is the mentality of individuals who have more or less lost their nerve as individuals, abandoning any claim to have a distinctive viewpoint of their own and merely opting for safe conformity instead. As an overcoming of the 'unhappy consciousness', the truth of the Gospel is an equally universal counter-affirmation of the infinite intrinsic value of every individual as such. Picture-thinking, however, can only communicate this by presenting us with the image of one *particular* representative individual.

And then, within Christian thinking, the 'unhappy consciousness' is able to reassert itself by focusing entirely on the particularity of that image, in such a way as to obscure the proper universality of the true idea represented. So, instead of being understood as an affirmation of the infinite value of human individuality in general, faith in the Incarnation is reduced, by the resurgent 'unhappy consciousness' within Christianity, to being simply an affirmation of the infinite significance of this one particular individual, Jesus of Nazareth – not so much here in his properly primary role as a representative of human individuality in general, but rather in his properly secondary role as the founder of the church. In which case, instead of functioning as a symbolic incitement to free-spiritedness, the Incarnation is on the contrary ideologized into just another argument for conformity; only now a Christian conformity, in submission to church authority.

Hegel's profound originality as a Christian philosopher consists in his decisive identification of *this* as the absolutely primary sense in which Christianity needs to be informed by philosophy; on the grounds that philosophy is that form of thinking which, with systematic intent, transcends the inevitable ambiguousness of picture-thinking.

But then again he also argues that Christian philosophy can only assert its proper claims in an appropriate historic context; and that it is in fact only in his own day that such a context has at long last finally arrived. For what is first required is a widespread and thorough calling into question of all the old assumptions of Christian orthodoxy, driving the tradition's defenders right back to first principles, to start afresh. And that is just what now, as never before in church history, the Enlightenment has accomplished. He agrees with Hölderlin and Blake that the positive theology of the Enlightenment – with its all too sweeping devaluation of everything with real poetico-religious power – is nothing but a cul-de-sac. But that failure nevertheless remains a vital contribution to setting the scene.

Or rather, to be more precise, there are really two main types of general intellectual development which Hegel sees as setting the scene for the possibility of his own philosophic breakthrough. One is the Enlightenment, culminating with Kant and Fichte; and the other is 'Pietism'.[14] Note that 'Enlightenment' and 'Pietism' are both of them, for Hegel, very broad categories. In both cases, we have a radical shaken negativity towards the old traditional emphasis on proper church-institutional loyalties and doctrinal 'correctness'; more or less tending towards 'pure insight'. The difference is simply that, whereas the Enlightenment argues on the basis of a highly abstract, in the sense of de-poeticized, rationality, Pietism does not. Unlike the thinking of the Enlightenment, it remains rich in poetic pathos.

Hegel's discussion of 'Pietism' in his 1827 *Lectures on the Philosophy of Religion* is primarily determined by a polemical concern to defend himself against the recent attack on his work by the young Pietist theologian F. A. G. Tholuck.[15] What Tholuck represented was in fact quite a conventional form of Pietism; a Pietism, one would have to say, at the very furthest possible remove from the cheerful unconventionality of 'pure insight'. This was Pietism as a mass movement: a whole culture of Bible study groups and dramatic conversion experiences; the prevailing ethos of the University of Halle, indeed, where Tholuck had recently been appointed professor of theology.

But is there not also a sense in which – given Hegel's extremely broad definition of the term – this same category further includes such altogether less conventional figures as Hölderlin and Blake? Of course, they represent a polar opposite sort of 'Pietism' from Tholuck's. They are maverick Pietists; for theirs is a Pietism which represents 'pure insight' at its purest. Yet here is where they surely belong in the grand Hegelian scheme of things. If 'pure insight' appears at its religiously crudest in the Enlightenment, then its Pietist version is the immediate antithesis. And true 'speculative' philosophy, then, is just the translation of what is thereby arrived at, back into a more discursively rational form.

VI

Meanwhile, in terms of Hegelian aesthetic theory one would equally have to say that Hölderlin and Blake are amongst the most 'romantic' of poets.

This theory traces a progressive progression through three species of art: the 'symbolic', the 'classical' and the 'romantic'.[16] Each of these species is primarily illustrated by the art of a different period, or range of cultures; but in essence they embody three contrasting relationships between the art work and what Hegel calls the 'Idea'. By which, again, he means the true idea of 'Spirit' – in its universal character as sheer shaken creativity. Or: that whole spiritual appropriation-process, infusing fresh subjective life into the objective data of tradition, out of which any form of artistic originality springs, as well as all true religious faith; the ultimate source of poetic truth, in general.

When Hegel speaks of 'classical' art he means the species best exemplified, he thinks, by the sculpture, the epic poetry and the drama of ancient Greece. And in one sense, even in his later thought, he still agrees with Hölderlin that this represents an unsurpassable achievement. It is unsurpassable in its combination of two qualities:

First, such art is shaped by a powerful drive towards sacramentality – although he does not use this actual term, sacramentality is very much a crucial aspect of the Hegelian aesthetic ideal. The religion of ancient Greece was as a whole, he thinks, a 'religion of art': a beautiful artistic celebration of the sacredness of the beautiful as such, for which art had therefore become 'the supreme mode of our knowledge of the Absolute'.[17] The beautiful anthropomorphism of the Greek gods, shown in their statues, was directly symbolic of the infinitely expansive potential of the liberated human spirit – the beauty of the 'Idea' – which it then became the whole task of art both to celebrate and to embody.

Second, what the Greeks produced was at the same time also a profoundly consensual art. Ancient Greek drama, to be sure, does register certain radical conflicts between different levels of the prevailing ethical consensus. (*Antigone* is a prime example.) But it seldom does so in campaigning fashion; or only as the most cheerful sort of comedy. At all events, it is never prophetic in tone. Classical art is most truly classical, in Hegel's sense of the term, where it is least polemical and most celebratory, best integrated into the larger ethical life of the surrounding culture. So that here we have an art which, with unique effectiveness, expresses the 'Idea' as the quite untroubled, governing and unifying sacred ideal of a whole culture.

'Symbolic' art, by contrast, is art which has not yet arrived at the perfection of the classical, because it lacks an environment which would encourage the necessary sacramentality. The examples Hegel has in mind are, in the first instance, the monumental buildings, the sculptures and the poetry of ancient Egypt, India, Persia and Israel. In fact, it seems to me to be a major weakness of the argument that he lumps the prophetic poetry of ancient Israel into this category without proper recognition of its radical ambivalence – in his own terms, precisely as regards its special relationship to the 'Idea'. But what he is concerned with is just the difference of all these cultures from that of ancient Greece. They none of them have gods that are fully anthropomorphized: this, for Hegel, is the key factor. And as a result, he argues, their sacred art is altogether less *directly* celebratory of the 'Idea'. However original its creativity, in other words, it falls short of a proper celebration of that originality for its own sake, as an expression of freedom. The 'Idea' is, to this extent, a much less self-reflective – and therefore less 'determinate', more 'abstract' – presence than in classical art. Symbolic art plunges off in all sorts of directions. It may be quite sublime and mysterious in its symbolizing of the sacred. And yet, in the end, the essential difference is that it still lacks that radically free-spirited *self-identification* with the sacred which is the distinctive hallmark of the classical.

'Romantic' art, on the other hand, departs from the classical ideal in another way. For it is, in effect, defined by its loss of background-consensuality. This is, pre-eminently, the art of Christendom/post-Christendom, at its most original and distinctive, and above all in its later forms; Hegel is thinking especially of its painting, music, drama and literature, although nowadays one would also have to include its architecture and sculpture.

The visual art of romanticism begins with a quite unclassical attitude of religious polemic, against the 'worldliness' of the surrounding world. Whereas the statues of the ancient Greek gods are a splendid sensual celebration of this-worldly values, the icons of Byzantium and its successor-cultures are polemically anti-sensual, other-worldly; and not even the inspired would-be neo-classicism of Renaissance visual art was ever able at all effectively to subdue the intrinsic recalcitrance of the crucifixion, as a central theme.

The romanticism of romantic art essentially consists in its quality as a vehicle for discontent. Romantic music is music which yearns.[18] Drama and literature become romantic to the extent that the author is ill at ease with the world, or at war with it – poets like Blake and Hölderlin are just the most extreme sort of example. In the sense that art's 'highest vocation' is to articulate the sacred values of a whole culture, romantic art is thus the art of a world for which, in Hegel's phrase, 'art, considered in its highest vocation, is and remains . . . a thing of the past'.[19]

But why? I think one might put it as follows. Symbolic art is art in which the demands of the Idea are still too weakly appropriated. But in romantic art the situation is the exact reverse: the demands of the Idea are so vigorously appropriated, they are pressed to the point where they simply *overflow* the capacities of any consensual form. The 'Idea', in artistic terms, is first of all the drive towards an ever more effective consensual affirmation of creative freedom, as in classical art; but then, more deeply, the drive towards an ever more intense pathos of shakenness, in the exercise of such freedom – which however shatters consensus. Romantic art goes beyond classical art in that it rises to this latter level.

Or, again, it would appear that these three species of art represent three quite different levels of aesthetic relationship to the 'unhappy consciousness'.[20] Symbolic art at its most sacred tends towards an unreserved endorsement of the 'unhappy consciousness', investing the 'unhappy consciousness' with extravagant pathos of glory. This pathos of glory may be imperialistic, reinforcing a thoroughly conservative form of the 'unhappy consciousness', as in the case of the pyramids, tombs and temples of ancient Egypt; or it may be revolutionary, as illustrated by the word-portraits of Yahweh in the traditions stemming from Hosea. Either way, though, where symbolic art lays claim to serious authority it is always an intimidatory authority. Classical art differs, in that it is the art of a culture relatively free of any sacralization of the 'unhappy consciousness'. The artistic portrayal of the gods of ancient Greece is not intimidatory – even as one reverences them, one can also joke about them. But romantic art, at any rate potentially, goes one step further. For such art, at its truest – as in the work of Blake or Hölderlin – is not just free of the 'unhappy consciousness'. It is a direct polemic *against* it: highlighting its unhappiness, mocking it, deploring its destructive consequences. In principle, this is what Christian religious art does, with its focus on Christ's passion. And then the secular art that comes afterwards, in various ways, extends the same critique; not just in its critical content, but more and more in its experimentation with nonconformist style as well.

There are, it is true, certain forms of romantic art which Hegel criticizes for going too far. He by no means approves of the more nihilistic forms of romanticism, for which nothing is sacred – or nothing except the ego of the solitary artistic genius. And so, for example, he rejects the fashionable cult of romantic 'Irony' promoted above all, in the Germany of his day, by Friedrich von Schlegel; since that is certainly how he sees this.[21]

But, I think, in its basic thrust his argument needs primarily to be understood very much as a move beyond his own earlier standpoint, which he had shared with Hölderlin.

Although in his *Aesthetics* lectures he does not actually refer to Hölderlin – whose work at that time was still largely unknown – what he is first and foremost concerned to refute is, nevertheless, nothing other than

Hölderlinian nostalgia. It seems in fact that Hölderlin agreed with Schiller's argument in his *Letters on the Aesthetic Education of Man*, where Schiller hints at a spiral grand narrative: beginning from the recognition that the splendour of ancient Greece was indeed irretrievable – in that it was a culture of comparatively un-self-conscious, spontaneous harmony with nature – the hope held out here was for an eventual return to some equivalent harmony, only now one which was finally self-conscious.[22] Yet still, according to this scheme, the highest art would be a return to some sort of classicism; art restored to what Hegel also calls its 'highest vocation', the articulation of the sacred values of a new consensus. Hölderlin is thus a profoundly romantic artist who, however, laments the fact – and dreams of being what Pindar or Sophocles had been instead.

Hegel's whole argument surely originates out of his fundamental, if regretful, repudiation of that dream. In effect, it seems, he sides with what is evidently Blake's view, against Hölderlin: that the most truthful art is, and *always will be*, dissident – and that even to dream otherwise is to confuse the issue. Art 'in its highest vocation' is *not* the highest art. The truth of Hölderlin's vision lies in its shakenness; not its nostalgia, which is something else.

There is, in short, no need to be nostalgic for a lost 'natural' consensus, Hegel is arguing. (And he would no doubt want to argue the same, today, against some of the more one-sided forms of contemporary anti-modernism.) But, far rather, all that is required is a proper, poetically rich religious culture of forgiveness.

Notes

1 Faith: poetry versus metaphysical opinion

1 Francis Bacon, *The Essayes or Counsels, Civill and Moral*, ed. Michael Kiernan (Oxford: Clarendon Press, 1985), p. 7.

2 Consider, in particular, the very clear opposition between the absolute certainty, by definition, of *fides* and the constitutive uncertainty of *opinio* in the thought of Thomas Aquinas. The certainty of *fides* here is not the opinionated certainty of the bigot, but far rather (I think one might say) the certainty of an authentically thoughtful self-knowledge, as mediated through the poetic resources of the Christian tradition.

   On the larger history of the word 'faith', see for example Wilfred Cantwell Smith, *Belief and History* (Charlottesville: University Press of Virginia, 1977), and *Faith and Belief* (Princeton: Princeton University Press, 1979).

2 Confessions of a traitorous *clerc*

1 For a general survey of Benda's work, see Robert J. Niess, *Julien Benda* (Ann Arbor: University of Michigan Press, 1956).

2 Published in Paris by Grasset, 1927; 2nd edn, ibid., 1947 (but dated 1946). The English translation by Richard Aldington actually came out under two different titles: *The Great Betrayal* (London: Routledge, 1928) and *The Treason of the Intellectuals* (New York: Morrow, 1928).

3 Paris: *Les Cahiers de la Quinzaine*, series 12, cahier 3 (1911); and Gallimard, 1928.

4 *The Treason of the Intellectuals*, pp. 202–3.

5 Francis Fukuyama, *The End of History and the Last Man* (London: Penguin, 1992).

3 The 'pathos of shakenness': its three defining marks

1 The trouble with the usual translation, as 'kingdom', is just that this is a word which has nowadays acquired very different connotations from those it once had. In a democracy, even one which is a constitutional monarchy, 'kingdom' has ceased to mean what *basileia* meant for the gospel writers. It has lost too much of its original flavour of authority.

2 Thomas Aquinas, *Quaestiones disputatae de veritate*, qu. 1, art. 1.

3 *Vom Wesen der Wahrheit* (4th edn, Frankfurt am Main: Klostermann, 1961). There are two English translations: by John Sallis, in Martin Heidegger, *Basic Writings*, ed. David Farrell Krell (London: Routledge and Kegan Paul, 1978); and

by R. F. C. Hull and Alan Crick, in Martin Heidegger, *Existence and Being*, ed. Werner Brock (Chicago: Henry Regnery, 1949). The argument is a development of section 44 of *Being and Time*, first published three years earlier in 1927; translated by John Macquarrie and Edward Robinson (Oxford: Blackwell, 1962).

4 Section 3; *Basic Writings*, p. 125.

5 Ibid., section 3, p. 126; section 4, p. 130.

6 Ibid., section 4, p. 127.

7 Ibid., section 5, p. 132.

8 Ibid., section 6, p. 132. My emphasis.

9 Ibid., section 6, p. 134.

10 The final flourish of this puritanism comes when, towards the end of his life, Heidegger actually renounces the modern word '*Wahrheit*', 'truth', itself: condemning it as a sheer mistranslation for *aletheia* in its deepest sense – even though he also quite frankly acknowledges that, even in ancient Greek, that deepest sense was never altogether clear. Thus, he ends up saying that the ultimate *telos* for thinking is not 'truth'! It is (what he calls) *aletheia* – instead. See *Zur Sache des Denkens* (Tübingen: Max Niemeyer Verlag, 1969); translated into English by Joan Stambaugh as *On Time and Being* (New York: Harper and Row, 1972), pp. 69–71.

11 See the discussion in both *God and Modernity* (London: Routledge, 2000) and *Civil Society, Civil Religion* (Oxford: Blackwell, 1995).

12 Cf. *Civil Society, Civil Religion*, Chapter 4. (I hope, in future, systematically to develop this approach to Trinitarian theology.)

13 Martin Luther, *Selections*, translated into English and edited by John Dillenberger (New York: Anchor Books, 1961), p. 503.

4 'Mythic theology'

1 Benda's most comprehensive critique of poetry is to be found in the final section of *Du Poétique* (Geneva and Paris: Editions des Trois Collines, 1946). But this is part of an ongoing campaign, traceable through a whole series of works including for example *Dialogues à Byzance* (Paris: Editions de la Revue blanche, 1900), *Délice d'Eleuthère* (Paris: Gallimard, 1935), *Précision* (Paris: Gallimard, 1937), *La France byzantine* (Paris: Gallimard, 1945) and *Du style d'idées* (Paris: Gallimard, 1948).

2 The new element is the attack, in paragraphs 595–602, on poetry as a form of artistic 'imitation', *mimesis*. Here the poet is contrasted unfavourably with the craftsman. The latter – so the argument goes – makes things that are at any rate useful (beds and tables are mentioned by way of example). The one who actually gets closest to the true reality of the ideal Forms in question (such as Bed and Table) is in fact the reflective *user* (of beds and tables and suchlike) for whom the craftsman works, and who instructs him in what is required: the contemplative man of leisure, in other words. And the craftsman then approaches that reality at one remove. But, by contrast to what the craftsman produces, the poet's work is at yet a further remove from reality – because it is not even useful. It is merely *mimesis*.

This however is really not so much an argument as just a somewhat elaborate declaration of war! Of course poetry is 'useless' – if you arbitrarily demand that it serve purposes that are intrinsically alien to it. So Homer is also criticized here on the grounds that he was no legislator, no statesman, no inventor, no community-founder (paras 599–600). But then, why should these be relevant criteria?

3 *Republic*, para. 607.

4 Cf. in particular *Republic*, paras 604–5. The only sort of poetry ever likely to make a real persuasive impact on the public, it is argued here, is that which focuses on, and awakens sympathy for, the most unstable, emotionally self-indulgent and impulsive characters – for the simple reason that their activity is so much more dramatic, and their motivation so much more easily communicable in poetic form, than that of the tranquil wise man.

5 As he himself in effect acknowledges, citing various poetic counter-attacks: ibid., para. 607.

6 *Essai d'un discours cohérent sur les rapports de Dieu et du monde* (Paris: Gallimard, 1931).

7 Among his other work, Benda edited two anthologies of Kant's writings.

8 The *Dialogues à Byzance* of 1900 have a distinctly positivist quality. And the turning point, back to positivism, in his later work comes in *Exercice d'un enterré vif* (Geneva and Paris: Editions des Trois Collines, 1946).

9 The surviving fragments of Varro's work are collected and discussed in Burkhart Cardauns, *M. Terentius Varro: Antiquitates Rerum Divinarum, Fragmente und Kommentar* (Wiesbaden: Abhandl. Akad. Mainz, Geistes- und Sozialwiss. Klasse, 1976). See also Godo Lieberg, 'Die "theologia tripertita" in Forschung und Bezeugung', in H. Temporini (ed.), *Aufstieg und Niedergang der römischen Welt* I (iv) (Berlin: Walter de Gruyter, 1973), pp. 63–115; Burkhart Cardauns, 'Varro und die römische Religion', ibid., II, 16 (i) (1978), pp. 80–103; Jean Pépin, 'La théologie tripartite de Varron', in *Revue Augustinienne*, vol. 2 (1956), pp. 256–94; Pierre Boyancé, 'Sur la théologie de Varron', in *Revue des études anciennes*, 57 (1955), pp. 57–84, and 'Les implications philosophiques des recherches de Varron sur la religion Romaine', in *Atti del Congresso Internazionale di Studi Varroniani* (Rieti, 1976), pp. 137–61.

10 Augustine, *The City of God*, English translation by Henry Bettenson (London: Penguin, 1984).

11 *The City of God*, VI, 6.

12 Paul Avis, *God and the Creative Imagination* (London: Routledge, 1999).

13 There is certainly a fine lyric swagger to much of the surviving Gnostic literature; although, I would say, quite heavily tainted by a continually latent sectarian pathos of glory, glorifying the enlightened community's leadership elite. But the Montanist literature was effectively suppressed, so that it is impossible to judge its quality. Hippolytus (*Refutation of All Heresies*, VII, 19) refers scornfully to the 'infinite number' of Montanist prophetic books circulating in early third century Phrygia. And yet almost nothing has survived from them.

14 Nietzsche, *The Will to Power*, English translation by Walter Kaufmann (New York: Vintage, 1968), § 1067.

15 *On the Genealogy of Morals*, English translation by Walter Kaufmann (New York: Vintage, 1969), I, § 16.

16 *The Will to Power*, § 129; and cf. §§ 104 (Napoleon compared with Goethe), 128, 751, 975, 1018 (Napoleon set alongside Dante, Michelangelo). All of this furthermore links into Nietzsche's extensive rhetoric about the rulers of the future, who will be great 'breeders' of a new humanity.

17 *On the Genealogy of Morals*, III, § 25.

18 He campaigns against it both in the form represented by Nietzsche and in that represented by Bergson. In fact, it is Bergson who is his real *bête noire* – largely due to the phenomenal popularity of Bergsonism in the French intellectual world of his youth; and even though Bergson's actual politics are so much milder and more liberal than Nietzsche's.

19 See for example Mark Warren, *Nietzsche and Political Thought* (Cambridge, Mass. and London: MIT Press, 1988), and Laurence Lampert, *Nietzsche's Teaching: An Interpretation of* Thus Spoke Zarathustra (New Haven and London: Yale University Press, 1986).

20 "Nur noch ein Gott kann uns retten", *Der Spiegel*, issue no. 23, 31 May 1976; date of interview: 23 September 1966. English translation by Lisa Harries in G. Neske and E. Kettering (eds), *Martin Heidegger and National Socialism: Questions and Answers* (New York: Paragon House, 1990).

21 It is Heidegger himself who speaks of this as *the* turn in his thinking. Alternatively, one may identify it as the third of three crucial such turns: the first in 1917–19, a conversion away from the fervent Catholicism of his early years, to the Kierkegaardian Protestantism which still remains the latent religious background to *Being and Time*; the second in 1928–9, which is when he first adopted the revolutionary Prometheanism; culminating in 1933, his 'Nietzschean' phase.

So, for example, John Caputo argues in his *Demythologizing Heidegger* (Bloomington: Indiana University Press, 1993), pp. 178–9. (Of all the critical literature on Heidegger, this book of Caputo's seems to me to be one of the most penetrating.)

5 The heritage of Amos

1 Translation from Francis I. Andersen and David Noel Freedman, *Amos: A New Translation with Introduction and Commentary* (New York: Doubleday, Anchor Bible series, 1989).

2 See the detailed discussion by Andersen and Freedman, pp. 245–50.

3 Still more speculatively, they associate the prophecies collected in Chapter 5, all together, with the period of the first vision; and those in Chapter 6 with that of the second: ibid., pp. 83–5.

4 Andersen and Freedman associate Chapters 3–4 with the third vision, Chapters 1–2 with the fourth. They imagine Amaziah as being provoked into action by the oracles of 2: 6–16. And then they envisage the fifth vision, in which the earthquake brings down a temple, presumably that of Bethel, coming to Amos whilst he was (supposedly) under arrest there.

5 Karl Jaspers, *The Origin and Goal of History*, translated into English by M. Bullock (New Haven: Yale University Press, 1953).

6 Samson was said to have been a Nazirite (Judges 13: 5, 7; 16: 17); also, apparently, Samuel (1 Samuel 1: 11). There was also apparently a whole clan bound by Nazirite vows: namely, the Rechabites (Jeremiah 35; cf. 2 Kings 10: 15–17).

7 'Yahweh-aloneism': I take this phrase from Morton Smith, *Palestinian Parties and Politics That Shaped the Old Testament* (New York: Columbia University Press, 1971). And see also Bernhard Lang, *Monotheism And the Prophetic Minority* (Sheffield: Almond Press, 1983), Chapter 1.

8 Reading Hosea 13: 4, for example:

> Yet I am Yahweh,
> your God since the days in the land of Egypt;
> you know no God but me,
> there is no other saviour

one is immediately reminded of the opening words of the Decalogue, in Exodus 20: 1–2 and Deuteronomy 5: 6–7: 'I am Yahweh your God who brought you out of the land of Egypt, out of the house of slavery. You shall have no gods except me.' But this may well be more a matter of the Decalogue tradition echoing Hosea than vice versa.

9 Or perhaps two wives: there is no clear link between the text in Chapter 1 and that in Chapter 3.

10 Translation from *The Jerusalem Bible* (London: Darton, Longman and Todd, 1966).

11 It is also possible that it is the other way round, and that Amos 6: 14 was originally framed as a response to an earlier prophecy of Jonah's. But here I follow Andersen and Freedman, *Amos*, pp. 585–8.

12 Or it may be that the second speaker is a lone survivor from among those who were in the house. In which case, the initial question is: 'Are there any others of you still left alive?'

13 Cf. the extensive discussion of sacrifice in the work of René Girard: *Violence and the Sacred*, translated by P. Gregory (Baltimore: Johns Hopkins University Press, 1977); and *Things Hidden since the Foundation of the World*, translated by Stephen Bann and Michael Metteer (London: Athlone, 1987).

14 This is indeed the one point where Hosea does, quite strikingly, echo Amos: Hosea 6: 6.

15 Moreover, he also adds weight to this call by the following quite extraordinary invocation of the legendary glory-days of the exodus: in Chapter 5, verse 25, Yahweh asks, 'Did you bring me sacrifices and gifts for forty years in the desert, O house of Israel?' The clear implication being that no, they did not – a picture of the exodus, be it noted, in complete contradiction to the whole tradition later written down in the Pentateuch.

16 This is what Andersen and Freedman suggest: pp. 434–5. Lo-Dabar and Qarnaim were two towns in Transjordan, evidently both captured by Jeroboam.

17 Although it is also true that they do have something in common with Israel: in that they too have experienced – and in Amos's day were still experiencing – oppression by Egypt.

18 An alternative reading would be that this is just another comment on the degradation of sinful Israel – which is thereby rendered as alien to Yahweh as the utterly alien Cushites. Such a reading, however, would obviously destroy the parallelism with the second question; and therefore seems unlikely.

19 Translation taken from the New Revised Standard Version (Cambridge: Cambridge University Press, 1989).

20 Isaiah 41: 1–5; 41: 21–9; 43: 8–15; 44: 6–8, 21–2; 45: 20–5.

21 Already in the first year of his reign in Babylon, 538, Cyrus did just what the prophet had said he would do: he issued a decree permitting the return of Jewish exiles to their homeland, and the resumption of the public cult of Yahweh there.

22 And the puzzlement goes back a long way: cf. for example Acts 8: 26–35.

23 That is: following the more immediate autobiographical self-reflectiveness of Jeremiah's laments, complaining about the anguish of his own prophetic calling and calling on Yahweh for vengeance. There is in fact something of the flavour of these in both the second and the third of the servant songs.

6 A shaken sacramentalism: Hölderlin and Blake

1 The terrible weakness of the actual French Revolutionary festivals, on the other hand, was their dishonesty. Thus, the Festival of the Supreme Being for example appears to have been premised on a belief that the acute cultural disunity then afflicting France might best be eased by averting one's gaze. Hence it became a symbolic celebration of the natural, biological unity of the species. It turned the world inside out: making a systematic public display of the citizenry's private life,

at its most decorous and wholesome. Throughout the country, the processions gave pride of place to pregnant women, on their husbands' arms; young mothers giving suck to their infants, especially if male, or leading small children by the hand; maidens with baskets of flowers, or sheaves of corn, and flowers in their hair; shepherds carrying lambs with pink ribbons on; labourers and craftsmen of every sort, carrying the tools of their trade; chariots heaped high with agricultural produce. The aim was to present a living picture of a-historical Arcadian fecundity, peace and contentment. All evil was elsewhere – symbolized by a cardboard statue of 'Atheism', or some equivalent, which was ceremonially burnt.

Then consider David's anguished self-portrait, painted in a spare moment during his period in power. David: the impresario behind the festivals, an artist of undeniable genius – yet at the same time Robespierre's right-hand man on the Committee of General Security, running the police; whose signature is to be found on over 400 extant arrest warrants, and who was directly involved in innumerable guillotinings, often of men who had previously been his own friends and allies. It is a truly haunting work of art.

2 Edmund Burke, *A Philosophical Enquiry into the Origin of our Ideas of the Sublime and Beautiful*, ed. J. T. Boulton (London: Routledge and Kegan Paul, 1958); Immanuel Kant, *Critique of Judgement*, translated by J. C. Meredith (Oxford: Oxford University Press, 1956).

3 On Blake's London, see in particular Peter Ackroyd's biography, *Blake* (London: Minerva, 1996).

4 For Blake's writings, see *The Complete Poetry and Prose of William Blake*, ed. David V. Erdman (New York: Anchor, 1988).

5 *Blake Records*, ed. G. E. Bentley (Oxford: Oxford University Press, 1969), p. 540.

6 See also the two short texts, etched together perhaps in 1820, 'On Homer's poetry' and 'On Virgil' in Erdman, pp. 269–70. 'The Classics', Blake here exclaims, 'it is the Classics! & not Goths nor Monks, that Desolate Europe with Wars.'

He admired Classic sculpture: as his extraordinary annotated engraving of the Laocoön, in particular, bears witness. (But even then he felt impelled to attribute it to Greek borrowings from a higher, lost artistic culture of the Middle East; just as the writings of 'Homer & Ovid; of Plato and Cicero' are in his view 'stolen' as well as 'perverted'.)

7 Klopstock is one German poet of whom Blake was aware, thanks to the translations by his patron William Hayley. And his response in 'When Klopstock England defied' is far from complimentary!

8 Blake appears, briefly around the year 1789, to have become a member of the Swedenborgian 'New Church', or at least a fellow-traveller. But his first great work of religious prophecy, *The Marriage of Heaven and Hell*, is also his polemical renunciation of that church.

9 Milan Kundera, *The Unbearable Lightness of Being*, translated by Michael Henry Heim (London: Faber and Faber, 1984), p. 248.

10 Ibid., p. 253. In the novel, the context of this formula is a dream. The dreamer is Tereza. And the dream is in fact a nightmare: she dreams she is one of a group of naked women being marched around a swimming pool and forced to sing cheerful songs, while corpses float just below the surface of the pool:

> Tereza could not address a single question, a single word, to any of the women; the only response she would have got was the next stanza of the current song. She could not even give any of them a secret wink; they would immediately have pointed her out to the man standing in the basket above the pool, and he would have shot her dead.

11 It is perhaps worth noting that these speeches are widely regarded as one of a number of later additions to this book, and are by no means necessarily consonant with the original author's intentions.

12 Letter to Thomas Butts, 6 July 1803. Erdman, p. 730.

13 Erdman, p. 660.

14 Everything, we are told, has its own vortex – but in what sense? The traveller through eternity passes them – through them or by them? Seen in retrospect, each one looks like a sun, a moon, a universe – or 'like a human form, a friend'. The heaven is a vortex already passed, the earth a vortex not yet passed. 'Thus is the earth one infinite plane, and not as apparent / To the weak traveller confin'd beneath the moony shade' – who lives by the 'Corporeal Understanding'.

No kidding.

Not surprisingly, this passage has been much puzzled over by the critics. But cf. especially the discussion in Vincent Arthur De Luca, *Words of Eternity: Blake and the Poetics of the Sublime* (Princeton: Princeton University Press, 1991), pp. 80–4.

7 Blake: shakenness in confrontational form

1 *Jerusalem* 4: 5.

2 *Milton* 3: 3–4.

3 *Jerusalem* 98: 45–6.

4 *Milton* 40: 20–1.

5 In the earlier *Book of Urizen*, he speaks not of a wheel but of 'the Net of Religion', like a spider's web. In *The Four Zoas* he speaks of 'Mystery'. Elsewhere he personifies this 'wheel' or 'net', of mystificatory sacred ideology, especially in the figure of 'Rahab'.

6 *Jerusalem* 77: 21–3.

7 *The Everlasting Gospel* (k), 21–2.

8 *Jerusalem* 77: 20.

9 Ibid. 7–11.

10 *A Vision of the Last Judgment*, Erdman, pp. 565–6.

11 'Those who Martyr others or who cause War are Deists, but never can be Forgivers of Sin. The Glory of Christianity is, To Conquer by Forgiveness. All the Destruction therefore, in Christian Europe has arisen from Deism': *Jerusalem* 52. Here in fact the term 'Deism' has evidently taken not one, but two quite distinct leaps from its conventional sense: first, as noted earlier, to be identified with the Anglican establishment-mentality of Blake's day, in its hostility to monkish or Methodistical enthusiasm – and then to become a more or less a universal term for aggressive establishment-mindedness of every sort. A prime example of Blake's characteristic grasshopper logic!

12 *A Vision of the Last Judgment*, p. 564.

13 All these works are to be found in Erdman.

14 How much did Blake actually know about Gnosticism, though? He does refer to the traditional notion of '*adam qadmon* in his address 'To the Jews', which prefaces *Jerusalem*, Chapter 2. And he may have acquired some sketchy knowledge of Christian Gnosticism from the English translation of Mosheim's *Ecclesiastical History*. But the resemblances are perhaps more a matter of coincidence than anything else.

15 This is only true of the Lambeth prophecies. In the post-Lambeth period Orc does become an altogether more ambivalent figure. In *The Four Zoas* VIII, page 101 in Blake's manuscript (Erdman, p. 373), we are in fact shown

Jesus and Orc directly juxtaposed, now as two *opposing* manifestations of the same basic 'Zoa' – namely, Luvah. In this context Orc has actually become the glittering bejewelled serpent whom Blake elsewhere calls 'the Covering Cherub': one of his prime symbols for the Antichrist. His original transformation into this form happens in VII, p. 93 (Erdman, p. 365) – which is perhaps an allegory of the collapse of the French Revolution into tyranny.

16 *A Vision of the Last Judgment*, Erdman, p. 564.

17 Ibid., p. 562.

18 This story of the 'Horses of Light' is merely alluded to, in several places: *The Four Zoas* 10: 11–13 (Erdman, p. 305); 39: 2–3 (p. 326); 50: 28–30 (p. 334); 93: 11–13 (p. 365); 119: 26–7 (p. 388).

19 *Jerusalem* 66: 15 is perfectly specific: 'Luvah is France'. But this identification is also fundamental to the whole structure of political allusion in Blake's myth, *passim*.

20 See especially *The Four Zoas* 48: 11–20 (Erdman, p. 332).

21 Ibid. 51: 12–20 (Erdman, p. 334):

> Now all comes into the power of Tharmas . . .
> The Eternal man is seald never to be deliverd
> I roll my floods over his body my billows & waves pass over him
> The Sea encompasses him & monsters of the deep are his companions
> Dreamer of furious oceans cold sleeper of weeds & shells
> The Eternal form shall never renew my uncertain prevails against thee
> Yet tho I rage God over all.

Tharmas's fallenness consists in his 'uncertainty'. Unlike Urizen and Luvah, he does not *want* to be God (line 29) – but is no less trapped in the illusion.

22 Ibid. 4: 6 (Erdman, p. 301); 69: 11 (p. 346).

23 *Jerusalem* 63: 5.

24 *The Four Zoas* 68: 28–69: 6 (Erdman, p. 346); 77: 1–4 (p. 352).

25 *Jerusalem* 14: 4–9; *Milton* 2: 10–13.

26 *The Four Zoas* 85: 26–86: 11 (Erdman, pp. 367–8). 'Be assurd I am thy real Self', says the Spectre to Los. And 'if we unite in one, another better world will be / Opend within your heart & loins & wondrous brain'.

27 Jeremiah 20: 7–20.

28 *Jerusalem* 5: 68–11: 7; 17: 1–47.

29 Northrop Frye, in his classic study, *Fearful Symmetry* (Princeton: Princeton University Press, 1947), p. 127, defines the difference in terms of 'objectivity' and 'subjectivity': 'The word "emanation" in Blake means the object-world. . . . "Spectre" means the subjective counterpart to this.' But what are we ever 'fallen' into, if not 'objective' alienation? Both Emanation and Spectre alike are surely modes of subjectivity become falsely objective to itself. The Spectre, in another sense, is clearly more 'subjective', the Emanation more 'objective', in relationship to the masculinity of a male individual; but in relationship to the femininity of a female individual, the reverse is true.

30 *Jerusalem* 49: 47; 88: 10–11; 90: 1–2.

31 See for example ibid. 90: 1–13.

32 Ibid. 92: 13–14. And see also 30: 14–15; 79: 73–7. In Blake's work as a whole, 'sexual' is generally a term for relationships of manipulativeness.

33 See for example ibid. 18: 29–30; 30: 2–9.

34 Erdman, p. 2.

35 Besides being the name of a prostitute, 'Rahab' is also the name of a sea monster, sometimes associated in the biblical literature with Egypt, and as such

in the Authorized Version translation of Psalm 87: 4 directly juxtaposed to Babylon.

36 For the source of this conception see the Authorized Version translation of Ezekiel 28: 14–16.

37 In *Milton* 37: 8–9 the Covering Cherub is described as including both Satan and Rahab. Elsewhere, however, 'Satan' is the inclusive term.

38 See for example ibid. 101: 33–7 (Erdman, p. 374).

39 *Milton* 10: 1.

40 Cf. his famous remark in *The Marriage of Heaven and Hell*, Erdman, p. 35: 'The reason Milton wrote in fetters when he wrote of Angels & God, and at liberty when of Devils and Hell, is because he was a true Poet and of the Devil's party without knowing it'. In this context, of course, Blake is in effect identifying Milton's 'Devil' with the liberating Orc of his own Lambeth myth.

41 Milton, *Paradise Lost* IX, 494–526.

42 Cf. *Jerusalem* 74: 10–13. 'The Spectre is the Reasoning Power in Man' – in the Urizenic sense which, in effect, identifies true rationality with whatever the ruling classes complacently regard as common sense.

43 The star symbolism is especially interesting in this regard. Elsewhere in Blake's writing stars are typically associated with Urizen. See for example *The Four Zoas* 33: 16–36 (Erdman, p. 322). And at the climax of the Last Judgment there they are therefore 'consumed like a lamp blown out' (138: 24; Erdman, p. 406). No doubt the logic of this association is quite closely related to Plato's reasons, in his *Laws*, for advocating a star-worshipping religious-cult, the better to promote the political prestige of the wise: astronomy being regarded as symbolically representative of scientific knowledge in general. In Blake's terms, that is the purely Urizenic aspect of Platonism. Or again one might also cite Kant, with his reverential coupling of 'the starry skies above and the moral law within'. Not that Blake would probably have been very aware of Kant. But whenever the vastness of the starry skies is invoked in any sort of authoritative conjunction with morality – what else is this, deep down, if not a symbolic manoeuvre to belittle, and so intimidate the human individual, as a potential dissident? Which is for Blake the very essence of false sublimity.

(Hegel, incidentally, appears to have felt similar misgivings to Blake's. The evidence is Heinrich Heine's little anecdote: 'One fine evening when the stars were shining we two stood side by side at the window, and I, a youth of twenty-two, I had just dined well and had my coffee, and I spoke of the stars with some fervour, calling them the abode of the blessed. The master, however, muttered: "The stars, hum! hum! The stars are nothing but a gleaming leprosy on the sky."')

Yet here the stars are, so to speak, redeemed. These star-studded angels are also the 'seven eyes of God': for Blake, a symbol for the whole of human thought in its necessary experimental passage through diverse erroneous visions of reality, towards the truth. (Cf. Zechariah 4: 10; Revelation 5: 6.)

44 *Jerusalem* 16: 28–60; 71: 10–49.

45 *Milton* 3: 42–3.

46 When he lived in Lambeth, his home was in fact not far from the famous Albion Mill. See Peter Ackroyd, *Blake* (London: Minerva, 1996), pp. 130–1: this

was the first great factory in London, designed by John Rennie to run upon steam-engines and supposed to produce some 6,000 bushels of flour a week. It was one of the 'sights' of the metropolis, which Erasmus Darwin described as 'a grand and successful effort of human art'. But in March 1791, just after Blake had moved to Lambeth, it was burnt down – some believe it to have been arson, and the rejoicing millers on Blackfriars Bridge made no secret of their feelings. 'Success to the mills of ALBION', one placard was inscribed, 'but no Albion Mills'. The factory was destroyed, and remained as a black ruined shell until 1809. Blake passed it every time he walked into the City, with the hills of Highgate and Hampstead in the distant smoky air.

8 Hölderlin: towards releasement

1 The play is called *Der Tod des Empedokles*. Hölderlin produced first a preliminary outline sketch of the whole; then two different unfinished draft versions, following another pattern; then an essay (*Der Grund zum Empedokles*) setting out the theoretical basis for the project, as reconceived following the abandonment of both of those; then, finally, a third unfinished draft; and another outline sketch for this third version.

2 Textual references here are to Hölderlin's *Sämtliche Werke, Große Stuttgarter Ausgabe*, ed. Friedrich Beißner and Adolf Beck, 8 vols (Stuttgart: Cotta/Kohlhammer, 1943–86). The translations in the text are my own. But cf. Michael Hamburger's complete English version: *Hölderlin: Poems and Fragments*, 3rd edn (London: Anvil Press, 1994).

'Wie wenn am Feiertage' is to be found in the *Sämtliche Werke*, vol. 2, pp. 118–20.

3   Und wie im Aug' ein Feuer dem Manne glänzt,
    Wenn hohes er entwarf, so ist
    Von neuem an den Zeichen, den Thaten der Welt jezt
    Ein Feuer angezündet in Seelen der Dichter.

4   uns gebührt es, unter Gottes Gewittern,
    Ihr Dichter! mit entblößtem Haupte zu stehen
    Des Vaters Stral, ihn selbst, mit eigner Hand
    Zu fassen und dem Volk ins Lied
    Gehüllt die himmlische Gaabe zu reichen.
    Denn sind nur reinen Herzens,
    Wie Kinder, wir, sind schuldlos unsere Hände,

    Des Vaters Stral, der reine versengt es nicht
    Und tieferschüttert, die Leiden des Stärkeren
    Mitleidend, bleibt in den hochherstürzenden Stürmen
    Des Gottes, wenn er nahet, das Herz doch fest.

5   Doch weh mir! wenn von

    Weh mir!

       Und sag ich gleich,

    Ich sei genaht, die Himmlischen zu schauen,
    Sie selbst, sie werfen mich tief unter die Lebenden
    Den falschen Priester, ins Dunkel, daß ich
    Das warnende Lied den Gelehrigen singe.
    Dort

6   Und daher trinken himmlisches Feuer jezt
    Die Erdensöhne ohne Gefahr.
                     (lines 54–5)

7 *Sämtliche Werke*, vol. 6, pp. 425–8.

8 The other subject he had earlier considered for his drama was actually the death of Socrates. One way or another, he was determined to celebrate philosophy.

9 See Heidegger, *Gesamtausgabe* (Frankfurt am Main: Klostermann): *Erläuterungen zu Hölderlins Dichtung*, ed. Friedrich-Wilhelm von Herrmann, is to be found in vol. 4 (1981); *Hölderlins Hymnen 'Germanien' und 'Der Rhein'*, ed. Susanne Ziegler, in vol. 39 (1980); *Hölderlins Hymne 'Andenken'*, ed. Curd Ochwadt, in vol. 52 (1982); *Hölderlins Hymne 'Der Ister'*, ed. Walter Biemel, in vol. 53 (1984).

10 See the extensive discussion in my previous books: *Civil Society, Civil Religion* (Oxford: Blackwell, 1995) and *God and Modernity: A New and Better Way To Do Theology* (London: Routledge, 2000).

11 The English version, *Being and Time*, translated by John Macquarrie and Edward Robinson (Oxford: Blackwell, 1962), gives marginal page references to the 7th German edition: this formulation is to be found on p. 305, in this reckoning.

12 Ibid., p. 297.

13 *Gelassenheit* (Pfullingen: Neske, 1955); translated into English by John M. Anderson and E. Hans Freund (New York: Harper and Row, 1966) as *Discourse on Thinking*; originally written 1944–5.

14 *Hölderlins Hymnen 'Germanien' und 'Der Rhein'*, *Gesamtausgabe*, vol. 39, p. 214.

15 For an extended critique of Heidegger on poetry, in general, see especially Véronique Fóti, *Heidegger and the Poets: Poiésis, Sophia, Techné* (Atlantic Highlands: Humanities Press, 1991). Also Gerald Bruns, *Heidegger's Estrangements* (New Haven: Yale University Press, 1989).

16 There is a clear imbalance, already, in his initial choice of hymns on which to comment.

17 This attitude to all things German is still very apparent, not least in his novel *Hyperion*, written during the period 1792–9.

18 'Der Einzige', first version: *Sämtliche Werke*, vol. 2, pp. 153–6.

19   Mein Meister und Herr!
        O du, mein Lehrer!
        Was bist du ferne
        Geblieben? und da
        Ich fragte unter den Alten,
        Die Helden und
        Die Götter, warum bliebst
        Du aus? Und jezt ist voll
        Von Trauern meine Seele
        Als eifertet, ihr Himmlischen, selbst
        Daß, dien' ich einem, mir
        Das andere fehlet.

        Ich weiß es aber, eigene Schuld
        Ists! Denn zu sehr,
        O Christus! häng' ich an dir.
20   Es hänget aber an Einem
        Die Liebe. Diesesmal
        Ist nemlich vom eigenen Herzen
        Zu sehr gegangen der Gesang,
        Gut machen will ich den Fehl
        Wenn ich noch andere singe.
        Nie treff ich, wie ich wünsche,
        Das Maas.

21 *Sämtliche Werke*, vol. 2, p. 170.

22   Wenn aber einer spornte sich selbst,

Und traurig redend, unterweges, da ich wehrlos wäre
Mich überfiele, daß ich staunt' und von dem Gotte
Das Bild nachahmen möcht' ein Knecht –
Im Zorne sichtbar sah' ich einmal
Des Himmels Herrn, nicht, daß ich seyn sollt etwas, sondern
Zu lernen . . .

(There is in fact an ambiguity in this: it is left unclear whether the presumptuous slave is the poet or his assailant. I think the former is more likely – but *mutatis mutandis* the basic point remains in either case.)

23 For a discussion of the various literary forms of Hölderlin's verse – especially the elegies and 'hymns' – see for example David Constantine, *Hölderlin* (Oxford: Clarendon Press, 1988).
24 *Sämtliche Werke*, vol. 2, pp. 96–9.
25   Vieles bat ich, zu lieb dem Vaterlande, damit nicht
     Ungebeten uns einst plözlich befiele der Geist.
26   Wenn wir seegnen das Mahl, wen darf ich nennen und wenn wir
     Ruhn vom Leben des Tags, saget, wie bring' ich den Dank?
     Nenn' ich den Hohen dabei? Unschikliches liebet ein Gott nicht,
     Ihn zu fassen, ist fast unsere Freude zu klein.
     Schweigen müssen wir oft; es fehlen heilige Nahmen,
     Herzen schlagen und doch bleibet die Rede zurük?
27   Sorgen, wie diese, muß, gern oder nicht, in der Seele
     Tragen ein Sänger und oft, aber die anderen nicht.
                                        (lines 107–8)

(Again, these lines are ambiguous: 'die anderen' *might* refer to other cares, rather than the other people around the dinner table, 'the relatives' to whom the poem is dedicated. However, I think it is at any rate more interesting to take it in that second sense.)

28 *Sämtliche Werke*, vol. 2, pp. 90–5.
29   Drum an den Isthmos komm! dorthin, wo das offene Meer rauscht
     Am Parnaß und der Schnee delphische Felsen umglänzt,
     Dort ins Land des Olymps, dort auf die Höhe Cithärons,
     Unter die Fichten dort, unter die Trauben, von wo
     Thebe drunten und Ismenos rauscht im Lande des Kadmos,
     Dorther kommt und zurük deutet der kommende Gott.

     Seeliges Griechenland! du Haus der Himmlischen alle,
     Also ist wahr, was einst wir in der Jugend gehört?
     Festlicher Saal! der Boden ist Meer! und Tische die Berge,
     Wahrlich zu einzigem Brauche vor Alters gebaut!
30   wir kommen zu spät. Zwar leben die Götter,
     Aber über dem Haupt droben in anderer Welt.
     Endlos wirken sie da und scheinens wenig zu achten,
     Ob wir leben, so sehr schonen die Himmlischen uns.
     Denn nicht immer vermag ein schwaches Gefäß sie zu fassen,
     Nur zu Zeiten erträgt göttliche Fülle der Mensch.
     Traum von ihnen ist drauf das Leben.
31 Indessen dünket mir öfters
     Besser zu schlafen, wie so ohne Genossen zu seyn,
     So zu harren und was zu thun indeß und zu sagen,
     Weiß ich nicht und wozu Dichter in dürftiger Zeit?
32 [Aber indessen] kommt als Fackelschwinger des Höchsten
     Sohn, der Syrier, unter die Schatten herab.

Seelige Weise sehns; ein Lächeln aus der gefangnen
Seele leuchtet, dem Licht thauet ihr Auge noch auf.
Sanfter träumet und schläft in Armen der Erde der Titan,
Selbst der neidische, selbst Cerberus trinket und schläft.

('The Syrian' is a nice touch: partly, perhaps, a half-identification of Christ with Adonis; partly a little alienation effect – the geographical imprecision of an outsider, whose spiritual home is very much elsewhere!)

33 *Sämtliche Werke*, vol. 2, pp. 165–72.

34   denn nie genug
Hatt' er von Güte zu sagen
Der Worte, damals, und zu erheitern, da
Ers sahe, das Zürnen der Welt.
Denn alles ist gut. Drauf starb er. Vieles wäre
Zu sagen davon. Und es sahn ihn, wie er siegend blikte
Den Freudigsten die Freunde noch zulezt,

        Doch trauerten sie.

35   Denn izt erlosch der Sonne Tag
Der Königliche und zerbrach
Den geradestralenden,
Den Zepter, göttlichleidend, von selbst,
Denn wiederkommon sollt es
Zu rechter Zeit.

36   Wenn aber stirbt alsdenn
An dem am meisten
Die Schönheit hieng, daß an der Gestalt
Ein Wunder war und die Himmlischen gedeutet
Auf ihn, und wenn, ein Räthsel ewig füreinander
Sie sich nicht fassen können
Einander, die zusammenlebten
Im Gedächtniß, und nicht den Sand nur oder
Die Weiden es hinwegnimmt und die Tempel
Ergreifft, wenn die Ehre
Des Halbgotts und der Seinen
Verweht und selber sein Angesicht
Der Höchste wendet
Darob, daß nirgend ein
Unsterbliches mehr am Himmel zu sehn ist oder
Auf grüner Erde, was ist diß?

        Es ist der Wurf des Säemanns, wenn er faßt
Mit der Schaufel den Waizen,
Und wirft, dem Klaren zu, ihn schwingend über die Tenne.

(Note the description of Christ here as a 'Halbgott': Hölderlin's Hellenizing impulse at its most directly heretical!)

37 *Sämtliche Werke*, vol. 2, pp. 533–8.
38 Strophe 9, p. 536.
39   Viel hat von Morgen an,
Seit ein Gespräch wir sind und hören voneinander,
Erfahren der Mensch; bald sind wir aber Gesang.

40   Reif sind, in Feuer getaucht, gekochet
Die Frücht und auf der Erde geprüfet und ein Gesez ist
Daß alles hineingeht, Schlangen gleich,

Prophetisch, träumend auf
Den Hügeln des Himmels. Und vieles
Wie auf den Schultern eine
Last von Scheitern ist
Zu behalten. Aber bös sind
Die Pfade. Nemlich unrecht,
Wie Rosse, gehn die gefangenen
Element' und alten
Geseze der Erd. Und immer
Ins Ungebundene gehet eine Sehnsucht. Vieles aber ist
Zu behalten. Und Noth die Treue.
Vorwärts aber und rükwärts wollen wir
Nicht sehn. Uns wiegen lassen, wie
Auf schwankem Kahne der See.

    Wie aber liebes? Sonnenschein
Am Boden sehen wir und trokenen Staub
Und heimatlich die Schatten der Wälder und es blühet
An Dächern der Rauch, bei alter Krone
Der Thürme, friedsam; gut sind nemlich
Hat gegenredend die Seele
Ein Himmlisches verwundet, die Tageszeichen.
Denn Schnee, wie Majenblumen
Das Edelmüthige, wo
Es seie, bedeutend, glänzet auf
Der grünen Wiese
Der Alpen, hälftig, da, vom Kreuze redend, das
Gesezt ist unterwegs einmal
Gestorbenen, auf hoher Straß
Ein Wandersmann geht zornig,
Fern ahnend mit
Dem andern, aber was ist diß?

    Am Feigenbaum ist mein
Achilles mir gestorben,
Und Ajax liegt
An den Grotten der See,
An Bächen, benachbart dem Skamandros.
An Schläfen Sausen einst, nach
Der unbewegten Salamis steter
Gewohnheit, in der Fremd', ist groß
Ajax gestorben.
Patroklos aber in des Königes Harnisch. Und es starben
Noch andere viel. Am Kithäron aber lag
Elevtherä, der Mnemosyne Stadt. Der auch als
Ablegte den Mantel Gott, das abendliche nachher löste
Die Loken. Himmlische nemlich sind
Unwillig, wenn einer nicht die Seele schonend sich
Zusammengenommen, aber er muß doch; dem
Gleich fehlet die Trauer.

(The most significant ambiguity here is in the penultimate line: 'aber er muß doch'.
I have taken this to be a fatalistic 'must': one 'must' do what one is driven to do,
even if the gods disapprove. It might, though, on the contrary be a moralistic
'must', meaning 'one must obey'.)

9 'After Auschwitz': the case of Nelly Sachs

1 Theodor Adorno, *Negative Dialectics*, English translation by E. B. Ashton (London: Routledge and Kegan Paul, 1973), p. 367.

2 Ibid., p. 362.

3 She had in the past corresponded with the celebrated Swedish author, Selma Lagerlöf, and Lagerlöf's intervention with the Swedish authorities, just before her death, appears to have been a crucial factor in their obtaining their entry visas.

4 See the rather moving biography, *Nelly Sachs*, by Ruth Dinesen, originally in Danish but also translated into German (Frankfurt am Main: Suhrkamp, 1992).

5 Letter to Gisela Dischner, quoted in Bengt Holmqvist (ed.), *Das Buch der Nelly Sachs* (Frankfurt am Main: Suhrkamp, 1977), p. 311.

6 These are collected in *Zeichen im Sand* (Frankfurt am Main: Suhrkamp, 1962).

7 Bahr, *Nelly Sachs* (München: Beck, 1980), p. 130. Enzensberger, 'Über die Gedichte der Nelly Sachs', in Holmqvist (ed.), *Das Buch der Nelly Sachs*, p. 356.

8 In her own appendix to *Eli*, Sachs speaks of having written it 'in flames . . . over a period of several nights'; and on the title page of the first edition she dated it 1943–4. As a matter of fact, the writing appears to have extended over several months, and was not finally completed until November 1945. But, looking back, what she remembered was just the original dramatic moment of traumatized inspiration. See Dinesen, op. cit., pp. 154–61.

9 The whole story of this friendship is told in Dinesen, pp. 210–54.

10 There is therefore some irony in the fact that the chief collection of her work in English translation, in the Penguin Modern European Poets series, brings her together with Abba Kovner: *Abba Kovner and Nelly Sachs: Selected Poems* (Harmondsworth: Penguin, 1977). For Kovner, who led a guerrilla band of Jewish resistance fighters against the Nazis in Lithuania during the war, was also a leading advocate of terrorist revenge action against Germany thereafter.

11 Except perhaps, by implication, in one early poem: 'Auch der Greise . . .'

12 Bengt Holmqvist, 'Die Sprache der Sehnsucht', in *Das Buch der Nelly Sachs*.

13
O die Schornsteine
Auf den sinnreich erdachten Wohnungen des Todes,
Als Israels Leib zog aufgelöst in Rauch
Durch die Luft –
Als Essenkehrer ihn ein Stern empfing
Der schwarz wurde
Oder war es ein Sonnenstrahl?

O die Schornsteine!
Freiheitswege für Jeremias und Hiobs Staub –
Wer erdachte euch und baute Stein auf Stein
Den Weg für Flüchtlinge aus Rauch?

O die Wohnungen des Todes,
Einladend hergerichtet
Für den Wirt des Hauses, der sonst Gast war –
O ihr Finger,
Die Eingangsschwelle legend
Wie ein Messer zwischen Leben und Tod –

O ihr Schornsteine,
O ihr Finger,
Und Israels Leib im Rauch durch die Luft!

(All the translations here are my own.)

14   Wer aber leerte den Sand aus euren Schuhen,
Als ihr zum Sterben aufstehen mußtet?
Den Sand, den Israel heimholte,
Seinen Wandersand?
Brennenden Sinaisand,
Mit den Kehlen von Nachtigallen vermischt,
Mit den Flügeln des Schmetterlings vermischt,
Mit dem Sehnsuchtsstaub der Schlangen vermischt,
Mit allem was abfiel von der Weisheit Salomos vermischt,
Mit dem Bitteren aus des Wermuts Geheimnis vermischt –

O ihr Finger,
Die ihr den Sand aus Totenschuhen leertet,
Morgen schon werdet ihr Staub sein
In den Schuhen Kommender!

15 Both 'Psalm' and 'Mandorla' belong to the collection entitled *Die Niemands-rose* (1963): in Paul Celan, *Gedichte* I (Frankfurt am Main: Suhrkamp, 1975). So too in 'Tenebrae', from *Sprachgitter*, the poet blasphemously urges God to pray to us mortals; perhaps to be honourably readmitted into the domain of valid poetry, from which the catastrophe seems to exclude him.

16 The full text of this poem, entitled 'Zürich zum Storchen', runs as follows:

Vom Zuviel war die Rede, vom
Zuwenig. Von Du
Und Aber-Du, von
der Trübung durch Helles, von
Jüdischem, von
deinem Gott.

Da-
von.
Am Tag einer Himmelfahrt, das
Münster stand drüben, es kam
mit einigem Gold übers Wasser.

Von deinem Gott war die Rede, ich sprach
gegen ihn, ich
ließ das Herz, das ich hatte,
hoffen:
auf sein höchstes, umröcheltes, sein
haderndes Wort –

Dein Aug sah mir zu, sah hinweg,
dein Mund
sprach sich dem Aug zu, ich hörte:

Wir
wissen ja nicht, weißt du,
wir
wissen ja nicht
was
gilt.

The talk was of the too-much, of the
too-little. Of Thou
and Thou-again, of
being troubled by clarity, of

Jewishness, of
your God.

Of
that.
On the day of an ascension, there
stood the Minster, and sent
a little gold across the water.

The talk was of your God, I spoke
against him, I
let the heart, that I had,
hope:
for his highest, death-rattled, his
squabblesome word –

Your eye looked at me, looked away,
your mouth
addressed itself to the eye, and I heard:

We
just don't know, you know,
we
just don't know
what
counts.

17 Bahr (*Nelly Sachs*, pp. 81–2) does in fact find a hint of dubious theodicy in 'O the chimneys'. But I am not at all convinced.

Note also, in this connection, Sachs's enthusiastic admiration for Simone Weil: closely bound up, surely, with the radical anti-theodicy at the heart of Weil's thought. See Peter Sager, *Nelly Sachs: Untersuchungen zu Stil und Motivik ihrer Lyrik* (Bonn: Rheinische Friedrich-Wilhelms-Universität, 1970), pp. 24–5, 277; citing letters to Walter Berendsohn dated 7 June 1952 and 9 June 1952. And there is also an abandoned poem, 'In memory of Simone Weil', printed in an appendix to Sager's book, p. 332.

18   In der Flucht
welch großer Empfang
unterwegs –

Eingehüllt
in der Winde Tuch
Füße im Gebet des Sandes
der niemals Amen sagen kann
denn er muß
von der Flosse in den Flügel
und weiter –

Der kranke Schmetterling
weiß bald wieder vom Meer –
Dieser Stein
mit der Inschrift der Fliege
hat sich mir in die Hand gegeben –

An Stelle von Heimat
halte ich die Verwandlungen der Welt –

19 This phrase, *Fahrt ins Staublose*, is the title both of her fifth collection, and of the volume, published by Suhrkamp in 1961, including all her major poetry up to that point.

20 Dinesen, p. 104.
21 Ibid., p. 109.
22 Ibid., pp. 200–9. The *Zohar* cycle appears in her 1957 collection *Und niemand weiß weiter*.
23 *Fahrt ins Staublose*, p. 204.
24 Ibid., p. 353.
25   Mit Wildhonig
       die Hinterbliebenen
       nährten
       in frühen Gräbern
       einbalsamierten Schlaf
       und ausgewanderte Pulse
       gossen Dattelwein
       in die Bienenwabe
       der Geheimnisse.

       Im schwarzen Kristall der Nacht
       die eingeschlossene Wespe
       der ausgetanzten Zeit
       im Starrkrampf lag –

       Aber du,
       aber du,
       wie nähre ich dich?

       Alle Meilensteine aus Staub
       überspringt die Liebe,
       wie die geköpfte Sonne
       im Schmerz
       nur Untergang suchend.

       Mit meinem Untergang
       nähre ich dich –
26 Dinesen, p. 104.
27   Schritte –
       In welchen Grotten der Echos
       seid ihr bewahrt,
       die ihr den Ohren einst weissaget
       kommenden Tod?

       Schritte –
       Nicht Vogelflug, noch Schau der Eingeweide,
       noch der blutschwitzende Mars
       gab des Orakels Todesauskunft mehr –
       nur Schritte –

       Schritte –
       Urzeitspiel von Henker und Opfer,
       Verfolger und Verfolgten,
       Jäger und Gejagt –

       Schritte
       die die Zeit reißend machen
       die Stunde mit Wölfen behängen,
       dem Flüchtling die Flucht auslöschen
       im Blute.

       Schritte

die Zeit zählend mit Schreien, Seufzern,
Austritt des Blutes bis es gerinnt,
Todesschweiß zu Stunden häufend –

Schritte der Henker
über Schritten der Opfer,
Sekundenzeiger im Gang der Erde,
von welchem Schwarzmond schrecklich gezogen?

In der Musik der Sphären
wo schrillt euer Ton?

(This is included in Sachs's second collection *Sternverdunkelung: Eclipse of the Stars*.)

28   Wieviele Meere im Sande verlaufen,
wieviel Sand hart gebetet im Stein,
wieviel Zeit im Sanghorn der Muschel
verweint,
wieviel Todverlassenheit
in den Perlenaugen der Fische,
wieviele Morgentrompeten in der Koralle,
wieviel Sternenmuster im Kristall,
wieviel Lachkeime in der Kehle der Möwe,
wieviel Heimwehfäden
auf nächtlichen Gestirnbahnen gefahren,
wieviel fruchtbares Erdreich
für die Wurzel des Wortes:
Du –
hinter allen stürzenden Gittern
der Geheimnisse
Du –

29 See Martin Buber, *I and Thou*, English translation by Ronald Gregor Smith (Edinburgh: T. and T. Clark, 1937). Buber was an important influence on Sachs's thinking generally; especially his apologia for the Hasidic tradition.

30   Wer zuletzt
hier stirbt
wird das Samenkorn der Sonne
zwischen seinen Lippen tragen
wird die Nacht gewittern
in der Verwesung Todeskampf.

Alle vom Blut
entzündeten Träume
werden im Zickzack-Blitz
aus seinen Schultern fahren
stigmatisieren die himmlische Haut
mit dem Geheimnis der Qual.

Weil Noahs Arche abwärts fuhr
die Sternbilderstraßen
wird
wer zuletzt hier stirbt
den Schuh mit wasser angefüllt
am Fuße haben

darin ein Fisch
mit seiner Rückenflosse Heimwehsegel

die schwarz vertropfte Zeit
in ihren Gottesacker zieht.

31 Völker der Erde
ihr, die ihr euch mit der Kraft der unbekannten
Gestirne umwickelt wie Garnrollen,
ihr, die ihr in die Sprachverwirrung steigt
wie in Bienenkörbe,
um im Süßen zu stechen
und gestochen zu werden –

Völker der Erde,
zerstöret nicht das Weltall der Worte,
zerschneidet nicht mit den Messern des Hasses
den Laut, der mit dem Atem zugleich geboren wurde.

Völker der Erde,
O daß nicht Einer Tod meine, wenn er Leben sagt –
und nicht Einer Blut, wenn er Wiege spricht –

Völker der Erde,
lasset die Worte an ihrer Quelle,
denn sie sind es, die die Horizonte
in die wahren Himmel rücken können
und mit ihrer abgewandten Seite
wie eine Maske dahinter die Nacht gähnt
die Sterne gebären helfen –

32 Diese Jahrtausende
geblasen vom Atem
immer um ein zorniges Hauptwort kreisend
aus dem Bienenkorb der Sonne
stechende Sekunden
kriegerische Angreifer
geheime Folterer

Niemals eine Atempause wie in Ur
da ein Kindervolk an den weißen Bändern zog
mit dem Mond Schlafball zu spielen –

Auf der Straße mit Windeseile
läuft die Frau
Medizin zu holen für das kranke Kind

Vokale und Konsonanten
schreien in allen Sprachen:
Hilfe!

Glühende Rätsel is included in Nelly Sachs, *Späte Gedichte* (Frankfurt am Main: Suhrkamp, 1968).

33 *Abram im Salz* was written over the period 1946–56, *Nachtwache* chiefly in 1952, on the basis of earlier materials. Both are included in *Zeichen im Sand*. Sachs's source for the Abraham legend was Herder's translation, first published in 1781. See Dinesen, pp. 162–79.

34 Fortgehen ohne Rückschau –
das letzte Zittergras aus dem Auge reißen
Als Tsong Khapa seinen Meister verließ
wandte er sich nicht nach ihm um
Der Abschied wohnte in seinem Schritt
Die Zeit flammte aus seinen Schultern –

Der Verlassene rief:
»Werft seine Hütte in den Abgrund –«
Und die Hütte schwebte über dem Abgrund
von fünffarbigem Licht durchstochen –
Und der ohne Abschied schritt
in den abgezehrten Ort der nur Geist ist
Und sein Haus war kein Haus mehr
Nur Licht –
35   Diese Nacht
ging ich eine dunkle Nebenstraße
um die Ecke
Da legte sich mein Schatten
in meinen Arm
Dieses ermüdete Kleidungsstück
wollte getragen werden
und die Farbe Nichts sprach mich an:
Du bist jenseits!

36 The passage in question describes an Hasidic vision:

> The Holy Baal Shem in glory. At the bottom red, then yellow, then around the head blue, but above that white like nothingness. These are the searching colours of Babylonian towers. Next to the earth red. At the top blue. But where the divine dwells – the colour "Nothingness".

Quoted in Sager, *Nelly Sachs*, p. 162. (And cf. also *Fahrt ins Staublose*, p. 351.)

37 Ibid., pp. 170–7, 307–8. This double symbolic reference, both to divinity and to death, is the same as in her sea-imagery.

38 Gershom Scholem, ed. and trans., *The Zohar, The Book of Splendour* (New York: 1949), p. 27.

10 Incredulity and liturgy

1 So let us, just by way of a beginning, note the following birthdays: William Blake's was 28 November; Friedrich Hölderlin's, 20 March; Nelly Sachs's, 10 December.

Appendix 1

1 I am talking here about *systematic* philosophy, as such; that is, philosophy at its most different from poetry. The more philosophers like Nietzsche or Heidegger start aiming at something closer to poetry, the more difficult it becomes for them to sustain a plausible negotiating strategy. (Of course, Nietzsche never had any interest in even trying to do so!)

2 Hobbes did, as it happens, write poetry as well. His second published work was a Latin poem, *De Mirabilibus Pecci* (1636), describing a tour of the Peak District. And in his old age he translated the whole of Homer into English. But, still, his shakenness is all in his prose.

3 See Carl Schmitt, *The Leviathan in the State Theory of Thomas Hobbes*, translated into English by George Schwab and Erna Hilfstein (Westport: Greenwood, 1996), Chapter 1.

4 Hobbes, *Leviathan*, Chapter 17; ed. C. B. Macpherson (Harmondsworth: Penguin, 1968), p. 227.

(In Job the sea-monster Leviathan is juxtaposed to the land-monster Behemoth; and in Jewish tradition they had often been portrayed in conflict, symbolizing the conflict between various Gentile powers. For Hobbes, Behemoth becomes a symbol for anarchy – such as only Leviathan can hold in check. See his 1656 polemic, *The Questions Concerning Liberty, Necessity and Chance.*)

5 This text appears both on the title page, and at the end of Chapter 28.
6 *Leviathan*, Introduction, p. 81.
7 *Milton* 2: 1–16; *Jerusalem* 4: 3–5.
8 *Milton* 30: 12–20.
9 Ibid. 30: 1–3.
10 *The Four Zoas* 5: 29–32 (Erdman, p. 303). But see also for instance *Jerusalem* 69: 14–33.
11 *Milton* 37: 16.
12 *Jerusalem* 37: 14.
13 *Milton* 30: 14.
14 And cf. 1: 2; 3: 4.
15 Erdman, pp. 24–5.

Appendix 2

1 This comes from a letter of Hölderlin's to his brother: *Sämtliche Werke*, vol. 3, p. 367.
2 The earliest registering of the shift comes in the fragment 'eine Ethik', in which for example one finds the affirmation, 'I am now convinced that the highest act of Reason . . . is an aesthetic act'. In the past it was widely supposed that this fragment originated as part of an essay perhaps jointly written by Hölderlin and Schelling, sent to Hegel shortly before his move to Frankfurt, and copied out by him. H. S. Harris however, following Otto Pöggeler, questions this: *Hegel's Development: Towards the Sunlight 1770–1801* (Oxford: Clarendon Press, 1972), pp. 249–57. The fragment nevertheless remains quite Hölderlinian in tone; and Harris also suggests that Hegel wrote it, in the first instance, for his friend.

   And then, at Frankfurt, he wrote his first decisively post-Kantian essay, 'The Spirit of Christianity and its Fate': translated in T. M. Knox's edition of Hegel's *Early Theological Writings* (Philadelphia: University of Pennsylvania Press, 1948).

   (Harris generally plays down the revolutionariness of Hölderlin's actual influence on Hegel at this point; which Dieter Henrich, on the other hand, sees as far greater. See for example, Henrich's essay, 'Some Historical Presuppositions of Hegel's System', in Darrel E. Christensen, *Hegel and the Philosophy of Religion*, The Hague: Martinus Nijhoff, 1970.)
3 Hegel, *Phenomenology of Spirit*, English translation by A. V. Miller (Oxford: Clarendon Press, 1977), para. 535.
4 It is above all what faith in the Holy Spirit, philosophically interpreted, points towards: ibid., paras 530–5.
5 Ibid., para. 537.
6 The whole section 'Faith and Pure Insight' is about various forms of what begins as a shaken 'flight from the world', in this sense: the same is in fact equally true of the 'faith' in question, prior to 'pure insight'.
7 Ibid., para. 537: 'This pure insight is thus the Spirit that calls to *every* consciousness: *be for yourselves* what you all are *in yourselves – reasonable*'. Again, 'reasonable' here essentially means responsive to Spirit. All of us ('in ourselves') have the potential for such responsiveness. But to be reasonable 'for oneself' means self-consciously and unambiguously acknowledging this to be one's highest vocation.
8 Ultimately, there is no serious faith-tradition without at least some such element; no tradition entirely devoid of any shaken impulse could develop or survive at all. That is the basic point of the typically tortuous argument in ibid., paras 547–8.

9 Faith's 'kingdom' is a kingdom of dreams, the kingdom of heaven. But here faith 'has been expelled from its kingdom; or this kingdom has been ransacked, since the waking consciousness has monopolized every distinction and expansion of it and has vindicated earth's ownership of every portion of it and given them back to earth': ibid., para. 573.

10 Ibid., paras 660–71.

11 So it is that the final reconciliation between the judgemental 'universal consciousness' and the dissident 'evil consciousness' in para. 670 is described as the essential breakthrough to '*absolute* Spirit'.

12 For a discussion closer grounded in the actual texts (and also further spelling out the contrast with Anselm) see my *Hegel's Political Theology* (Cambridge: Cambridge University Press, 1991), Chapter 1.

13 Hence the situating of the original account of this phenomenon in the *Phenomenology of Spirit*: in Chapter 4, well before the analysis of inter-cultural differences as such, which only begins in Chapter 6. Much of the difficulty of the *Phenomenology*, throughout, derives from the veiledness of the illustrative allusions; a veiledness which is Hegel's rather awkward homage to the intrinsic generality of what he is discussing. And here the tensions are especially acute: his thinking on this topic flows directly out of his earlier thought about Christian history, which is still alluded to; but he is, at the same time, all the while struggling to get beyond that level of discussion, to a properly systematic approach.

14 For the parallelism here, see in particular his *Lectures on the Philosophy of Religion*, English translation edited by Peter C. Hodgson, vol. 3 (Berkeley and Los Angeles: University of California Press, 1987), pp. 342–7.

   In these lectures Hegel is dealing with religious movements as such; in his earlier writings he deals with more or less the same attitudes, far rather, as defended by specific philosophers, or philosophically minded theologians – above all Jacobi, but also Schleiermacher.

15 Tholuck was the chief pioneer of the charge that Hegelianism is false because it is 'pantheist'. He was also very hostile to any sort of trinitarian theology, arguing that this was an alien intrusion into Christianity from older pagan traditions, mediated through Greek philosophy. Both of these arguments appear in his book *Die speculative Trinitätlehre des späteren Orients*, first published in 1826. Hegel nowhere accords Tholuck anything like the detailed direct critical attention he had earlier given Jacobi; but, by way of response, his writings from this time onwards are peppered with scornful references to the hazy concept of 'pantheism', and he also becomes increasingly concerned to accentuate his own commitment to Trinitarianism.

16 Hegel, *Aesthetics*, English translation by T. M. Knox (Oxford: Clarendon Press, 1975), vol. 1, pp. 75–81.

17 Ibid., p. 10.

18 In the Hegelian sense, perhaps the most truly romantic of all music would be the 'tintinnabulism' of Arvo Pärt, today; or the work of Henryk Górecki.

19 *Aesthetics*, p. 11.

20 Hegel himself does not, in fact, speak of the 'unhappy consciousness' in the *Aesthetics*; so that what follows is my extrapolation from his argument rather than what he actually says. However, I am only extrapolating in the sense of drawing out some of the (surely quite clear) implicit connections that there are between the *Aesthetics* and the *Phenomenology*.

21 See for example *Aesthetics*, pp. 64–9; in which Schlegel is bracketed with K. W. F. Solger and Ludwig Tieck – as well as being closely identified with the legacy of Fichtean metaphysics. Also, the *Philosophy of Right*, §140.

22 See especially Schiller, *Über die ästhetische Erziehung des Menschen* VI; in *Werke*, vol. 20 (Weimar: Hermann Böhlaus Nachfolger, 1962). Hölderlin, *Hyperion Fragment*, in *Sämtliche Werke*, vol. 3 (Stuttgart: Kohlhammer, 1957).

(In his introduction to the *Aesthetics* lectures, Hegel praises Schiller as the first aesthetic theoretician to arrive at something like a proper theoretical understanding of the 'Idea': pp. 61–3. Schiller's work was first published in 1795, and was clearly at that point a major influence on the thinking of both Hölderlin and Hegel.)

Index